Dear reader — may you be greatly blessed and inspired by reading this true story of the wonderful grace and mighty manifestations of our great ~~God~~ that are chronicled in this book!

Sincerely,

Rev. Gail B. ___

Jeremiah 29:11

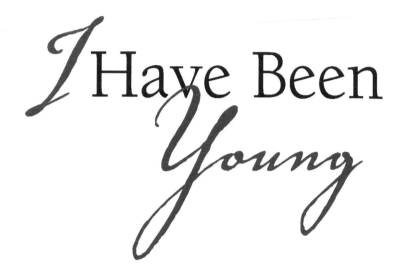

I Have Been Young

"I have been young, and now am old;
yet have I not seen the righteous forsaken,
nor his seed begging bread."

—*Psalm 37:25*

TABLE OF CONTENTS

FOREWORD

In January 1951 I had just received Jesus as my Lord and Savior and, along with a brother named Louie Ott, was active in lay ministry at The Church by the Side of the Road in Seattle, Washington. That following summer, Louie got word that his kid brother, Gail, was headed toward the Northwest in a chartreuse Plymouth convertible. Louie had invited Gail to come stay with him and had great concern for his welfare and salvation. Being the same age as the young Kansas farmer who was now barreling his way north, I promised Louie I would welcome Gail when he arrived and make a sincere effort to befriend him.

Of course, the enemy of our souls tried his best to keep Gail in spiritual darkness, but eventually Jesus won his heart. How was I to know then that the man in that chartreuse Plymouth convertible would become a Christian and, indeed, was also destined to become my closest friend? Following his conversion, Gail and I traveled throughout the Midwest doing evangelistic work, learning God's ways and enjoying one another's company, as well.

One afternoon as we traveled through northwestern Missouri, hoping to find a quiet place to fast and pray, we came upon a huge rainstorm. Gail pulled our Oldsmobile car off the road and veered us into a rest stop where we could wait out the deluge. Locking the car doors, we soon dropped off to sleep.

Gail awoke first—and *with a start!* He noticed that my car door was open and saw a man standing there as if talking to me (I was still asleep, having a vivid dream). Gazing transfixed at this mysterious visitor, Gail suddenly realized that the man outside our car door was a being from another world. Simultaneously, in my dream I saw a large field, ripe for harvest, and saw Gail and me running through it with two girls . . . who seemed to be sisters. In my vision, a strong, piercing voice thundered from the clouds.

"Go preach," it said.

The images of this mysterious visitor, the harvest field and the sound of that voice has remained very real and vivid to my mind. Yet it was not until later in life that I realized the two women in the dream I had that day were our wives, who are, by the way, sisters. Our meeting and marrying them was confirmation of the prophetic visions we had both seen that day. Indeed, these ladies have served in the harvest fields with us for all of the years since.

This experience brought Gail and me even closer in a mutual calling to the ministry. We have been like blood brothers, notwithstanding brothers-in-law, for nearly fifty years now! Hence I feel well-qualified to introduce you to Gail Ott—my friend, my brother, and my true yokefellow in Christ.

A book of this nature is dependent upon the true record of history. That said, I bear witness to the events described herein and to the faithful ministry of its author. You will find many miracles recorded within these pages and will read of a life lived for and with God that will thrill your heart and encourage you to live more fully for Him. I trust that traveling for a few days in the "chartreuse convertible" through Gail's life history will bless you as it has me and cause you to trust God for all your needs to an even greater degree.

—Chaplain Art Morlin

FOREWORD

In the course of a lifetime you can usually count on the fingers of two hands the number of people who have treated you lovingly, fairly, decently, and with consistency. It is those people who stick with you and continue to stand by your side—no matter what comes. I have found Gail Ott to be just such a person. His decency and sincerity are matched by few men. His willingness to suffer in order to advance the purposes of God in people's lives in also unparalleled. As you read about his life, perhaps you may discover how even a youth born in obscurity can be used of God in powerful ways that impact their generation.

By the grace of God, I was born and raised Jewish, becoming a Christian while in college after a "Damascus Road" encounter with Christ. I graduated from the University of California at Los Angeles in 1986 and received my Juris Doctrine from the University of Santa Clara in 1989. I have been a practicing attorney since that time, and, after studying to become an ordained minister and pastoring for a time as well, am now an international church conference speaker. By God's grace I am married to my beautiful wife, Maribeth, and have four wonderful children.

Shortly after my wife and I moved to Oregon in 1989, we met Reverend Gail Ott for the first time. As a fledgling "minister in training," I wasn't very good at *anything* ministerially, but Gail was faithful to "take me under his wing" and help me grow in the things of God and the ways of public ministry. He continually provided me both opportunities to preach at his church and encouragement to open my life more to the revelation of God's will for me.

Since that time, Gail has served faithfully on the Board of Compassionate Hands International, a worldwide Christian humanitarian aid organization that is active among the most needy peoples across the globe. As its founder and president, I can say that his prayers and support been a valuable asset to our organization in many ways, as well.

Hence it is without hesitation that I recommend to you *I Have Been Young*—not only for the story that unfolds within its pages, although it makes for great reading, but for the man who wrote— *and lived*—it. What you hold in your hands is a reflection of Gail Ott's integrity and the blessing of God on a life in response to a heart that is faith-full and overflowing. *Enjoy!*

—Randall J. Wolfe
Lake Oswego, Oregon

PREFACE

From time to time across the years, I have related some of the experiences chronicled in this book to family members, fellow ministers, and close friends. Again and again I heard these words: "You need to write a book about the miracles you've seen!" Rarely, however, did I give even casual consideration to the suggestion that I do so. Rather, I would reply simply, "Oh no, not me; I'm not a writer! Who would want to read something written by an unknown like me?"

This went on for a number of years, even as new experiences were realized along the way. Again and again, people would urge me to consider writing a book but my response was usually somewhat the same: "I don't think so!" That is, until I began to sense in my spirit that the Lord would have me do just that—write and publish a book declaring His glorious deeds and make known the miracles that He has done, of which I am His eyewitness and humble co-laborer in Christ.

I first felt the prompting of the Holy Spirit concerning this matter in the summer of 1980. A nephew, Mike, and his wife were overnight guests in our home, and that evening Mike and I were engaged in a lengthy conversation in the family room. As the night wore on, I began to realize that Mike was "picking my brain" about some of the things I had experienced in my younger years. The more I shared with him, the more he wanted to know.

"Tell me more," he urged, often fighting back tears as he listened, holding on with rapt attention to every word. He was visibly stirred as he listened with sincere interest to the account of "His story" that I was quietly sharing with him. This went on until 2 A.M. the next morning—when I finally suggested that we needed to go to bed and get some rest!

Just before we split for the night, my nephew extracted a promise from me.

"I want you to promise me the very first copy of your book once it's published!" Although I had no plan or intention at that time to actually *write* a book, I happily agreed.

"Sure, Mike, when and if I ever decide to write that book, I promise that you shall have the very first copy of it. OK?" With that, we retired to an admittedly brief night's sleep.

Not long after my conversation with Mike, and in the following weeks, as I began sensing the prompting of the Holy Spirit to do just that, I said out loud to the Lord: "Me, write a book? You must be kidding! Lord, you know that I'm not a writer. I'm not a celebrity— I'm a virtually unknown person. Who would want to read anything written by a nobody like me? Nevertheless, if this is truly your will, Lord, I will do my best to obey. But You are certainly going to have to help me. And, Lord, if You will indeed help me, then by Your grace and enablement, I will attempt to write the book!"

Not long after I made that commitment, I started jotting down memos about some of the remarkable life experiences that God had so graciously permitted me across five decades of ministry. *But what would I call this book?*

"A Good Name Is Rather to be Chosen than Great Riches."

When I first began to sense that God wanted me to write, I began thinking about what the story's title should be. From time to time I would jot down phrases or impressions that might be suitable for a book title, but each time something seemed to be missing. This went on for many months, and the results were always the same: none of the titles I'd thought of seemed right.

Then one morning while in the shower, not thinking about the book or its title, a strong impression of a phrase from the Bible suddenly came to me: "I Have Been Young!" At once I recognized these words as part of David's proclamation, recorded in Psalm 37:25, when he said, "I *have been young*, and now am old; yet have I not seen the righteous forsaken, nor His seed begging bread."

While meditating upon this inspired phrase, these words suddenly came pouring into my spirit, as clearly as if I had heard an audible voice: "The title of this book shall be *I Have Been Young*."

At that moment I was fully aware that the Lord had just spoken through the "still, small voice of the Spirit," a voice I had heard on numerous occasions in the past. Just then a deep, settled peace came over my entire being. I was supernaturally emptied of all doubt and hesitation concerning the title of the book.

But a conflict emerged. From the very first time I'd said, "OK, Lord, with your help I will write this book," I had firmly purposed in my heart that the book would not be about me but rather about Him, "the Author and Finisher of my faith."

This resolve would seem to present a paradox, however, for while on the one hand I'd stated emphatically that this book was not going to be about me, yet on the other hand its title was to begin with the personal pronoun "*I*."

I was now faced with an apparent contradiction. How could I reconcile those two positions which, on the surface at least, seemed diametrically opposed one to the other?

While meditating upon this matter, reasoning it over and over in my mind, the thought occurred to me that since I am the person in whom the Almighty in His goodness chose to show forth His might and His glory, then of necessity this would have to be my story as well.

I am humbled to think that the God of the universe would condescend to reveal His glory and to manifest His supernatural power to one as insignificant as me—not to a celebrity; one with absolutely no claim to fame—a poor Kansas farm boy, one of ten children, essentially a "nobody" as far as this world is concerned. Yet, by virtue of the New Birth, I am indeed a child of the King of Kings and thus *somebody* in His sight!

While meditating on these matters, I suddenly thought of a chorus I had learned and had loved to sing when I was a younger man. It went like this:

> He's the Oak and I'm the ivy,
> He's the Potter; I'm the clay;
> He's the Oil and I'm the vessel,
> I'm the traveler; He's the way.
> I'm the flower and He's the fragrance,
> I'm the lamp and He's the Flame;
> I'm the words and He's the Music,
> I'm the bride who takes His Name!

Please indulge me a few brief disclaimers. Know that any and all personal references in this book are intended solely to glorify the *Great I Am*—not this author. He's *the message*; I'm only the messenger!

And although much of the content of this book relates to events, incidents, and experiences that transpired in conjunction with my sharing of the gospel with others as an ordained minister, it is not intended to be a synopsis of my ministry. This account of the miraculous is not simply an autobiography of one man, or any other of God's creatures, but is a chronology of the acts of the Creator. It has seemed necessary that I should include some detail of the events of my life that led up to the miracles of supernatural provision, intervention, protection, and guidance of God, yet it has been for the express purpose of proclaiming His glory by means of the written word that I have included those details in this writing.

Jesus once said to His disciples, "Many prophets and righteous men have desired to see those things which you see, and have not seen them" (Matthew 13:17). I've felt this way on numerous occasions as I've witnessed and experienced manifestations of the supernatural! For the past fifty years, I have traveled throughout the world for the purpose of ministry. My journeys have taken me to all six inhabited continents, to every country in the North American continent, to all fifty states of the USA, and to many other countries, colonies and islands of the seas.

But despite the fact that many of the notable miracles and mercies chronicled in this book happened in far off places, the mention of these travel destinations and locations is not intended to be a travelogue; rather, is wholly intended to glorify the Lord God. *To Him be all the glory, honor and praise, for He alone is worthy!*

"Publish with the Voice of Thanksgiving!"

Some months after my conversations with Mike and with the Lord, in the spring of 1980, my wife Bobbie and I were vacationing on the east coast of Florida. Sitting in a folding chair there at Daytona Beach, while Bobbie was looking for sea-shells, I began what would become a "long day's journey into the night" with reference to the writing of this book. It was there that I began jotting down topics for chapters as well as writing some sections of them.

I had heard the Rev. Robert Schuller say, "Getting started is half done!" And as a general rule I had found that to be true. However, that wasn't necessarily a fact with me concerning this project. Actually, I seemed to be completing it in starts and stops. That is to say, after the initial writing in 1983, I did not write again for some time. Perhaps the old Chinese proverb, "A journey of a thousand miles begins with a single step," would be more applicable to my project than Reverend Schuller's wise maxim!

During the times when I have really applied myself to the project, however, the Holy Spirit has illuminated and anointed my mind and spirit so that events and experiences about which I'm writing have become so crystal clear in my memory that it seems they happened just a week ago! Visual details and words that were spoken thirty-some years ago have come to my remembrance with such clarity that I knew they were coming from more than just a keen memory on my part. Truly, this has been the Lord's doing and it has blessed *me* immensely!

One of my most productive writing times was in August 2001 during a week's stay in Fort Lauderdale, Florida. Several chapters were written that week, especially about events and experiences that had taken place there in south Florida some forty-eight years earlier, in 1953. Alone in a hotel room, I wrote with such intensity and emotion that I found myself overcome at times. When the sacredness of those thrilling experiences and events gripped my heart, I often found myself sobbing, even weeping openly at times. It was a good feeling as I virtually relived the sacred times about which I was writing!

Yet not until February 2002, on the occasion of my seventieth birthday, did a strong conviction grip my heart that I must intensify my writing and complete the manuscript for this book, forwarding it for publication. In that month, it was as if the Holy Spirit were saying to me, "It's time to get serious about writing and completing the manuscript for this book!" Furthermore, I felt strongly impressed that I should try to have it complete and ready for publication within the next year or so. In obedience to the Holy Spirit, I pressed harder into the work—and discovered the joy of giving birth to the volume you now hold in your hands!

Another reason for writing this book is a deep-seated desire on my part to glorify the God of my salvation and to magnify His Beloved and Only Begotten Son, the Lord Jesus Christ. The beloved psalmist expressed the longing of my heart (as well as that of his own) when he exclaimed, "That I may publish with the voice [or pen] of thanksgiving, and tell of thy wondrous works" (Psalm 26:7).

"He must increase, but I must decrease" (John 3:30).

During my younger years I may well have succumbed to the temptation to "make a name for myself," as some young men do. I don't know that for certain, however, as the opportunity to do so never presented itself to me or, if it did, I was oblivious to it. As an older man, however, I do know that now my one desire and earnest prayer in recounting the events described herein is that these words might lift up and magnify the One who said, "And I, if I be lifted up . . . will draw all men unto me" (John 12:32).

Much of the content of this book chronicles spiritual experiences and supernatural encounters that occurred in the season of my youth. My present passion is to pass this account on to the youth of today, many of whom may never have experienced the supernatural or as yet had a personal encounter with the Lord Jesus Christ—and to all who hunger for the manifestation of God's power and glory in their own lives. If the true story you are about to read succeeds in that resolve, then our work will not have been in vain. May God bless you and increase your faith in Him.

—Reverend Gail B. Ott
Vancouver, Washington
March, 2004

ACKNOWLEDGEMENTS

I want to acknowledge and honor my family for without their understanding, patience, and sacrifice, this book would never have been written.

First, to my beloved and devoted wife, Barbara, with deepest gratitude and love I acknowledge that had you not been willing to stay behind in order that I might go, I would never have been able to travel the world in quest of souls through missionary evangelism. Quite probably your eternal reward will exceed any of which I may eventually be accounted worthy as it no doubt required greater grace and sacrifice on your part to stay behind as I traveled throughout the world. *Thank you, Bobbie, dear!*

Secondly, I wish to acknowledge our only daughter and first-born child, Sally Gail (Ott) Doss, who was without a father's touch for much of her infancy and early childhood. I left for Brazil on your first birthday. Returning three months later, I had to work hard to regain your trust and acceptance. By the time you were five years old, I had missed a total of one full year of your young life. Beloved and cherished daughter, I will always feel a debt of gratitude to you, Sally, for overlooking those months when I was an "absentee" dad.

Thirdly, I pay tribute to our son Andrew for always believing in me and for the encouragement you have freely given me across the years. While I was not away from you in the days of your childhood as much as I had been from your sister, I was away on several important occasions. Growing up, Andy, you were a real joy to your mother and me, just as was Sally. Attending baseball, football, and basketball games from your fifth birthday on through your college years made us very proud parents! For this and so much more, I acknowledge you as a vital and significant part of my life and ministry.

Fourthly, with love and devotion I acknowledge the role that each of my extended family members has played in my life: my son-in-law, Calvin Doss; daughter-in-law, Tristeen (Parker) Ott; and six grandchildren (one in heaven, Jaynece Gail Nevin), Doug Nevin, Alyssa, Megan, Sydney, and Drew Ott. I love each of you equally. You are my joy in these, my "sunset years."

Finally, the scriptural injunction, "Give honor to whom honor is due," certainly pertains to the publication of this book. Without the help, patience, and guidance I've received from Athena Dean and the editorial staff of WinePress Publishers, I could not have realized the fulfillment of my calling to publish. I am equally grateful to Susan Bramlette for all of her expertise and input in editing my manuscript. I shall forever be grateful for the kindnesses these professionals have extended to me.

Sincerely,
Reverend Gail B. Ott

Chapter 1

. . . .

IN THE BEGINNING . . .

M onday, February 8, 1932, was a cold and wintry morning in South Central Kansas. Mother had just been taken to Aunt Jennie's house on a farm five miles north of the town of Norwich. The time had come for her to give birth. Doctor Eugene "My Ford is always ready" Wallace had been summoned from his small clinic in town to assist with the delivery of the fifth of the Ott children. Big sister, Pauline, brothers Louie, Lloyd, and Lester waited anxiously to find out if the new sibling would be a sister or a brother. *There was no such thing as "ultrasound" in those days!*

Without complication, Gail Buel Ott emerged into the world and was named after a beloved minister, Reverend Gail W. Shultz. *Buel* was the middle name of Grandpa Bailey (Daniel Buel), my mother's father, and so was affixed to the first name. Thus in this humble fashion another "Depression baby" of British heritage drew breath in the Kansas dust bowl, the middle of ten children.

"Honor Thy Mother and Thy Father."

My parents, Lewis and Vera Ott, were poor, hard-working farm people. They never owned land and thus lived as tenant farmers (also then known as "sharecroppers.") The landlord generally

25

received one-third of their crops (mostly wheat) and they were permitted to keep the other two-thirds as their livelihood.

Tenant farmers knew no permanent security; hence the Ott family lived in nine different houses on as many different farms during my childhood. The Great Depression of the 1930s made it especially difficult for them to eke out a living. Immortalized in stories like *The Grapes of Wrath*, that decade was known as the "Dirty Thirties" in the Midwest as frequent dust storms threatened to wipe out everyone's crops and posed serious health hazards to its residents as well.

Through it all, the Ott family somehow managed to survive and in fact increased in number to twelve, with Dwane, Janice, Beulah, Gary, and Vera Jane all following me (Gail) and the older siblings in Mom and Dad's household.

Each of the nine different farmhouses my family lived in had a name—usually the name of the landlord. In the spring of 1937, we were living in the Richardson House near the small town of Adams, Kansas. One late afternoon in April of that year, a heavy rain had fallen, and then the sky cleared. A couple of my brothers and I were sitting on the porch of that house, along with Mother and baby sister, Janice. After the rain had ceased and the clouds had cleared, a beautiful rainbow appeared in the eastern sky. As a five-year-old boy, I recall asking Mother what this beautiful, colorful thing (the rainbow) was. In answer to my question, Mother told us kids the story of Noah and the great flood. She had become an ardent student of the Bible and knew the story very well.

She explained to us that because the people on the earth in that ancient time had become very wicked and had forgotten God, the Lord had decided to send a great flood to destroy them. I recall how we boys would interrupt occasionally to ask questions like, "Who is God," and "Why didn't Noah and his family drown, too?"

Mother carefully and patiently answered all of our questions, telling us that Noah was a good man who feared God and obeyed Him, therefore God chose to allow Noah to build a huge ark so that he and his family and two of all kinds of animals and birds could be spared from destruction.

Mother concluded the story by telling us that after the flood waters had subsided and the ground was dry again, so that Noah and his family and all of the animals and birds could come out of the ark, God put a rainbow in the sky to remind mankind that He would never again destroy the world with a flood of water.

"So," she said, "whenever you see a pretty rainbow in the sky, remember that it is a reminder of God's promise which He made to Noah."

For some reason I was particularly intrigued with that man, Noah, and so I asked Mother a number of questions about him. She explained to me and my siblings that God had called Noah to warn the people of his generation about the coming flood and to tell them that the ark he was building would be the only safe place for survival.

Then Mother proceeded to tell us kids that the next time God destroys the wicked people here on the earth will not be by a flood of water but rather by fire! She told us about heaven and hell, and said that the only hope we have to escape the "Lake of Fire," which is hell, and to go to that beautiful place where God lives, called heaven, is to believe in Jesus Christ, God's Son.

My next question was, "Would there be anybody, like Noah, whom God would send to warn people everywhere that He's going to destroy the wicked people with fire?"

"Oh, yes," she answered. "Only the next time there will be *many* men and women to warn the people of the world of coming judgment. They are called 'preachers' and 'Christians' and they are already warning people about hell and the Lake of Fire!"

"*Wow!*" I thought that was awesome and was so glad that Mother had taken the time to tell us kids that story. I would never forget it as long as I lived. It was following that time of sitting there with Mother that I experienced my first encounter with the Lord. I was so deeply stirred and touched by that story about Noah and the Great Flood and about a coming day of final judgment and impending doom for the wicked and ungodly, as well as the hope and prospect of going to heaven someday, that I went into the house and got inside a small closet under the stairway, then known as "the cubbyhole."

After closing the closet door, I just sat there on the floor in the dark (our house did not have electricity) going over the story of Noah and everything else Mother had just told us about the Great Flood, etc. I must have stayed in the cubbyhole for thirty minutes or more thinking it all over in my young mind.

Though I did not understand it at the time, I was somehow made strangely aware that God was speaking to me—not in an audible voice, but through a deep-seated impression upon my spirit that made me to know that He was calling me to one day warn the people of *my* day about the coming of judgment, even as He had called Noah to do in his day and time.

After crawling out of the cubbyhole, I don't recall telling anyone about what I had experienced, but I knew that I would never forget that moment. It has stayed with me ever since that April day in 1937!

Strangely enough, it was shortly after that first encounter with the Lord that I began having some "close brushes" with death. First, after noticing a chicken (hen) coming out of a small culvert that was probably no more than eighteen inches in diameter, I decided she must have a nest of eggs inside there, so I crawled, head first, inside the narrow opening—my arms out in front of me. But I'd failed to notice that the culvert was clogged with debris so that I could not see through to the other end.

Having "wormed" my way down into the culvert I did find a nest of eggs. With two eggs in each hand, I proceeded to crawl backwards. Just then fear gripped me and hysteria set in. My shirt was caught on a snag between my shoulders where I could not reach to loosen it. Unable to move further in either direction, I cried out in panic for help, but nobody was near to me.

I realized that I was beginning to suffocate. In my distress, I cried out, "Please help me, God!" And help me He did! No one could ever convince me that it was not the Lord that unhooked my shirt from the snag I was caught on because after numerous unsuccessful tries I was able to inch back out of that culvert alive (with four eggs in hand, also!)

To this day I sometimes shudder when I think of that ordeal. *What if I had suffocated inside that culvert? Would my family have ever found my body?* Each time I think about it, to this day, I simply have to say, *Thank you, Lord, for sparing my life!*

I had another close encounter with death in the winter of 1938. A heavy snow had fallen that year and, as a boy will, I played furiously in the white stuff with my pals during recess and lunch hour at school each day. Coming back into the warm classroom, then running back out to play in the snow again at the next break, produced a series of radical temperature changes that adversely altered my small body's immune system.

Within two days of the snow storm I was deathly ill with pneumonia in both lungs. Realizing how serious my illness was, my Dad called Dr. Wallace in Norwich, seven miles away.

"I'll come right away," the doctor said, and he did. After examining me that night, Dr. Wallace called my parents aside and spoke with gravity.

"I'm afraid you've called me too late. There is nothing I can do. He's too far gone."

"This boy will not be alive by morning," he went on to say. "I'm sorry, but that's just how it is." With that, the doctor left our home and returned to Norwich.

My parents sat grimly by my bedside—the light of a kerosene lamp flickering in the darkness and despair of that night. Dad, now thirty-three years of age, sat staring into space, dozing occasionally. Mother both sobbed and prayed at the same time. "Please don't let my Gail die, Lord. Let him stay with us awhile longer so that he can serve You!"

It was a long, dark night for my parents and siblings. The thought of losing one of their children was a most difficult prospect to them, as it might be to any caring parent. Then, to the surprise of both of my parents *and* to Dr. Wallace, who had called around daybreak to inquire about their deathly ill boy, I had begun to rally physically some time in the wee hours of the morning and was now showing strong signs of improvement.

In retrospect, I am convinced that Satan, the devil, wanted me dead and tried to kill me through that mortal sickness. But I am even more convinced that the Eternal God had a different plan, thus I survived that crisis, regaining strength and health.

By the time I reached the age of nine, our family had moved to the eighth farm—this time to the Bently Place—where we lived for eight years before making the final move to the Johnson Place near the town of Cheney in Sedgwick County.

In 1944, at the age of twelve, I experienced my second encounter with the Lord's presence. Although I had not yet come to a saving knowledge of Christ at the time, this experience was so vivid and powerful I knew that I would never forget it. Word had just reached our family that a prominent minister had died a sudden and premature death at the age of thirty seven. His name was Rev. Robert Parham, a son of the late Rev. Charles F. Parham (known by many as "the daddy of Pentecost in the twentieth century").

Robert Parham was one of only a very few ministers that I had ever heard preach, and that was only a short while before his passing away. It was very rare for Dad to allow Mother to go to church, although she longed to be able to do so, and especially to the little Apostolic Faith Church in Cheney, commonly known as the "Cheney Mission."

Knowing that Robert Parham was to be the guest speaker on that particular Sunday morning, Mother somehow got permission to go. Louie, her oldest son, volunteered to drive her there that morning and somehow I was allowed to go with them. I don't recall Rev. Parham's sermon topic, but I still remember the handsome, dark-haired young preach to this day. I was intrigued by his demeanor, his anointed preaching, and his sweet, gentle spirit.

Brother Parham made a lasting impression on a twelve-year-old farm boy that Sunday morning. I also recall his wife, Pauline, their twelve-year-old daughter, Roberta and six-year-old son Charles sitting on the front pew that day.

When the shocking news came that Robert Parham had died, I was stunned. Shortly thereafter, while standing between two mulberry trees, feeling the shock and keenly sensing the loss of a choice servant of the Lord, suddenly I was overshadowed by the Holy Spirit. Although I did not fully understand it at that moment, in that distinct and powerful encounter I was made to know that God was laying His hand upon me for service and calling me into the ministry.

I don't recall telling anyone about this experience. If I did tell anyone, it would have been my mother. Now, the encounter I had had in the "cubbyhole" of the Richardson house at age five began to make sense to me. By some mystery, it seemed that both encounters were parts of a whole. God had my number and for reasons known only to Him, had need of me. He was calling me to go work in His vineyard!

Mother had accepted Christ as her Savior two weeks after she was married to my dad, so she was always a devout Christian and a sweet, loving, gentle person. Dad was completely the opposite. His had been a very hard childhood. His father had died when he was only five-years-old. His mother, Bethel Ott, remarried after the death of his father and his stepfather was very mean, even cruel, to him.

My dad finally left home at the age of thirteen, working for pennies a day for several different farmers and sometimes just for room and board. Somehow his difficult childhood and adolescent years had caused him to become harsh and hard-boiled; even downright mean at times. He was a big, strong, handsome man who could be very nice and loving at times, but also quite volatile and unpredictable. His quick temper and fierce anger made him a feared and dreaded father at times. That is, until he surrendered his life to Christ at age forty-two.

Mother had prayed for Dad to be saved for over twenty years. But it seemed that the longer she prayed, the more hopeless the possibility of that ever happening became. Then one Wednesday afternoon (April 10, 1946), Dad came in early from the field. He had injured his fingers on the tractor, so he'd decided to quit work early. On the way home from the field, he stopped at our mailbox to pick up the mail for that day. Among other pieces of mail, there was a flyer from the Apostolic Faith Church in the town of Cheney, seventeen miles away, announcing a revival meeting that was in progress, with Rev. James Hosler serving as the evangelist.

I was fourteen-years-old at the time and I distinctly remember Dad throwing that flyer down on the kitchen table while saying to mother, "Get the kids ready, Vera. We're going to this revival meeting in Cheney tonight!"

A freshman at Belmont Rural High School, I had just walked into the house and will always remember the amazed look on Mother's face upon hearing those words come out of Dad's mouth. With a look of both disbelief and joy, she responded, "Alright Lewis, I'll have them ready!"

In retrospect, the small drama that played out that late afternoon in the kitchen of an old Kansas farmhouse reminds me of what happened to the Apostle Peter (recorded in Acts, chapter twelve). Peter was imprisoned in Jerusalem and was condemned to die the next day. "But prayer was made without ceasing of the church unto God for him" (Acts 12:5b). When prayer was answered and Peter stood outside knocking at the gate, no one could believe that it was indeed Peter himself!

So it was with my dear mother. Her many years of praying for Dad to be saved must have seemed futile at times, but she never gave up on him. And now, at a time when she least expected it, her prayers were about to be answered!

Why I was allowed to stay at home that night I do not recall—possibly I had a high school track meet, as I was the mile-runner for Belmont High School. Whatever the reason, I did not go to the revival meeting in Cheney that night and missed witnessing the conversion of my Dad.

Two nights later, (Friday, April 12, 1946), I did go to the revival meeting with my family. I remember the forceful, anointed preaching of Rev. James Hosler and how the power of Holy Ghost conviction gripped my heart. When the altar call was given at the end of the sermon, while the congregation sang *Just As I Am*, an elder of the church, Brother Johnny Peacock, came up to me and said, "Young man, wouldn't you like to go to the altar and give your heart to Jesus?"

With strong conviction gripping my heart, I responded, "Yes, I would," as I made my way out of the pew and down the aisle to kneel at the altar and cry out to God for His salvation. I know that Christ met me there at that altar for when I finally got up and stood on my feet again, I felt clean; even holy! The load of sin and guilt in my life had been lifted from me. The following Sunday afternoon, on April 14, my Dad, another new convert (Mr. Lloyd Rhodes) and I were baptized in the Ninnescah River south of Cheney. I felt a wonderful peace as I stepped into the water to be baptized by Rev. Hosler while the saints sang "*Shall We Gather at the River?*"

That was the beginning of a somewhat up and down walk with the Lord for the next six years. During the month of August, 1946, I attended a camp meeting, along with my family, in the city of Baxter Springs, Kansas. From April 12 to that time I had slipped away from the Lord, so again I went to an altar of prayer to ask God's forgiveness for my backsliding and to rededicate my life to Him.

Shortly after returning home from the camp meeting I was asked to speak at a youth rally at the little church in Cheney where I'd been converted. I do not recall what my topic for the rally was that day, but I do remember experiencing *stage fright* for the first time!

It seemed like my knees knocked for the whole five minutes of my "mini-sermon" that first time in the pulpit. *How could I know this was just the beginning?*

Chapter 2

. . . .

THE DOG HOUSE EPISODE

I suppose that volumes could be written about my childhood and adolescent years, as about those of others, but I'll limit the inclusion here of anything that strays too far from my stated purpose of glorifying God. Perhaps the following account represents a slight departure from that resolution, but because of the somewhat comical nature of this true story I've decided to relate it in this book.

When I was about three years old, a farmer friend of my dad's gave us a cute little tawny colored puppy. We named him "Jiggs," and for the next eleven years, Jiggs was a part of our family. Whenever we moved, Jiggs moved with us. My brothers and I loved Jiggs and would do anything to protect him and make him happy.

An example of this devotion was when I decided to install a small string of tiny six-volt Christmas tree lights in Jiggs' doghouse. *With Jiggs' dog-house situated up next to our house, I wondered how I might get those lights to light up.* Then I speculated that the source of power would be the telephone line coming into our house from a pole along the road in front. I postulated that every time phones rang on the "600" line, Jiggs' doghouse would light up!

What a lucky dog old Jiggs will be! I thought.

At age eleven, it was apparent that I had a lot to learn about electricity, for I was of the opinion that the phone line would be the "positive" source of energy that I needed to light up the Christmas tree lights. I also knew that there had to be a negative (or "ground") line in order to get the results I so desired; thus I drove an iron rod into the ground next to the doghouse, then clamped an insulated wire onto it. I then connected one line of the Christmas tree lights to a wire running up to the phone line and the other line to my "ground" wire. *Voila!*

Everything was in place—all that had to happen next was for someone to use their phone on the 600 line! Or so I thought. All through the night, whenever a phone was used on that line, Jiggs' doghouse would indeed light up! What I didn't understand, however, was that after making the final connection, none of the patrons on the 600 line of the Belmont Telephone Exchange had phone service any longer!

Mr. Warrell, the owner and manager of the BTE, had driven up and down all the miles of road along which the 600 line ran—looking for anything that might be grounding out the line (like a tree limb that may have fallen across the line or a broken glass insulator on a telephone pole).

After about ten days he began calling on each residence in our rural area, checking each phone to see if it might be the one that was shorting out. Ours, naturally, was the very last phone to be checked. Now, these phones were the old box types with a crank on the side that were mounted on the wall. When the crank was turned, a magnet inside the box caused the phones on that line to ring. A combination of long and short turns of the crank indicated to all hearers who the call was for. For instance, to reach the Lewis Ott residence one would crank out one long and two shorts.

Of course, everyone's phone on the line rang every time so oft times, just for entertainment, an eavesdropper would pick up his receiver and listen to his neighbor's incoming call. For anyone on the line to call "central" (the operator), they rang (turned the crank) just one time. The magnet inside the phone box generated enough electrical energy to make every phone on the line ring, as well as the line in the central operator's office. That is, until the lights in Jiggs' doghouse were connected! Apparently the phone's magnet was not designed to light up doghouses.

Mr. Warrell opened up the phone box in our house and tested everything for a shorted circuit, then closed it back up and went back out to his service truck. Standing on the sidewalk in front of our house, he spoke to Dad grimly.

"Mr. Ott, I'm totally exasperated! I've searched for ten days trying to figure out what is short-circuiting this 600 line and I'm at a complete loss as to where to look next. I'm worn to a frazzle trying to solve this problem," he blustered.

Just after making that statement, I noticed that his eyes were suddenly attracted to the wire running down from the incoming phone line and into Jiggs' doghouse. He lunged quickly over to it and spotted the ground rod driven into the dirt with a wire leading from it into Jigg's doghouse. He then got down on one knee and looked inside the doghouse.

"Oh my God," he exclaimed. "I think I've found the problem!"

Thus, upon making that amazing discovery, Mr. Warrell and my dad both began to inspect my ingenious installation of "electric lights" inside Jiggs' doghouse. Up until that time I had stood nearby listening to the conversation between the two men, but when I heard Mr. Warrell say to my dad, "Lewis, I ought to sue you in court for all the time I've lost and for the days of misery this has caused me," I knew I was in big trouble!

Dad apologized to him several times and begged for mercy.

"I'm a poor man," he said, "I cannot afford being sued in court. I could lose everything I have if you do that."

"Well," Mr. Warrell replied, "I guess you can't always be responsible for everything your kids do, so if you'll promise me that when you find out which one of them did this you'll give him the whipping of his life, I'll let it pass this time. I'm just glad I've found the cause of the problem."

Upon hearing those words I quickly did a disappearing act, knowing that judgment was about to fall! After Mr. Warrell drove away, very tired and disgusted, but relieved, Dad looked around for me. He didn't bother to interrogate any of my brothers, any one of whom was capable of something like this. Rather, in his loud, raspy voice, he roared, "Gail, where are you?"

By this time I was several hundred yards removed from the scene of the crime. Chills ran up and down my spine when I heard Dad calling my name. Again, he bellowed, "Gail, you'd better get yourself up here to this house immediately if you know what's good for you!" Hence, I knew that this eleven-year-old boy was in big trouble!

As I timidly approached my dad, with brothers Lloyd, Lester, and Dwane looking on, he asked me, "Do you know anything about those Christmas tree lights in that doghouse and who it was that connected them to that telephone line?"

"You'd better not lie to me, either," he added.

Knowing I was caught hands down, I confessed that it had been me. Handing me his sharp pocketknife, Dad ordered me to go to one of the mulberry trees and cut off a gad (a switch, if you please!) When I returned with the switch, I handed him back his pocketknife, which he folded and returned to his pocket. Dad took the switch from me, grabbing me by my right arm and started meting out the punishment he had promised Mr. Warrell he would inflict on the guilty party.

As he switched me across my back, my buttocks, and the back of my legs, Dad said, "I'm going to teach you a lesson you'll never forget, you little devil you!" His policy was to wear the switch out until it was shredded before the punishment was considered complete. By the time he had vented his anger toward me for the doghouse episode, I believed I quite possibly would die! There were welts up and down my backside from my ankles to my neck for several days following.

Poor Mother—she could only watch through the screen door as one of her offspring was being so severely punished again. Tears filled her eyes as she hurt for me, realizing that I meant no harm when I wired up Jiggs' doghouse and connected it to the phone line. One thing was certain: I did indeed learn a lesson that I would never forget, just as Dad had promised, as he worked me over with that mulberry gad! It would take me several years, and a greater understanding of God's mercy, to unlearn it and to forgive my earthly father. "With God, all things are possible" (Mark 10:27).

Chapter 3

....

THE REVOLVING GLASS DOOR

In April 1945 I was thirteen-years-old and just about to graduate from the eighth grade at Golden Rule Elementary School, a country schoolhouse. The graduation ceremony was scheduled to be held in the gymnasium of Belmont High School, three miles away. Even with the eighth grade graduates of Belmont Elementary School combining with us for the occasion, it would be a small group. But despite how few graduates there were (six or seven), the ceremony would contain quite a bit of pomp and pageantry—something I definitely wasn't accustomed to, for sure!

My older sister Pauline, now married and living in the big city of Wichita, felt sorry for me because I didn't have a suit to graduate in, so she came out to the farm one Saturday to propose a bigger idea than I had ever heard before.

"Come on with me, Gail. We're going into town to buy you a suit for your eighth grade graduation!"

I had been to the big city of Wichita only four or five times before that day, so was excited, especially at the prospect of getting my very own new suit to wear for the graduation ceremony! It seemed like an enormously big city to me—especially compared to the town of Belmont, population 50. For a thirteen-year-old country bumpkin like myself, this was really a major event!

Pauline had always been a refined, proper young woman with high ideals, so she went over some "protocol" with me after she parked her car curbside in Wichita so we could begin the search for just the right suit for me.

"Be sure to zip up the fly of the pants before you come out of the dressing room," she told me, as well as stating other special pointers on how to act.

There was, however, one "how-to" she failed to educate me about—that was entering and exiting a large department store through "revolving glass doors!" Out in Belmont, I had never seen or heard of a *revolving glass door*, much less passed through one!

"We're going to look in Inis' Department Store first," Pauline announced confidently. It was a huge store with a large selection of clothing for people of all ages. Sis again went over the manners she expected of me as we walked from the parking place to the store. She certainly did not want to be embarrassed by her country "hayseed" kid brother in such a sophisticated place as Inis'!

Not considering that I had never seen a revolving glass door in my life before, much less entered a building through one, Pauline stepped into the first triangular, moving space in the unit as one is supposed to do, expecting that I would step into the next space as the door turned. But, to her surprise and embarrassment, I tried to jump into the same space she was in and, of course, got caught, causing the big door suddenly to *stop!*

Pauline quickly grabbed me by the arm and yanked me out of the door, trying to avoid further humiliation by this uncivilized farm boy. She kept a close eye on me thereafter and we eventually found just the right suit for me, plus a shirt and tie, which she purchased with great flourish at the store counter.

Was I ever proud of my new attire and grateful to my big sister Pauline for her kindness and generosity! Prancing around in my dandy, new "clothes make the man" attire at graduation, I felt just about like I had "died and gone to Heaven!"

Did God somehow know, even then, the life's work that He would one day call me to and clothe me with attire suitable to it? I expect so.

Chapter 4

THE BARN BURNER

roubles again seemed to plague me following my second encounter with God's Spirit—the most notable being the "barn burner" incident. It was late October 1945. My brother Dwane and I had just gotten our twelve milk cows into the large barn and were set to do the morning milking. But before beginning the milking process, we had decided to "torch" a huge swarm of flies that had clustered in a small building nearby. As we were returning to the dairy side of the huge barn, I accidentally dropped my torch next to the foundation of the building where some dry hay was sticking out between the two large barn doors. Dad, my brothers, and I had just filled the middle section of the large barn to capacity with hay a couple of months earlier in preparation for the coming winter. Hurriedly I threw the two large doors in the center of the barn open, trying to put the fire out. This was a gross mistake, however, for the oxygen flooding into the barn poured the flames forward across the dry hay. In a matter of seconds, the barn had become a blazing inferno.

Our twelve cows were all fastened in their stalls and held in place by stanchions. On the other side of the barn, four or five workhorses whinnied in their stalls, enjoying a generous helping of hay.

Just then, I panicked and in great fear ran to the house to call the Norwich Fire Department, which was pointless, at best. By the time they could have gotten there almost everything would have been destroyed anyhow. Of course, they did not come at all.

In the meantime, Dwane, two years my junior, stayed cool, calm, and collected and at once began leading the animals out of the barn—just before the roof collapsed. He was unharmed, and to his credit none of the livestock was harmed. Dwane chased the animals away from the burning barn, down the lane, and out into the pasture.

Throbbing with fear as to what Dad might do to me when he heard about this, I set out running like a deer. Mother loaded up the younger children in the family car and drove five or six miles east of our farm to tell Dad what had happened. He was doing custom work for another farmer at the time. Before Mother ever got to where he was working, Dad had seen the thick billows of smoke rising skyward and his first thoughts were, "There goes my barn up in smoke."

Meanwhile, my heart pounding wildly, I ran for two or three miles without stopping, following a creek bed in order to stay out of sight. I finally stopped to catch my breath, wondering what to do next. Since he was never one to take foolish actions like this lightly, I was fearful that Dad might beat me to death for what I had done.

Finally, I decided to go up to the house of an elderly widow woman I knew who lived alone on a small farm. After telling her my story in a frantic litany, she invited me to come in, which I did. The dear old lady tried to calm my fears by asking me questions and giving me suggestions. She offered to prepare some food for me, but I told her I wasn't hungry.

After several hours of conversation with this kind lady, I was finally persuaded to go back home and "face the music." Slowly and reluctantly I walked across fields and cow pastures back to my home. With fear and trembling I walked into our house. Mother met me at the door.

"Are you alright, Gail?"

"I guess so," I said, "but I'm afraid."

Then, Mother said to me "Your dad is lying on the bed in our bedroom. You need to go in there and let him know you're here."

With my heart pounding wildly again, I stepped into the bedroom, expecting the very worst; namely, an unmerciful beating. To my surprise, Dad didn't even get up off the bed when I walked in. He just lay there like he was stunned, gazing at the ceiling.

"Dad, it's me," I announced meekly. Without ever making eye contact, he began telling me in a somewhat subdued voice what a terrible hardship I had brought upon him as most all the winter feed for the livestock had gone up in smoke.

"I'm not going to give you a whipping for what you've done, but I am going to make you drop out of school so you can work to help make up for this terrible loss," he said.

That pronouncement was like being thrust through with a dagger. I was a freshman at Belmont Rural High School, had already made a number of friends, and most of all really liked school. High school was so much different than the elementary school I had graduated from the previous April. I was having a lot of fun and was learning the ropes of high school life, so to be told I had to drop out was a terribly disheartening thing to me. Nevertheless, I did not talk back to Dad when he informed me of my punishment.

Dad went on to say that I'd be stripped of all privileges—no more driving the car or truck; not even a tractor. In fact, he said that "anything I enjoyed doing was out."

After two weeks of hard work on the farm (mainly harvesting the fall crops), Dad finally consented to allow me to go back to school, which lightened my spirit to an indescribable degree!

Even though I dreaded the razzing I'd no doubt face from my peers when I returned, I still was happy to be able to go back to school. To my surprise, everyone was nice to me when I made my reappearance. I reckon they figured I'd been punished enough already, so no one even brought up the barn-burning episode

In order to have somewhere to milk the cows, Dad built a small shed, using lumber from a deteriorating farm building close by. Of course, I assisted him in erecting the new cowshed. Things went reasonably well between Dad and me for about a month, and then it seemed like all hell broke loose.

One evening I had driven several miles from home to pick Dad up, as per his instructions on that particular day. He had been doing custom farm work for another farmer that day.

Upon arriving at the farmer's house, Dad and the farmer were engaged in a lengthy conversation, so I had to just sit and wait for their talk to end. Mind you, I still had cows to milk and other chores to do once we were back home again, so I was getting a little antsy. Finally, after waiting more than an hour, the conversation ended and Dad and I drove home. He didn't talk to me much on the way home but told me to get to the cowshed immediately once we were home to do the milking and other chores that awaited.

I had actually skipped school that day, and wondered secretly if this now had anything to do with Dad's uncommunicative demeanor towards me. *Did he sense it somehow?* After driving my younger siblings to school in Belmont that morning, I'd driven back home to help Mother with the laundry. She could never seem to get the small gasoline engine on the washing machine started or, if so, couldn't keep it running. I had agreed to come back home and help her after dropping the kids off at Belmont Elementary School.

As I headed for the cowshed to milk the cows Dad went into the house to eat his supper. He became suspicious about Mother doing the laundry that day, noticing a clothesbasket full of clean towels, etc.

"You washed clothes today, didn't you?" he said to Mother.

"Yes, I did, Lewis," she replied.

"So how did you get the engine started on the washing machine?" he probed. When Mother didn't answer that question, his anger flared and his fist hit the table in a furious rage.

"Gail skipped school today to help you wash, didn't he?"

46

Mother began to weep as she answered meekly, "I cannot lie about it; yes, he did."

At that, Dad immediately jumped up from the table and stomped out the door, heading straight for the cowshed, where I was milking a cow by lantern light. I could hear his heavy footsteps as he approached. Somehow I sensed that I was in big trouble again—and indeed I was!

Dad flew through the door of the cowshed and without saying a word to me, lunged at me in a furry, kicking me as hard as he could. In fact, he kicked me so hard that I toppled off the stool and rolled underneath the cow I was milking, while Dad continued kicking me. All of the cows in the shed were startled and began shifting their bodies back and forth. The milk bucket went rolling, spilling all of the milk inside.

In fright, one cow stepped on the upper section of my leg as I scrambled to get out of reach of Dad's kicking work boot. The cow's foot on my leg hurt so badly, I quickly freed myself from it, jumped to my feet and grabbed a nearby pitchfork, backing myself into a corner. Holding the pitchfork firmly with both hands aimed at Dad's stomach I screamed, "Leave me alone or I'll kill you!"

I had never fought back at my dad before, no matter how hard he was beating me, but this time he had pushed me beyond my limit.

"You'd better put that pitchfork down right now if you know what's good for you," Dad said to me. I hesitated momentarily, my heart pounding rapidly, and then dropped the pitchfork, slowly pushing the tines of the farm tool into the ground. The instant I did that, Dad landed into me again, kicking me with both feet while punching me in the head with both fists.

Evidently Dad had allowed bitterness to build up in his heart toward me for the barn fire I had caused, and now he was venting his fierce anger. It wasn't a pretty scene. Dad was a big man—six feet four, 240 pounds, and exceptionally strong. On the other hand, I was a scrawny thirteen-year-old kid weighing in at about half his mass. So now that he had me cornered he continued pounding me with his fists and kicking me with his heavy work boots until I thought he'd surely beat me to death before he would stop. Perhaps an angel of mercy helped me just then as the makeshift siding boards behind me suddenly gave way to the relentless impact of the beating I was getting; thus I escaped into the darkness of a nearby wooded area.

Dad didn't come looking for me as seemingly he had satisfied his anger toward me—at least for the time being. I eventually returned to the barn, feeling half dead, but finishing the milking and other chores assigned to me. Then I tiptoed back into the house and went to my bedroom. I had just endured the worst punishment of my entire life.

In the weeks that followed, I began to allow resentment and even hatred to build up in my heart toward Dad, for I had again been grounded from going to school. My future seemed so black and futile that I had little hope concerning life itself. Up until this time I had been able to bounce back from the numerous severe punishments inflicted upon me by my dad. But this time was different. My resentment toward him began to turn into hatred. I spoke to my mother about my feelings.

"You've put up with him and his meanness for over twenty years, Mom, but I'm not going to keep taking this kind of treatment," I told her. Mother had a look of grief on her face and she began to weep.

"Honey," she said, "the old devil is trying to poison your mind. God has a plan for your life and Satan desires to spoil it."

"Gail, you've got a tender heart, so don't you allow the devil to harden it through bitterness and resentment," she went on to say. "Your dad has had a hard life and we have to understand and be willing to forgive and forget those things that make for resentment and hatred. It's our choice—no matter what happens to us—how we will respond to it—with hatred or compassion."

How accurate Mother was! Satan was indeed at work poisoning my mind with a serious root of bitterness—so much so that I actually started to entertain the idea of loading our .22 caliber

Remington rifle and lying in wait for an opportune moment when I could draw a bead on Dad's head and shoot him to death! I am, to this very day, terribly ashamed to admit that I ever allowed Satan to push me to the brink of homicide through that bitterness I was harboring in my heart. But, I am compelled to confess that I had sunk to such depths of despair and hopelessness at the age of thirteen—the same age Dad was when he left home to escape the abuse and mistreatment of his own mean stepfather.

My rage, as I recall, was not so much because of the beating I had taken that late fall evening in 1945 as it was due to the grim prospect of continued mistreatment and abuse—not only to me, but also to Mother and my younger siblings. Thus I reasoned that it would be worth whatever punishment the law might exact upon me for doing my dad in. At least the rest of my family would have a reprieve from Dad's ongoing abuse!

Oh how glad I am that I did not follow through with that evil, vindictive plot! Without doubt, it was Mother's incessant prayer for me that caused me to dismiss that evil thought from my mind.

I know I've gone to great length in relating the "barn-burning incident" and the subsequent chain of events that followed it, but I've done so with good reason. You see, it may well have been (and I am convinced that it was) that the barn-burning incident figured prominently in bringing Dad to a realization that he needed God in his life. In any case, it was only about five months later that he announced he was going to that revival meeting in Cheney at which he was gloriously saved.

By way of contrast, before his conversion, church was the last place Dad wanted to go. He had no time for such nonsense, nor did he think that Mother should waste time going to church, although she longed to worship God along with fellow believers. About the only time Mother ever got to go to church was when her younger brother, Rev. Paul Bailey, came to visit us every summer.

Uncle Paul was a Pentecostal preacher who had pastored several Apostolic Faith churches in Kansas, Texas, Arkansas, and

California. He, too, had at one time been a farmer near the town of Cheney. He was a small but muscular and wiry young man and one whom many feared. As a younger ruffian, he had whipped a number of men in and around Cheney and Norwich. Then, after his conversion and some Bible school training, he'd entered into full time ministry.

Like Mother, Uncle Paul had a sweet, loving disposition that endeared him to most everyone he met. No doubt the great change that was wrought in his life after being converted had made an indelible impression upon Dad. How could he help but notice the happy, carefree, joyful person that his brother-in-law had become after becoming a Christian, even though he usually saw him only once a year?

Heaven alone will reveal the lives and events and perhaps greatest of all, the prayers that combined to bring Dad to the day of his surrender to Christ—the day when he was genuinely saved! For now, I like to think it had something to do with a barn-burning.

Chapter 5

My Darkest Hour: A Rendezvous with Death

fter my first encounter with the Lord at the age of five, Satan had tried to destroy me. Now that I was fifteen and a high school junior—just three years after my *second* encounter with the Lord between the mulberry trees—the devil would try to do me in again. This is how it happened.

In September, 1947, I was starting center for my high school football team. I had accepted Christ one year earlier but was having a hard time staying true to Him. I had played football in my sophomore year, the fall of 1946, despite the fact that I'd weighed in at only 126 pounds, loving every minute of each game. In fact, I'd played in every game the previous year, and loved playing defense even more than offense. Now a year older, a little heavier, and stronger as well, I could hardly wait for game one!

My brother Lester would start as a varsity fullback on the 1947 team (older brother Lloyd had gone on to play football at Garden City Junior College after varsity play on the first-ever football team at Belmont High in 1946). So the Ott brothers were very much involved with tiny Belmont High School's football aspirations.

Perhaps because Dad had ruled us boys with an "iron hand" at home, I wanted to take it out on the gridiron where it was OK.

Anyhow, I was involved in or made many of the tackles for our team. I hit the opposing ball carriers fearlessly and with all my might every time I made a tackle. And, curiously enough, I never got hurt in a game—that is, until the opening kick-off of the second half of that first game.

Friday night, September 19, 1947, was to be a home game against Norwich High School, always a formidable opponent. Our team had had a light workout under the lights on Thursday night and, after the workout, several of my teammates and I decided to drive into the city of Kingman, Kansas, for a bite to eat. The only restaurant still open at that hour in Kingman was an all-nighter, which unfortunately had a dubious reputation and was known as "Ptomaine Hollow." But since we were all hungry we ordered hamburgers and French fries before going back home. Our coach had admonished us not to be out late that night so that we could be at our best for the game on Friday night.

By game time twenty-four hours later, I had a severe stomachache. I was much too sick to be playing in a football game that night, but was determined to "tough it out" and play anyhow.

"Here, take a couple of *Tums*. It'll make you feel better," the dad of one of my teammates said. I did, and went out onto the football field to play ball, staying in the game the entire first half. By half time I felt even worse but was determined not to allow sickness to keep me out of the game. As the game resumed, I took my position back out on the field.

Norwich would kick off to us, beginning the second half. The football hurtled towards me. I tucked it in my arm and headed downfield with it. Suddenly, there was a breakdown in the "interference" runners ahead of me and I was tackled by two opposing players. One hit me at the ankles and another at chest height. Losing my balance, I went down, face up. At about the same instant my helmet hit the ground the foot of a third opponent plunged into my face, stomping me squarely in the mouth.

Since 1947 was prior to the time that helmets were required to have facemasks, this part of a player's head was quite vulnerable to injury. When my opponent's shoe struck me in the mouth it tore my upper lip loose clear up to my nose. I also had a serious nose-bleed from the blow. The pain caused by that foot to my mouth, coupled with the severe stomachache that had not let up, led me to the reluctant decision to come out of the game and play no more in the second half.

Hobbling to the dressing room, I showered and dressed, then went to my brother Lester's car, feeling really sick. As much as I'd hated leaving the game, afterwards I was even worse physically. My upper lip was swollen to twice its normal size and was throbbing with pain. It seemed like the longest second half of a football game I'd ever seen, especially since my team was getting trounced!

Lester drove me home and I went to bed as soon as we got there. Dad woke me at about 6 A.M. the next morning. I was scheduled to do some manual labor for Great Uncle George.

"I can't go, Dad," I said. "I am as sick as a dog!"

"Sure you're sick," Dad said, "Too much football is all that's wrong with you. You either get up and go to work with me or you won't be playing any more football—I'll see to that!"

With that ultimatum I forced myself to get up and dress for work that day. Dad was now a Christian. In fact, I considered him to be a "fanatical Christian." As such, he was convinced that all sports were both senseless and sinful; thus he never attended any of the sports events his sons played in (football, basketball, softball, or track.)

All the way to Uncle George's farm that morning Dad "preached" to me about the nonsense and evil of sports, stating how "worldly" football was. I don't recall responding to anything he was saying. I was a very sick young man.

Upon arriving at the Allen farm, Dad went to the cornfield with his implements while I was assigned to cover up a 400-foot-long ditch that had been dug to lay a water line in. My equipment for the job was a shovel! After shoveling dirt into that ditch for about an hour I suddenly began to shiver and shake almost uncontrollably. I felt like I was freezing to death. Finally I laid the shovel down and went up to the Allen's house.

When I knocked on the door, Great Aunt Maggie answered.

"I'm sick," I told her. "I just started shivering and shaking real bad and now I feel like I'm freezing to death." She reached out her hand and felt my forehead.

"Gail, you're burning up with fever. You'd better come inside and lie down. I'll cover you with some warm quilts," she said.

As I lay there shivering, almost violently, I was aware that there was something seriously wrong with me. I was thinking that there must have been ptomaine poison in that hamburger I had eaten in Kingman the previous Thursday night. What I did not realize, nor did anyone around me that morning know, was just how deathly ill I really was. As I continued to shiver and shake, Great Aunt Maggie finally brought a large "feather-tick" and placed it on top of the quilts. That seemed to help a little bit at least.

When evening finally came, Dad and I headed back home. He and Mother were planning to go to the town of Harper to do the grocery shopping. All the way home Dad preached at me again.

"You'd better get your heart right with God and give up all those worldly sports or you're going to die and be lost for all eternity," he told me. But I was so terribly sick I didn't respond to anything he said to me.

Home at last, I went straight to bed and my five younger siblings went to town with Dad and Mother to shop for groceries. Stores were always open late on Saturday night in those small towns in order to accommodate the farm people and, of course, to get their business.

After returning home from the town of Harper, Dad mixed up a solution of "Epson salt" which he had purchased there and told me to drink it, which I did. Then, shortly after drinking that solution I felt a strange sensation in my stomach. It was as if something *snapped*. Little did I realize that my appendix had burst!

After this, I did realize some relief from the terrible pressure and ache that had been building for more than twenty-four hours. After that strange sensation and a bout of diarrhea-like symptoms, I went to bed and fell asleep.

The next morning (Sunday, September 21, 1947) Dad came to our bedroom to see how I was doing. I told him I had felt some better after drinking his Epsom salts solution the night before, but that my stomach was aching again and that I was really sick.

"You ought to get out of bed and get dressed so that you can go to church with the rest of us this morning," he told me. The church in Cheney was seventeen miles away, but felt ever farther in my condition.

"I'm too sick to go to church today, Dad," I said.

Mother suggested that maybe she should stay home with me that morning, but Dad protested sharply.

Nonsense! It's that *football* he's been playing that's made him sick. He's going to have to learn sometime how worldly and sinful that is!"

Mother decided it wasn't a good idea to stay home with me, so she went to church with the rest of the family. But my brother Lester informed Dad that he was not going to church with them.

"Gail is bad sick," he said, "and I'm not going to leave him here alone."

Knowing that there was no use arguing with Lester (now seventeen, very strong, and somewhat stubborn), Dad conceded.

"Whatever you say," he replied, and then went on to church with Mother and the younger kids. Not long after my family left for church in Cheney I called my brother Lester into the bedroom where I was.

"Lester, I'm deathly sick," I told him. "I'm afraid I'm going to die. You'd better take me to see a doctor in Kingman just to be sure."

"I will," he responded. "You get dressed and I'll pull my car up to the sidewalk and pick you up so we can get going right away."

The pain was now so severe that I had almost lapsed into a state of unconsciousness. I managed to get into his car and we started out toward Kingman. About three miles from home we crossed a railroad track and as we did, the slight bump nearly caused me to pass out with pain. This frightened Lester noticeably.

"Maybe we should stop in Belmont and let Coach Junkins know what's going on," he said, though I was now unable to respond to him.

Coach Junkins was genuinely concerned and insisted that he drive us on to Kingman, thus I got out of Lester's Model "A" Ford coupe and into Coach Junkins' roomier sedan. I laid down in the back seat and soon we were on the road again—heading speedily to Kingman. Again, as we crossed over another railroad track, I felt a bolt of pain that nearly took my breath away.

It was almost high noon as we arrived in the city of Kingman. As we drove down the "main drag" on the south side of town, headed toward Memorial Hospital, my brother spotted Doctor Harry Haskins' medical office on the right side of the street. It was a hot September day and for reasons unbeknown to us Dr. Haskins had gone there to attend to some matter and was only going to be there for a few minutes, thus his office door was open.

"Let's stop here," Lester said to Coach Junkins, "and I'll run in there and see if he'd be willing to see Gail!" So Coach Junkins parked there in front of the doctor's office and Lester jumped out and ran inside, quickly telling Dr. Haskins about me.

"Bring him in," the doctor said, "and I'll take a look at him."

It was at once obvious to this doctor that I was very sick.

"Help me get him up on my examination table," the doctor said, "so I can check him out." Lester then gently lifted me up and placed me there. Dr. Haskins loosened my belt, pulled my shirt up and tapped on my stomach with his fingers a few times, then shouted, "Oh my God! Get this boy to the hospital at once. His appendix has ruptured. There's no time to waste!"

Dr. Haskins arrived at Memorial Hospital right alongside of us and thus went into the receiving room to alert the staff as to the dire emergency. When Lester informed him that Stella Settle, the superintendent of nurses there, was Dad's sister and our aunt, the doctor said to him, "Can you go get her right away?"

Lester left immediately to go to the Christian Church to get Aunt Stella. He had noticed their family car in front of the church as we drove past it on our way to the hospital. Notifying an usher that this was an emergency, the man went into the sanctuary and whispered to Aunt Stella.

"I'll come immediately," she responded as she got up out of the pew and quickly made her way out of the sanctuary and into the foyer where Lester was anxiously waiting for her.

By the time Aunt Stella and Lester arrived at the hospital I had been admitted and was in a side room being prepped for an emergency appendectomy. Since I was a minor, one of my parents' consent was required before the surgery could be performed.

"Do you know how to get in touch with Lewis?" Aunt Stella asked Lester.

"They're at church in Cheney," he responded.

"Well, see if you can contact them by phone and tell your Dad it's a dire emergency. There's no time to waste!"

Lester got to a phone quickly and put in a call to the Apostolic Faith Church in Cheney. Of course, there was no phone in the church building but there was one in the parsonage next door. The operator called the number and the phone began to ring. After it rang seven or eight times my brother began to panic.

"Would anyone hear that phone ringing?" he wondered. When the operator told him, "I am sorry, there's no answer," he urged her to let it keep ringing.

Since it was an unusually hot day that Sunday a window had been opened near the back of the sanctuary on the side next to the parsonage. The pastor's son happened to hear the phone ringing and ringing, so he decided to run over to the parsonage and answer it.

When C.W. Aikens picked up the receiver and said, "Hello," Lester breathed a sigh of relief as he asked the boy, "Could you go and get Lewis Ott and have him come to the phone? This is a *life or death* emergency."

Quickly, C.W. ran back to the church and summoned Dad to the phone. When Dad said, "What is it, Lester?" he told him it was imperative that he get to the Memorial Hospital in Kingman as fast as he could.

"Gail's appendix has burst and if they don't operate on him soon he's not going to make it!" Lester told Dad.

"It's seventeen miles from Cheney to Kingman," Dad told Lester, "but I'll get there just as fast as I can!" With that, Dad quickly summoned Mother and the younger children out of the church service.

"There's no time to lose. Gail is dying and they can't operate on him until we get to the hospital to give our consent," he told Mother. Once on U.S. Highway 54, Dad drove the family car at breakneck speeds, upwards of a hundred miles per hour. Mother feared for their lives and so was praying for Divine protection as they sped toward Kingman . . .

Before continuing the account of the greatest crisis of my life I choose to pause to reflect upon two unquestionable miracles of Divine Providence. First, what was the probability of Dr. Harry Haskins being in his medical office on that Sunday—with a window of time not more than fifteen minutes? Did he just "happen" to go to his office that forenoon to check on something and thus be there at the exact time that Coach Junkins and my brother Lester arrived in Kingman with a desperately ill young man?

Was it mere coincidence that he left his door open after entering his office a few minutes earlier? Was it just "chance" that my brother Lester happened to spot that medical office door open at that exact time? *I don't think so!* In fact, I'm absolutely certain that it was an act of Divine Providence! The Lord God, in His great mercy, had coordinated these events in precise time—and no one can ever convince me otherwise.

Then, too, what were the chances that September 21 would be such a hot day that a window next to the parsonage would be opened for ventilation, thus allowing the pastor's son to hear the continual ringing of the phone in his house? In my mind this was also unquestionably a matter of "Divine Intervention!"

Back to the scene at Memorial Hospital in Kingman. When Aunt Stella arrived at the hospital she came at once into the room where I was, bent over me, took my hand, and tried to settle my fears.

"You're going to make it, Gail," she assured me. She had talked with Dr. Haskins as she came in, who'd informed her that he had called Dr. Ned Burkett to come and assist him with the surgery since I (the patient) was merely "hanging on by a thread."

Aunt Stella was a very loving and caring person who had distinguished herself as one of the most competent nurses in the state of Kansas. She would be assisting the two doctors performing the surgery and assured me that they were both very good, competent doctors. She knew that my parents were on their way to Kingman and would soon be there.

"As soon as your parents get here and sign the consent form we can get started with the operation," she told me.

In a short while my parents did arrive and came immediately to my room. When Aunt Stella told Dad that he needed to sign the consent form, he asked what kind of anesthesia they were planning to use. When Aunt Stella told him that the only sensible anesthetic to administer was a "spinal block," Dad balked.

"I won't consent to that," he told her.

"Why won't you, Lewis?" she asked.

"Because it could cause him to have back problems for the rest of his life. I insist that they put him out with ether," Dad went on to say.

"Lewis, don't be so stubborn," Aunt Stella said. "Gail's resistance is already so low. He would never be able to recover if we use *ether* as an anesthetic." Then she added, "His blood count is already sky high." (It was at 2800 if I remember correctly.)

Finally, after Aunt Stella had convinced Dad that she and the doctors knew more about the right procedures than he did, he agreed to sign the consent form. Then he asked if he and Mother could have a few moments alone with me before they took me into surgery. Advising them to come into my room one at a time, she consented and left the area. So, while Mother waited outside my room in the hallway, Dad came into the room and started to talk to me.

"Gail," he said, "you're in critical shape. There is a chance you won't make it through this surgery. You'd better give your heart to the Lord while you can!" For some reason I just turned my head toward the wall and did not respond to his appeal. Finally Dad went out of the room and I heard him speak to Mother out in the hallway.

"Vera, you'd better go in there and talk to that boy. He won't listen to me." So Mother came in and stood by my bedside. She sweetly took my hand in hers and calmly said, "Gail, honey, wouldn't you like to give your heart to Jesus? He loves you and cares for you!"

When I looked up and saw the tears in her eyes and that sweet but concerned look on her face, all of my resistance broke down and I said, "Yes, Mommy. Will you pray with me?" As she prayed with me I again asked God to forgive me of my sins and to save my soul. Soon a sweet peace came over me and a calm assurance seemed to flood my whole being. Fear was instantly banished. I knew that the Lord Jesus Christ had heard my plea and had forgiven me of all my sins!

As soon as Mother went out of my room two nurses entered it with a gurney. Once I was on that gurney they wheeled me to the operating room, where the two doctors and Aunt Stella were waiting for my arrival. As soon as I was moved from the gurney onto the operating table I was rolled over onto my left side and asked to "hump" my back as much as I possibly could. When the desired posture was achieved one of the doctors injected the "spinal block" serum into my spinal area (about the middle of my back as I remember it).

After the injection I was rolled over onto my back again. A "blinder" screen was fitted around my mid-section, apparently to prevent me from seeing the doctors cut me open. The doctors kept telling me to "wiggle my toes." After several directives to that effect, I said, "I can't even feel my toes any more!" That was their signal that the operation could begin.

During most of the surgery Aunt Stella stood at my side, holding my hand and watching my countenance. The only time I felt the doctor's knife was when they'd cut through a blood vessel. My parents waited in a hallway outside of the operating room, praying for me and trusting for the best while bracing for the worst. I do not recall the duration of the operation—perhaps thirty or forty minutes. I do, however, remember Aunt Stella exclaiming, "Oh my goodness, that's awful!"

This was after the doctors had cut all the way through to my stomach cavity, where the infectious substance was located. That "gangrene" began gushing out of my side, flowing onto the operating table and on down to the floor—approximately a *quart* of it! At one point, I glanced down at the floor on my right side and saw that intensely unpleasant looking "puddle." It was a sickening sight to say the least!

Little did I know, but the two doctors performing the surgery had almost no hope that I would make it through the procedure. As stated a few weeks later, both actually expected that I would expire during the operation. But, of course, they continued working on me as long as I still had vital signs (heartbeat and breathing).

It was during this time of severe crisis that I experienced a spiritual encounter of another kind. Although I could not see them, I began to sense the presence of what I have come to catalogue as "demons of death" dancing around my body there on the operating table. For a moment fear gripped my heart. I momentarily became oblivious of the surgery that was being performed on me, and of the presence of my Aunt Stella and the two doctors who were operating on me. There must have been six or seven of these revolting, evil beings in the room at that time. It was as if they were just *waiting* for me to die.

But just as these wicked spirits were lurking around my body in cruel anticipation of my death, I suddenly sensed the presence of the Holy Spirit. I did not hear an audible voice, nor did I see any written words, but at that instant, as the Blessed Holy Spirit overshadowed my whole being, I sensed the sudden departure of those "demons of death" and then experienced a vivid reminder that God had called me to the ministry.

"Oh, Lord God, if you will spare my life I will answer your call to the ministry," I prayed. I'm not sure whether I did or did not utter these words out loud because at that moment I scarcely had strength enough to breathe. But I know that in my spirit I said and meant them.

At the exact instant that I made that promise to God, all fear incited by those revolting, wicked demons of death vanished. And although I was by no means "out of the woods" with reference to my physical condition, I never again feared dying as a result of my ruptured appendix and the subsequent health hazards that accompanied that whole ordeal. The Holy Spirit had supernaturally emptied me of all fear of dying!

Because the two doctors who had performed the appendectomy on me held virtually no hope whatever that I could or would survive, based on numerous other cases similar to mine, they did not bother to sew me up as per the normal procedure. Hence, I bear in my body to this day the physical evidence of that faithless decision—a hideous, ghastly-looking incision!

As good doctors do, the two men talked with my parents after the surgery, admitting they were amazed that I survived the operation. They also cautioned them that the worse was probably yet to come. Apparently in those days, when medical science was not even close to being as advanced as it is today, it was quite common that after the space of some forty-eight to fifty hours following an appendectomy a severe crisis would occur that was almost always fatal. In fact, a neighbor had died just a few years before my ordeal in this same manner—some forty-eight to fifty hours after the surgery, in a syndrome first marked by high fever, then delirium and finally *death*.

Sure enough, in about the space of forty-eight hours, this whole scenario began to unfold in my body. My parents were summoned and told the grim prospects.

"It's just a matter of time," Dr. Ned Burkett told my parents, "and he'll be gone. He doesn't have even *one chance in a thousand* to survive this crisis. There is nothing more we can do but to try to make him as comfortable as we can until he succumbs."

He further told my parents, "If you have any relatives living any distance from here who might want to attend his funeral, you might as well contact them and set a day for his memorial service. He simply is not going to make it!"

Of course, that was a terrible prognosis for my parents to hear, but they knew the doctor was just being honest and realistic with them. Dad went to the nearby telephone office and called his mother in Seattle to tell her the grim news. She called the train station in Seattle and made reservations to come to Kansas to attend my funeral, to be held a few days later.

My brother Lloyd, a freshman at Garden City Junior College in Garden City, Kansas, was also contacted concerning my condition. He left immediately to drive home, hoping to see me once more while I was still alive. But in spite of all the gloom and despair, my parents contacted the saints from their church in Cheney, as well as some from the sister church in Kingman. They all came to "pray the prayer of faith" for me!

On the afternoon of Tuesday, September 23, 1947, my condition suddenly worsened. I had been taken from the intensive care unit to a private room and until that afternoon seemed to be doing reasonably well.

My first symptom was a rapidly elevated fever. In a short while, the fever shot up to 105 degrees and *stayed there* for several hours. I was in a state of delirium most of the time, but I do remember coming out of that state of being for several minutes. I furtively looked around me and there in that hospital room, forming a circle around my bed, were my parents, several ministers, and some lay members holding hands and interceding for me, determined to pray the "prayer of faith" on my behalf. There must have been a dozen of them fervently and earnestly praying that God might spare my life. I lapsed back into delirium for some time still, yet the fever eventually broke and I started to rally.

Aunt Stella returned to the hospital and was keeping a vigil over me, carefully monitoring and recording my condition. By the following morning, I was 100 percent better and continued to improve daily.

Looking back on that decisive night when I was supposed to die, I can still see in my "mind's eye" all those godly, praying saints in that hospital room. They almost seemed more like angels than human beings. Their faces seemed to glow with radiance as they "did battle" for my very life! I was informed later that they prayed there in my room non-stop for more than an hour and I am totally convinced that it was the effectiveness and power of those prayers that "snatched me as a brand from the burning."

My brother Lloyd told me in recent years of the terrible, sinking feeling that came over him when Dad called for him at the college in Garden City that Tuesday afternoon, informing him that, "your brother Gail is dying and not expected to live through the night."

I remember sensing the presence and power of God that night in the hospital room, although I remained in a state of semi-unconsciousness most of the time. I know that it was only the effectiveness of intercessory prayer that brought me through that dark crisis. After a twelve-day stay in the hospital, I was released and assigned to the care of Aunt Stella. She and Uncle Weldon graciously took me into their home in Kingman to care for me and nurture me back to health. In fact, they invited me to stay with them for the balance of the 1947–1948 school year, which I did.

Aunt Stella had to convince my parents that to go back out on the farm, where there was no electricity or running water and where no readily accessible medical attention was available, definitely was not the right thing for me at that time. She explained to them that it would take at least six months for me to return to normal and regain health and strength. Realizing that all I had just gone through was no ordinary ordeal, they reluctantly consented for me to remain in Kingman, which I did.

For my part, the decision to stay in town created feelings of mixed emotions. On the one hand, I knew that life would be much easier for me living in town with my aunt and uncle. On the other, I knew I would miss my family, even though they lived just sixteen miles away. What I would miss most was being in high school with my brothers, Lester (two years older) and Dwane (two years younger). Of course, I knew that football and basketball would be out of the picture for me the rest of that school year, so this made the decision a little easier.

I did not relish the idea of having to switch to another, much larger high school, but that was part of the arrangement. I would have to adjust to it. I'd been out of school for five weeks due to my illness so when I enrolled at Kingman High School on Monday, October 27, 1947, I had a lot of catching up to do. This was further complicated by the fact that I had to drop some classes I'd been taking at Belmont High School that were not offered at Kingman, then take up some new classes at the new school. I somehow made it, finishing my junior year of high school in Kingman, and then heading home.

My life and faith had been forever changed at this crossroads. Now, with my health and strength regained and pretty much back to normal by September, 1948, I found myself back on the farm and a senior at Belmont High School, preparing to graduate in May, 1949.

Chapter 6

My Jonah Days: Running from God

The first year out of high school I bounced around from one temporary job to another. My family had moved from the Bently Farm in Kingman County to the Johnson Farm near Cheney in Sedgwick County, Kansas, where they lived and farmed until our parents' passing from this life.

In the summer of 1950, I finally landed a permanent job with a wealthy farmer and worked for him steadily up through October of 1951. On this place I was hired to work six and a half days a week for the great sum of twenty-five dollars per week, plus room and board (but not laundry service).

Regrettably, by this time I had drifted away from the Lord and, little by little, had slipped into a life of all-out sin. I had become almost a chain smoker and had also started drinking alcoholic beverages—first beer, then wine, and finally hard liquor. Although I knew this was wrong, I somehow seemed trapped by the devil and found myself doing things I had vowed never to do.

The summer of 1951 was a "turning point" in my life. During those many hours working out in large, open fields on a tractor, I had sufficient time to think about and reflect upon the direction in which I was headed. At times I would find myself singing out loud,

I suppose in an effort to drown out the haunting memories of the crisis times in my life and of the vows I had made to God during those times that I would serve Him and would answer His call to the ministry.

I had certainly come to realize the truth of God's Word, which declares, "The gifts and callings of God are without repentance" (Romans 11:29). Thus, just because I had turned to my own ways and had walked away from God and had put His call on my life on the "back burner," He still did not lift that call nor rescind it. Of course, this haunted me almost continually.

Now it so happened that my oldest brother, Louie, and his family had returned to Kansas from Seattle, Washington, where they had lived from January, 1949, to that present time. It was their summer vacation and their first time back home since leaving Kansas. I must confess that before Louie moved to Seattle in 1949 I was ashamed to take any of my friends around him. That was because he was so foul-mouthed. He seemed to curse and swear with every breath he breathed—especially in four-letter words. Although I am ashamed of myself for it now, I regarded Louie as an "ignoramus," even though he was a brilliant auto mechanic.

During their first two and a half years in Seattle something wonderful had happened to Louie and his wife, Irene. A friend had invited Louie to a home Bible study. Just how it was that he ever *consented to attend* a home Bible study was nothing short of a miracle, for up to that point in his life (age twenty-six), he had only darkened the door of a church a few times, much less attended a home Bible study.

I am told by the Christian gentleman who eventually led Louie to accept Christ, a brother named Bob Iverson, that Louie would sit and argue with the Christians who were conducting that home Bible study until he was becoming obnoxious. Brother Iverson told me that God had spoken to him and said, "You've got to love this man," which he said was not easy to do at the time.

On the night that Louie stopped arguing and surrendered his heart and life to God there was a glorious celebration among the attendees (as well as the angels in Heaven!) Not only was Louie gloriously saved, but he was also supernaturally delivered from the tobacco habit! For even though he had stopped smoking six months previous to this, the craving for nicotine had never left him—until *that night*, that is.

After his conversion Louie and his family started attending an independent Pentecostal church on Seattle's South End. It was called, "The Church by the Side of the Road," and was situated along U.S. Highway 99 at South 148th Street. As Louie and Irene increasingly *sold out to God* in the weeks and months that followed his conversion, blessing began to be poured out upon them—not only spiritual blessing, but material, as well. Incredibly, they built a new house (debt-free) and paid cash for a new Chevrolet just before coming on vacation to Kansas that summer of 1951.

I will always remember driving to my parents' home from the farm where I was working to see Louie and his family. My brother Dwane was with me since he was now working for the same farmer I was. When we arrived at Dad and Mom's house, a "new" brother greeted us. If I had not known Louie by his physical appearance I would never have recognized him! There seemed to be such a glow on his countenance that he was almost like an angel to me.

Without any explanation on his part or questions on my part, I at once knew that Louie had been genuinely saved and was now a totally changed person. For the first time, in his adult life at least, I heard him talk intelligently. It seemed strange but great to me not to hear him cursing and swearing, as had so often been the case in the past. Now *I* was the one who had to be careful what came out of my mouth because, sad to say, I had fallen so low that I often breathed out curse words, especially when I was angered by someone or by a situation.

Louie now talked about the blessed life of being a Christian, free from sin and strife. He seemed to be so happy and carefree, and that first visit made an indelible impression on me. It was very apparent that my dear brother had found the "Pearl of Great Price!" It was also vividly apparent that life had real purpose and meaning for him. All of this made a deep-seated impression on me, and even though I was not yet willing to surrender my heart and life to Christ, I knew for sure that what Louie and Irene now had was exactly what I needed and wanted in my life! Not that their spiritual experiences were superior to those of my parents; it was just that such a dramatic change had happened in their lives in the two and one-half years since I had last seen them.

As I visited with Louie that Sunday afternoon in August 1951, he invited me to come to Seattle.

"You'd love the Pacific Northwest," he assured me. "And there are a lot of good-looking girls in our church," he went on to say. "And you've got a place to stay if you decide to come. We have a spare bedroom for you!" I thanked Louie and Irene for the invitation and assured them that I'd give it some "serious thought."

After Louie and his family left to go back to Seattle I decided I was going to do some reforming. First of all, I decided I would quit smoking. And I did—for two weeks. It was a fierce battle; one that I lost. The craving for nicotine was relentless—hounding me every waking hour. Finally, in mid-afternoon on a hot August day, while working in a field with a big Case tractor and a field cultivator, even that "fizzled" out.

A bolt had loosened on the cultivator, allowing a disc to turn sideways. I stopped to correct the problem. While pulling with all my might to tighten the bolt, the wrench slipped off and I scraped the knuckles of my right hand on the frame of the cultivator. The flesh was torn open and my hand bled profusely—the searing pain acute at that moment.

That's when I lost my cool. My short-lived reformation crumbled. Although I am ashamed to admit it now, in a fit of temper I started swearing, kicking dirt up into the air, and even kicking the tires and fender of the tractor. After ranting and raving, I finally settled down. Now I was trying to find the wrench I had thrown as far as I could when the accident first happened. I am not sure if I ever found that wrench, but I do know one thing—I had to have a cigarette. Without a doubt, it was the continual craving for nicotine that had me on edge and flighty that day. Even though I had not puffed on a cigarette for two weeks, the craving had not gone away and demanded gratification!

So, at the risk of being fired from my job, I disconnected the tractor from that cultivator and went a mile to the farmer's house where my car was parked. With no springs on that big Case tractor, it was like riding a bucking horse across the rough terrain of that grain field. The machine could travel at seventeen miles per hour in high gear!

As I approached the turnout onto the county road and made a left turn with the tractor, I suddenly spotted a partially used cigarette that some smoker had flipped out along the roadside. I quickly slammed on the brakes, jumped off of the tractor, and hurried to pick up that "snipe." It was only about one-third gone, so there would be enough left to at least temporarily satisfy my nagging desire.

Of course my intention was to break off the burned end of the cigarette and then light the other end (the end that the previous smoker had had between his lips).

"What an idiot," I then thought. "I don't have a match to light that cigarette butt. Why did I stop to pick it up?"

Just then an idea struck me—why not pull up a dry weed along the road, break off the roots, and then dip it in the gas tank, which I did. Then, removing a spark plug wire and allowing the spark to jump across while holding it close to the spark plug and, at the same time, holding the gasoline-soaked end of the weed near the spark, it would ignite the gasoline on the weed and thus provide me with a "light!" *What a slave I had become to the tobacco habit!*

After lighting up my "snipe," while smoking away on it, I again set the big tractor at full throttle and was soon at the farmer's house. Upon arriving in the area where we parked the farm implements, I slammed on the brakes, shut off the engine, and parked the tractor. My next move was to jump into my car, start the engine, and take off for the town of Murdock (seven miles away) to buy a carton of cigarettes.

God in His mercy must have protected me, for I soon kicked my little 1940 Plymouth convertible up to speeds as high as one hundred miles per hour—on dirt roads! En route to Murdock, driving foolishly and dangerously, I could see a "rooster tail" of dust behind me that must have been one hundred feet high.

Upon arriving in Murdock I went to a small grocery store where I had a charge account and purchased a carton of Kool cigarettes and then headed back to the farm to continue my work in the field. My return to the farm where I worked was at a much safer speed than the trip into the town.

From that August afternoon in 1951 until the day I was supernaturally delivered from the tobacco habit I was more bound than ever by the nicotine craving. I was definitely addicted! Three hours was about the maximum time I could go without "lighting up." At times I would light up another cigarette with the fiery end of one I had been smoking when it got too short. *What a terrible, binding habit smoking is!* Looking back, I often realize that the cigarette actually did the smoking. I was just the "sucker!"

My younger brother Dwane and I had actually bought the 1940 Plymouth convertible together although I had traded my previous car in on the Plymouth, hence I usually referred to it as "my car," even though we were co-owners. It was registered in my name. One Saturday night in September, 1951, Dwane and I went to Murdock and picked up a friend, then decided to go "cattin' around."

"Why don't we go to Zenda," our friend, Lonnie, said. "We can buy some 'home brew' there." Home brew is illegally made and marketed beer. It was unlawful to sell beer in the state of Kansas if it contained over 3% alcohol—except in liquor stores, but we were too young to buy booze there anyway.

At the moment, Lonnie's suggestion seemed like the thing to do, so off we went to Zenda in quest of some "home brew" (something I had no experience with before nor have I since!) Besides the allurement of the "home brew," there was a dance in the town of Zenda that night, so our plans were to go to the farmhouse where the home-brew could be purchased, buy some of the stuff, and then go into town to take in the dance. Perhaps we could meet some girls at the dance—so we thought.

We located the farmhouse where the home brew was being sold and pulled into the long, U-shaped driveway, stopping in front of the house. As soon as we got out of the car we heard someone yell out.

"Who are those SOBs in that green convertible?" It was obvious that a rowdy bunch of young men were there buying home brew and looking for a fight, so we decided we'd better just get on out of there as we were greatly outnumbered.

Just as I jumped into the driver's seat and the other two guys landed in the passenger's side, one of the young men threw a can of beer, which struck the sun visor just above my head (we had the top down that night). We soon took off from that farm, but had crashed our Plymouth convertible between two other parked cars, nearly ripping the right rear fender off. We were soon being hotly pursued by a carload of angry young men bent on "working us over," especially after we had crashed into two vehicles in our haste to get away from the place. This gang of guys had been drinking and were eager for a fight.

Because the half-torn-off right rear fender was dragging against the rear tire on that side of the car, we could not reach a high speed. The guys in the other car soon caught up with us and were trying to force our car off of the road and into a ditch.

We reached U.S. Highway 54 and turned right toward Kingman. In a short while the loose fender had cut completely through the casing of the tire, causing a blow out.

When we pulled off of the road and stopped the car, the angry gang pursuing us pulled up and stopped behind us. Dwane and Lonnie jumped out of the car and took off running *for dear life!*

At that point, I got out of our car and went to the rear of the vehicle intending to face this gang, not knowing whether they might beat me to death or what they might do. I felt I had no other choice. *At least Dwane and Lonnie escaped the wrath of these thugs,* I thought.

"Don't you guys think you've done us enough damage already," I said, as the two carloads of guys jumped out and rushed towards me.

"Look at my car," I said. "It's wrecked. Now, is it going to make you feel better for a whole gang of you to unfairly attack one person?"

Now, even though that whole ordeal was a foolish and ungodly situation we had gotten ourselves into, I have to believe that only God in His mercy caused all of these young men to turn around, get back into their cars, and leave without striking me even once. As soon as they left, I started calling for Dwane and Lonnie.

We had stopped just before a bridge, thus were close to a river. Lonnie soon emerged from the shadows of the bridge, but no Dwane. I panicked momentarily. As I continued calling out his name. I finally heard him calling out, "Help! I'm drowning!" He had stumbled, then rolled down an embankment and into the edge of the river. He was in the water, holding onto a fence post, when Lonnie and I located him. After freeing him from the fence (his clothes were caught in the wire), we went back to our car to assess the damages.

We were sick inside when we saw, in the moonlight, what a mess our little car was! After taking the wheel off where the tire had blown out, we put the spare tire on the car and drove slowly on to Kingman, about five miles away. Of course, we first pried the badly damaged fender away from the tire enough to prevent the same thing from happening to the spare as had popped the other tire.

Arriving in the town of Kingman we found a body shop that was still open, so we pulled up in front, then summoned the owner to come out and give us an estimate to repair the damages.

Although the estimate included a complete paint job, as well as a new cloth convertible top, it amounted to a sum equal to what we had paid for the car just a couple of months earlier. We had no insurance on the car, so we'd have to pay for all of the damage done that night with our hard-earned cash. We left the car with the body shop and found someone to take us back to our respective destinations, miserable and defeated.

In essence, Dwane and I had blown our whole summer's wages—earned by working long, hard days during wheat harvest—in one night of folly and nonsense. What a shame! We agreed to pay the body shop owner one hundred dollars down payment on the work and then thirty dollars per month until the balance was paid. He, in turn, agreed to have the car ready in two weeks.

It was after that incident and night of madness that I really began to seriously think about the direction my life was going and about how far from God I was getting. Somehow I began to realize at that point in my life that God was trying to get my attention. For the first time since my *rendezvous with death* at Memorial Hospital in Kingman four years previous to this, I was starting to face the fact that I'd better make up my mind as to what I was going to do about the call of God on my life. Though I had never considered refusing to acknowledge or to reject that call altogether, yet I was procrastinating, dangerously so, and at last I was beginning to come to grips with the folly of continuing to go my own way.

It was just a few days after that "night of horror" near Zenda that my brother Lloyd came to visit me. He and his wife Erna had just returned from a trip to Seattle to visit Louie and his family. At the time they were in Seattle (September, 1951), Billy Graham was conducting an evangelistic crusade at Seattle's Civic Stadium. Since Louie had previously agreed to serve as an usher for the crusade and had taken the training for same, he went to the crusades each night. For whatever reason, Lloyd and Erna had declined to attend any of the night services with Louie and Irene, yet were deeply stirred by the awesome reports they brought back after each night's service.

Neither Lloyd nor I had ever heard of *Billy Graham* before, so on that night when Lloyd came to visit me (having heard of the "night of horror" Dwane and I had experienced a week earlier), we sat in his car talking at length about our lives and the direction we were both headed at that time. He, too, had once had a genuine experience with the Lord while staying with our Uncle Paul in Center Point, Texas.

Still deeply stirred about the Billy Graham Crusade in Seattle and the fact that movie stars, doctors, lawyers, etc., were coming to Christ in those crusades, we both agreed that we needed to reconsider the claims of Christ on our own lives. The conversation with my brother Lloyd that night was yet another indication that it was *high time* for me to get serious about the vow I had made to God on the operating table in Kingman as the "demons of death" danced around my body, desiring to end my life right then! As terrible as that "night of horror" near Zenda had been, it seemed that the "*last straw*" with reference to the direction my life was now falling into place.

Shortly after Lloyd's visit that night I decided conclusively that I not only *should*, but also *would* make a major change in the direction my life was headed at that time. Underlying that decision was the haunting remembrance of the vow I had made to God on that operating table in Memorial Hospital in Kingman, Kansas, that Sunday afternoon of September 21, 1947. Indeed, it was high time that I stop ignoring (or more accurately, postponing) God's call on my life and get turned in a different, right direction!

The decision I soon made was that I would give up my farm job and move to Seattle, Washington, to start a new (or at least different) life for myself. I talked this over with my brother Dwane, hoping that he might decide to come along with me on this new adventure. At the time, he concurred with my decision and agreed to accompany me in the move to Seattle. We notified our employer of our decision. Mr. Kostner seemed somewhat stunned. He had come to trust Dwane and me and leaned heavily on us to attend to all of the work that needed to be done. Now, suddenly, he was without any employees. He suggested that I probably was desirous to get married and that a farm job wouldn't be very appealing to a prospective bride, so he made me a very attractive offer if I would stay on with him.

There was a vacant house on a 160-acre plot of land that he owned. It was situated just one-half mile east of his home.

"I'll have that house completely remodeled for you and will also let you have the crops from that quarter-section of land if you will stay on with me," he offered. Of course, I won't deny that this was a very appealing offer to a nineteen-year-old young man. However, I did not flinch nor hesitate to say, "No, thank you," to him.

"Then, how about if I sweeten the offer enough to tear down that older house and have a brand new house built there for you. . . . Then would you consider staying on with me?" he asked.

"No, Earl," I replied. "It's very gracious and generous of you to make me such an attractive offer. I really feel honored and flattered by such an excellent offer," I said. "But even if you were to double or *triple* the offer, I would still decline. I'm sorry, but my mind is made up. I'm going to move out to Seattle, so I'll be ending my employment with you come November 12."

At that point Mr. Kostner had a bewildered look on his face. He couldn't believe that anyone my age would turn down an offer like he had just made to me.

"What more can I say? It looks like you've pretty much made up your mind to move off to Washington State. We hate to see you go, but we can't stop you, so we hope it all goes well for you. However, if you should happen to change your mind, just let me know. My offer still stands."

Although I had only worked for the Kostners for a little more than a year, I had become almost like a family member there, so admittedly it was somewhat of an emotional time (at least for me) when my last day with them came and I would have to tell them good-bye. I had lived in their beautiful home with them, eaten at their table, shared in family conversations, etc.; thus there were sentimental ties that would be broken on parting day. This would not be easy . . .

After that final day of our jobs on the farm, Dwane and I began making preparations for the drive to Seattle—saying good-bye to friends and relatives, getting our car ready for the trip, etc. We were to leave on Monday, November 19, so we had only one week to attend to all of the necessary details.

On Saturday, November 17, Dwane came to me and informed me that he had changed his mind and would not be making the move to Seattle with me. He had met a young lady in Kingman and had fallen in love with her, so he'd decided to stay there in Kansas.

Dwane's sudden change of mind necessitated a new agreement with reference to our 1940 Plymouth convertible. We discussed the matter briefly.

"You pay off the balance still owing to the body shop in Kingman and you can have the car," Dwane said. "I'll get me another car, OK?"

Even though I wasn't very happy with him "chickening out" on me, I agreed to his suggestion and let him know that I would be leaving on Monday, the 19th, with or without him.

On the brisk Monday morning of November 19, 1951, I drove from my parents' home near Cheney to Kingman to see my brother Lloyd off. He had been drafted into the Army and was leaving by bus from Kingman with a number of young men who were to be inducted into military service at Camp Crowder, Missouri.

After saying so-long to Lloyd, I dropped by my Aunt Stella's house to say good-bye to her, then headed back to my parents' home to load up my belongings, bid farewell to Mother, and get on my way. Saying good-bye to my precious mother was by far the hardest farewell for me. She embraced me, kissed my cheek, and then held my right hand tightly as she admonished me.

"Honey, don't let Satan harden your heart. You've got a tender heart and the devil is bidding high for your soul. Just remember, God loves you and has a plan for your life."

With tears streaming down both our cheeks, I bade Mother good-bye and drove away. As long as I live I will never forget the look of love on her face as with her hand she waved good-bye to me until my car was out of sight. I will forever be grateful to God for allowing me to have such a wonderful, loving mother as she was!

To avoid winter road conditions I chose to take a southern route west to San Diego, California, and then head north to Seattle along the western seaboard. Because I had a girlfriend in Los Angeles, I would be spending a few days in that area before driving on north. I had met this young lady that summer, 1951, when she was in Kansas visiting relatives in the town of Murdock and had become quite fond of her. Thus, a stop in L.A. was a must for me!

Along the way en route to L.A. I stayed in motels in Wichita Falls, Texas; Carlsbad, New Mexico; and Blythe, California. My new life had begun!

Arriving in San Diego that first afternoon was quite an experience for me as it was my first time ever to see an ocean. The Pacific looked magnificent and intriguing. I arrived at my destination in Los Angeles around 5:00 P.M. that Thursday evening. I had figured out where Bernadette (my girlfriend) lived, so I checked into a hotel not far from her home. After getting cleaned up and dressed, I gave her a call. When she asked where I was, I told her the name of the hotel and the location.

"I can't believe this," she exclaimed. "You're only a few blocks from our house." She could hardly believe that I had made it there without getting special directions.

That evening we went to a movie, then out to Long Beach to ride the roller coaster. Friday night was "party night" at her home, usually spent with a number of family friends (and, of course, me that particular Friday night). Her younger sister, Terri, was quite disappointed that Dwane had not come along with me. She was hoping to be his "date" for those few days.

Saturday night found me all dressed up in my navy blue suit and bowtie—all set for a big date and night of fun at the Aragon Ball Room, dancing the night away to the "Champagne Music" of the Lawrence Welk Orchestra! It was fun, yes, but back in my hotel room there was a feeling of emptiness deep down inside. The call of God on my life was still there, strong as ever, thus a feeling of dissatisfaction and the sense of being *unfulfilled* haunted me.

Bernadette and her family (sister Terri and their mother—their father had perished when his ship was sunk by the Japanese in World War II) were devout Catholics and went to mass on Sunday morning. I was invited to go with them, but declined. Sunday night would be our last night together as I would be leaving for Seattle early on Monday morning.

After returning from mass Bernadette called me at the hotel suggesting some afternoon activities. We drove all over L.A. that afternoon—to Hollywood, Santa Monica, Pasadena, etc., ending up at Griffith Park. After visiting the planetarium and observatory there, we parked and just talked for awhile. Bernadette informed me that she was "madly in love" with me and hoped that I was also in love with her because she wanted to marry me.

It was at that point in our brief courtship that I had to break her heart, or so she claimed. I told her that it had been a serious mistake on my part to allow the romance to go as far as it had gone because of the fact that she was a devout Catholic and I was of a Protestant, evangelical persuasion. I further informed her that I had the call of God on my life for the ministry and that she definitely would not fit into the picture.

"I'm sorry," I said in short, "but it is over!" At that, she began sobbing almost uncontrollably, clinging to me tightly.

"I just can't live without you!" she said.

"Oh, yes, you can," I assured her.

At last I drove her to her home, walked her to the door of her house and (at her request), kissed her one more time, then bade her farewell as I turned and went back to my car. She waited on her porch, watching me drive away as I waved a final "so-long" to her. Soon I was out of her sight and, essentially, out of her life. Why? Because the call of God was weighing heavily upon my consciousness and I knew that I had done what I needed to do.

Early Monday morning, November 26, I checked out of the hotel after calling home to let Mother know where I was and that I was leaving Los Angeles, heading northward, bound for Seattle. I had made a promise to Mother that I would call her before leaving the Los Angeles area and was keeping that promise. I was very glad that I had called her, for in doing so I learned that my brother, Lloyd, had been sent to Camp Roberts at Paso Robles, California. Since I would be driving right through Paso Robles, I determined that I would try to get onto the base to see Lloyd.

It was with caution and a little fear that I drove up to the gate of the camp and told the military police guard that I would like to visit my brother who had just been sent there a few days prior to my arrival. It was during the Korean War, thus security was tighter than usual. But, after checking my ID and asking me a few questions, I was given clearance to enter. The guard told me which building I would need to check into in order to find out the barracks Lloyd had been assigned.

Lloyd was definitely *surprised* and also happy that I'd stopped to see him.

The only area we were allowed to visit in was the latrine, and we had only one hour for that purpose. Among other subject matters that Lloyd and I discussed during that hour was our brother Louie in Seattle. Although Lloyd was equally impressed with the great change that had taken place in Louie's life as a result of his conversion, he cautioned me to beware of "fanaticism," which he considered Louie now bordering on.

When our hour was up, I had to move on, so I bid Lloyd farewell and proceeded on my journey northward.

When I drove into the driveway of my brother's home at about 9 P.M. on that Thanksgiving evening both Louie and his wife Irene were somewhat astonished that I was able to find their house, especially at night, since neither Lloyd nor my parents had been able to do that when they'd visited earlier that year.

After greeting one another, Irene offered her hospitality.

"Boy, are you hungry?" she asked—to which I answered, "Do birds fly?"

"Well then, come on out here into the kitchen. There's plenty of turkey, dressing, mashed potatoes and gravy, along with other food items, including pies," she said. Irene then warmed up the food, left over from their Thanksgiving dinner with her parents, and I sat down and ate to my heart's content.

Finally around midnight we were all ready for bed. I was shown my room and, after unloading my belongings from the car, retired for the night.

"I'll have to leave early for work in the morning," Louie told me. "But you sleep in as long as you want to. You've come a long ways alone, brother!"

Chapter 7

· ·

COUNTDOWN TO SURRENDER

I t was the first of December, 1951. Knowing I was addicted to tobacco, Louie had told me that I could smoke in my bedroom, but requested that I not smoke in any of the other rooms of the house, to which I readily agreed. There was noticeable anxiety on my part concerning the next day, Sunday morning, and the inevitable invitation to God's house it would no doubt bring. Indeed, Louie soon invited me to go to church with him and his family but assured me that I was not required to do so.

"But," he said, "there'll sure be a lot of young ladies in our church who will be disappointed if you don't go with us!" Apparently he and Irene had been telling the young women of the church that I was coming to Seattle and, hopefully, would be coming to service with them. At that time, Louie was co-leader of the youth group. He was well-liked and respected by the young people there.

Well, after thinking about my brother's kind offer and comment, I did go to church with Louie and his family that Sunday morning—all decked out in my "Glen" plaid suit and flowered tie! I must confess that I was more "eyes" than "ears" that morning. I had seated myself about two-thirds of the way back in the sanctuary, along with Louie and Irene, and was, for the most part, an observer. Most of the eligible girls of the church were singing in the choir so I was able to look them over and, likewise, they could also see me sitting there alongside my brother. The hundreds of hours I'd spent on tractors out in the fields of Kansas had caused my skin to be very tanned, something that seemed to have special appeal to the girls!

I recall picking out several good-looking females in the choir that I thought I'd probably be interested in, especially a brunette whose name was *Barbara Bagby* (yet went by the nickname, "Bobbie"). Although I did not date her until a year and a half later, she would eventually become my wife.

For some reason a young lady, who happened to be Bobbie's best friend, had persuaded Louie to "fix her up" on a date with me. The occasion was a youth Christmas banquet at a very nice restaurant called "The Green Parrot Inn." Ironically, Bobbie had been asked by the co-youth leader to be his date for that banquet. That young man, Art Morlin, a student at Seattle Pacific College (now *University*) would become my best friend and colleague in ministry—and also would eventually marry Bobbie's older sister, Joan. It was Bobbie and Art's only date. As for me, I sort of felt obligated to continue seeing Bobbie's best friend after that Christmas banquet—at least for a few weeks.

Back to that Sunday morning service at "The Church by the Side of the Road," a large, independent, Pentecostal church. One thing that immediately caught my attention was the Presence of the Lord in that place and the powerful anointing of the Holy Spirit that could be almost palpably felt there. This was not unfamiliar to me. I had been exposed to that kind of atmosphere and ministry back at the little Cheney Mission in Cheney, Kansas, as well as at the camp meeting I'd attended with my family in Baxter Springs, Kansas, in 1946. Now, since my heart was not right with God at the time, I was gripped with Holy Ghost conviction as Rev. Frank McAllister preached God's Word that morning. Still, I did not respond to the altar call at the conclusion of his sermon.

In Bondage to Tobacco

That Sunday morning of December 2, 1951, was the beginning of a great change in my life. It was the start of a practice of attending church regularly—something I had not done for several years. It was, indeed, a step in the right direction for me. Regular youth services were held at the church on Sunday evenings an hour prior to the beginning of the evening church service. So, with Louie being co-leader of the youth department, I started going to those meetings and then staying for the evening church service. It was not easy for me to do since I was bound by the tobacco habit and could go about three hours maximum between cigarettes, otherwise tormenting anxiety and craving for nicotine ensued. The few times I had to go longer between "light ups" I'd become fidgety and my stomach would seem to knot up, making me feel miserable.

This went on for several weeks (all the way through the month of January, 1952), but I continued attending services each Sunday. I kept telling the Lord, "*Next* Sunday night I'm going to surrender my life to You." When "next Sunday" rolled around, I'd repeat that promise—*Why?* Because I was bound by the "demon of nicotine" and could not see how I could withdraw from the habit, having tried and failed the summer before in Kansas. And although no one had told me I could not be a *child of God* and be a *smoker* at the same time, I somehow had this concept keenly in my mind. Thus I kept procrastinating with reference to surrendering my life to the Lord God.

During the week, between Sundays, Louie and I engaged in many serious conversations about the Christian life, God's claim on our lives, and about the call of God that I knew was upon my life. As I look back, I am still amazed at the wisdom and understanding that my brother possessed at the age of twenty-seven. I had many questions ("hang-ups," to put it more accurately), but Louie seemed to have an answer every time that I could not refute! He was a tremendous help to me—truly God-sent!

"Don't be concerned about your smoking habit, Gail," he'd tell me. "God can deliver you from it in an instant of time. He did that for me, and He'll do the same for you whenever you are ready to put your trust in Him!"

These serious conversations became almost a nightly thing for several weeks. I had worked at a couple of temporary jobs before landing a good, permanent job as a warehouse manager in the second week of January. So, usually each night after our evening meal, we would sit around and discuss spiritual matters.

I had told Louie that the next time I went to an altar I wanted it to be forever—no more "up and down" or "in and out" experiences. We talked often and quite extensively about my concerns in this regard. In the meantime, the young woman I had been dating informed me that she felt compelled to tell me that she could no longer continue the courtship because, "The Bible says not to be unequally yoked together with unbelievers."

"I understand and respect you for acting according to your own convictions," I told her. "So let's agree to let bygones be bygones."

After I took her home that night, driving away from her house, I actually felt *relieved* because she wanted to be more serious about our relationship than I wanted to be. I certainly wasn't interested in or ready for matrimony, hence I felt "free again" after our breakup.

But, the breakup was short-lived on her part as she called me the next day at my place of employment, crying her heart out, asking me to forgive her for what she had done and beseeching me to take her back again as my girlfriend.

"I can't talk about it right now," I said finally. "How about I come see you tonight? We can park somewhere and talk it over in the car." She agreed and the phone conversation ended. By the time I picked Elsie up at her home that night my mind was made up.

"I think we should leave it this way," I said. "Let's just go our separate ways." And so, that was the end of the relationship.

Wrestling with God: The Dream

The following Thursday evening (after the break-up with Elsie) I came home from work very tired. Since my sister-in-law Irene did not have dinner quite ready, I told everyone I'd like to lie down on my bed and rest for a little while, if they didn't mind.

"No problem," Louie responded. "We'll call you when it's time to eat."

With that, I lay across my bed and soon fell fast asleep—*but not for long*. While lying there, I had a disturbing, even frightful, dream that startled me into wakefulness. In fact, I literally jumped up off the bed, coming down on the floor on my feet with a "thud." It seemed to shake the house, so Louie came running into my bedroom to see if I was OK.

"I guess so," I said, "but I just had a terrible dream and it startled me so much I literally *jumped up* off the bed."

"Do you want to tell me about your dream?" Louie asked.

"Well, I guess so," I replied, rather reluctantly. "In my dream I saw that terrible night of horror north of Zenda, Kansas, back in September. It was as if I were seeing the whole scene unfold on a giant movie screen until I felt as if I were literally experiencing that horrible nightmare all over again. But the scene suddenly changed," I continued. "What came next was really scary."

"What do you mean by that?" Louie interrupted to ask.

"Well," I continued, "It was as if I were now looking through a very thick glass when suddenly a tragedy happened. I'm not sure if it was a car wreck or something else, but I saw mangled bodies, gaping wounds, and dripping blood. Do you think this might be a warning from God?" I asked Louie.

"It might be," he answered. "What do you think?"

"Probably so," I said rather cautiously. After a moment of silence, Louie said to me, "Boy, it looks to me like God's got your number! Why don't we get down on our knees right here and you call out to God for mercy and salvation. He's just waiting to forgive you of all your sins and to make you His child again, Gail!"

I hesitated to respond to Louie's suggestion. My heart was pounding because there was a war going on inside of me. On the one hand, the "demon of nicotine" seemed to be screaming in my ears: *But how are you going to do that? That craving for tobacco will hound you to death. You'll never be able to give up your cigarettes!* On the other hand, God's Holy Spirit was speaking to me strongly: *Now is the time of salvation . . .*

Finally, I looked over at my beloved brother who was noticeably eager to pray with me that I might surrender my life to God and be delivered from all of my bondages. "Yes, Louie," I said, "I know I ought to do that and am quite sure I will do it sometime soon. I'm just not quite ready yet."

"Well, you know I'm not going to try to push you," Louie assured me, wisely. "But I want you to know that I'm ready to pray with you and for you when you do make that decision!"

To that I agreed, and then we sat down to eat our dinner. The subject was not discussed further at the dinner table, but my precious brother knew down deep in his heart that the moment of surrender was close at hand for me. And indeed it was! In fact, after considering the dream I had had that Thursday evening of January 31, 1952, over and over again for the next three days, I realized that I was nearing a "point of no return," a time when it would be "now or never!"

On Sunday afternoon, February 3, 1952, Louie asked me if I would deliver a car to his youth group co-leader, Art Morlin.

"You can take the car down to his house and then ride with him to the youth service this evening," Louie insisted.

"I guess I can do that for you," I responded, "After all, you've done a lot of favors for me, so why not?"

Before leaving to deliver the car to Art I went into my bedroom, closed the door, and lit up a cigarette, waiting as long as I could before leaving for Art's place with the car. In fact, I smoked that cigarette down so far that the fire nearly burned my fingers as I held it between the thumb and index fingers of my left hand. The butt of that cigarette was only about half-an-inch long when I suddenly dropped it on the floor, then crushed it with the sole of my shoe to extinguish it.

Next, I methodically laid my cigarette package out on top of a chest of drawers . . . with one cigarette protruding out of the opening about an inch . . . in anticipation of "lighting up" again as soon as I got home from church that night. I had also opened a book of matches so that I could "light up" quickly once I was back in my room that night, which meant that I was already putting off surrendering to the Lord until the next Sunday night (February 10.) I knew that after going without a smoke for three hours at church, by the time I got back home again I'd be about to have a "nicotine fit," so I was getting in position for a "quick fix" once we arrived home.

After my careful preparation for a smoke later that night, I took off for Art's house with the car he had purchased from Louie. Louie phoned Art to alert him that I would be there with the car shortly and would then ride to the church with him. When I got to his house, Art was waiting for me. We left for the church immediately as it was almost six o'clock and time for the youth service to begin.

"God is in this place!"

Following the youth service that night, Missionary Lester Morgan was to be the guest speaker in the Sunday night church service. Brother Morgan had planned to tell his incredible story of being delivered from certain death in the "town plaza" (city square) of Bogota, Columbia, where he had been tied to a stake with wood, old tires, etc., piled all around it and was soon to be doused with gasoline and ignited! But Lester Morgan would have to return a few weeks later to tell this incredible story of deliverance, for after being introduced to the congregation by Pastor McAllister, it was just if he and God had planned that part of the service together beforehand. It happened on this wise:

Once the pulpit was turned over to Brother Morgan, he stepped to the podium, looking to the right and then to the left. Without a single word of greeting, he slapped the top of the podium with the palm of his right hand and said, "Folks, I feel God in this place!"

That would be all that Missionary Morgan would say from the pulpit that night for at the exact instant he said that, the "fire fell" from heaven! Even an avowed atheist would have been unable to deny the supernatural Presence of God that suddenly fell upon that church body. It was as if a "cloud of glory" had descended upon that congregation. Suddenly people began to weep and cry out to God—some in praise and adoration, others in agony of soul. Soon the altar was lined with people weeping and crying out to God at the same time. Once the altar was filled, next the choir loft filled up with worshippers and seekers; then the seats all across the front of the sanctuary became altars of prayer, praise and worship! Certainly I had never been in an atmosphere like this before.

My brother Louie was among the seekers and worshippers who went forward to kneel and pray at the altar. He had been sitting beside me. How long Louie stayed at the altar, I do not know. But I do recall Art's mother coming to me and inviting me to go to the altar.

"No!" I quickly barked to her. She was startled and jumped back for a moment, and then preceded toward the front of the church to try to find a place to pray.

By this time almost everybody in the sanctuary was crying out to God in a great concert of prayer, praise, and worship. I must have "stuck out like a sore thumb" in that service. While seated close to the right aisle of the sanctuary, about two-thirds of the way back, a "war of the worlds" was going on within my being. I certainly knew that God had my number and that His Spirit was striving to draw me to a place of decision. Thoughts were racing through my mind—the dream I had had on Thursday night; the promise I had made to God on the operating table at Memorial Hospital in Kingman, Kansas, on that Sunday afternoon of September 21, 1947; the call of God to the ministry that was upon my life, etc. And, of course, that package of cigarettes lying there on top of the chest of drawers in my bedroom back at Louie's house was looming large.

In short, it seemed that there was an auction going on and my soul was the merchandise being bid upon. The devil was bidding high for me: *You'll lose all of your freedom! Your life will be so dull. You won't have any more fun. All you'll do is just go to church all the time!*

While others fervently prayed and cried out to God all over the sanctuary, Louie suddenly stood to his feet, walked down the aisle towards me, and then seated himself on my left side. He didn't say a word to me; not at first, anyhow. He just sat there with his face in his hands as if he were praying silently. Then he lifted up his head, put his right hand on my left knee, and said to me, "Boy, don't you think it's about time you go up there to that altar and get your share of this?"

At the exact instant that Louie made that gesture, as clear as if it had been spoken by an audible voice, these words came to me: "It's now or it's never!"

"Now or never" definitely meant "right now!" Just what never meant, I did not want to learn; however, I knew it did not mean a "blessing." The struggle was half over the moment I stood to my feet. As I literally ran forward and then slid into the altar—like a baseball player sliding into second base to avoid being tagged out. The hardness and resistance that had been building up in my heart for so long literally melted away, as if it had been a chunk of ice that had just had a torch turned on it. As I hit the altar bench, tears streamed down my cheeks and I cried out to God in agony of soul for His forgiveness of all my sins and backslidings and for cleansing by the Holy Spirit of all the "filth" that my spirit had collected in those four-and-a-half years since I had departed from the Lord. And, oh, how faithful and gracious the Heavenly Father was to hear my cry!

Just how long I stayed there at that altar, I don't know—perhaps an hour or more. Not only did I ask for forgiveness, cleansing, and restoration, but I also talked to the Lord about the call upon my life for the ministry, beseeching Him to keep me true for the duration of my life. I knew that I never wanted to fall into the devil's trap of backsliding again!

What an awesome work the Blessed Holy Spirit wrought in my life on that Sunday night, February 3, 1952! When I finally got up and stood on my feet, I felt like a brand new person. The air seemed fresher. I felt clean through and through. All around me were godly Christian people who were laughing and crying at the same time, who, one by one, came forth to hug me and to encourage me in my new walk with the Lord. Truly, it was "the night of nights" for me!

My sister-in-law, Irene, was not feeling well earlier and had stayed home from church that Sunday night. The moment Louie and I walked in the door she knew that something fantastic had happened—*and indeed it had!* Irene rejoiced with Louie and me as we related to her all that happened in the service that night.

I feel compelled to say that the nearest I can come to complete accuracy in describing that *night of nights* is to characterize it as a "blaze of Holy Ghost Glory!" Since that night I have been in numerous services in which "heaven came down" and touched many lives (including my own, of course), but never have I been in one quite the equal to that one! It was indeed a sovereign, holy move of God. *Period!*

One of the first things I did when Louie and I arrived back home was to go into my bedroom, turn on the light and then, with a deliberate, almost violent move, seized the package of cigarettes on top of the chest of drawers, literally crushing them. With a powerful grip, and mangling them in my hand, I said out loud, "I denounce nicotine and cigarettes in the name of Jesus Christ!" I then made this declaration: "By the grace of God, I will never put another cigarette between my lips!"

At the very instant I made this declaration, I knew that I was truly set free from a bondage that had held me captive for over four years! And my deliverance included freedom from the torment of withdrawal pains, also! *Praise God!*

My only test, or temptation, came on Monday morning as Louie, Irene, Delores, Jim, and I sat at the breakfast table before Louie and I would leave for our workplaces. We had been remembering the glorious night before as we ate together. Then, just as I finished eating my breakfast, I caught myself reaching into my shirt pocket for a cigarette. I had done this for so long after each meal that I was doing it simply by rote. For a split second the craving for nicotine made a last ditch attempt to further enslave me. But at that same instant my spiritual guard went up and I blurted out loud.

"Satan, I rebuke you in the name of Jesus Christ! I am now the property of the most High God and you have no more claims on my life; therefore I will never again smoke another cigarette as long as I live!"

With that response to Satan's temptation, my deliverance was complete. It was final! And, I can truly testify that I've never had a desire for a cigarette from that day forward. Truly, this was a supernatural deliverance for me—so much so, in fact, that if I am ever subjected to tobacco smoke (or even to nicotine on another person's breath) it makes me nauseated. I hate tobacco with a passion and still rejoice on occasion that the good Lord completely delivered me from its bondage.

By God's grace, I had been renewed in fellowship with Him.

Chapter 8

· ·

NEW LIFE IN CHRIST

When I drove to my job on Monday morning the whole world looked better to me. The skies looked brighter, the grass looked greener, and other people looked different to me. I now saw every person as a candidate for Christ's wonderful gift of salvation.

Arriving at my workplace, I went to the office to see what my assignment for the day would be. Truly, that job was a blessing from God, though it was quite seasonal. As warehouse manager for the Laclede-Christy Company, I had hundreds of free hours each month. The product was fire-clay bricks, mortar, etc. Sometimes we would go two weeks with no business. Then when orders would come in, I had to prepare pallets to fill them and then load them on a truck, or several trucks, with a forklift. It was a "feast or famine" type of business.

Orders usually came in the many thousands of dollars, but came fewer in-between. Still, someone had to be there to fill them. Many days I would be in the warehouse alone (just me and the Lord!); hence I had "paid time" during which I was permitted to read and study my Bible. And, when I say, "Read the Bible," I do not mean a chapter a day, but rather whole *books* per day. I mostly read the

New Testament to begin with. I read the entire Gospel of John on the first Monday after my re-dedication, as there was no business for the company that day. In fact, there was no business that entire week, so I literally "ate" the scriptures, as my spiritual appetite was very strong. I suddenly had an intense hunger for the Word of God.

Another thing I did on that Monday, February 4, 1952, was write a twenty-eight page letter to my parents, telling them in detail about my conversion and supernatural deliverance from the tobacco habit. To the day she died, that letter was one of Mother's "treasures." After her homegoing, my family gave that letter back to me, so I now have it in my "archives."

By the end of the week I had read a good part of the New Testament. Each time I sat down to read the Bible I would first bow my head and, in a simple but sincere prayer, ask the Lord to help me understand His Word as I read. I knew even then that I was not reading just an ordinary book. This was God's Holy Word and I would treat it with reverence, taking care never to place anything on top of my Bible.

Not only did I read and study the Bible by the hours, but I also built myself a small altar there in the warehouse where I could kneel and seek the Lord in prayer. A personal conviction had gripped my heart that the Word of God was the food for my hungry soul and that prayer was the water for my spiritual thirst. Because I had decided to follow hard after the Lord, I could sense that rapid growth was taking place in my inner being.

Friday, February 8, was a special day. It was my twentieth birthday and I was now happier than I had ever been in my life. I was twenty years old in the natural, but only five days old in my new walk with the Lord; hence I had two birthdays in one week! The following Sunday, February 10, was another glorious day in my new life with Christ. A lay preacher, Brother Bud Grasley, who is now with the Lord, was a guest speaker in the evening church service at our church. His topic was "The Baptism of the Holy Spirit with the Evidence of Speaking in Other Tongues."

I had had some knowledge of this experience and had heard several godly people at the little Cheney Mission in Cheney, Kansas, speak in heavenly languages as the Holy Spirit moved upon them. I remembered how it seemed like the hair stood up on the back of my neck as I witnessed (and heard) this spiritual phenomenon and I knew that I wanted to have that experience for myself someday. Now that *someday* had arrived, so I listened intensely, with great interest, to every word as Brother Grasley explained that this wonderful blessing that was experienced by the saints in the days of the Early Church was still valid and available to modern-day saints who would earnestly, fervently, desire to experience it. For sure I knew that was me. I wanted the experience of the Baptism and was determined that I would *not be denied.*

At the conclusion of his simple but very informative message, Brother Grasley invited any and all present who had never received this blessing and who were desirous of experiencing the infilling of the Holy Spirit to come forward and sit in the seats on the front row, directly in front of the podium.

I was quick to respond, hence was the first to come to the front to be seated, as he had instructed the seekers. Five others soon joined me there. Brother Grasley asked those who had already experienced their "Pentecostal blessing" to come forward to lay hands on the six seekers and pray for them to receive this wonderful Baptism of the Holy Spirit.

Unlike the other five seekers, perhaps, I first sought the Lord for an experience of entire sanctification. I wanted to be a totally clean vessel for the "White Dove of Heaven" to come and fill. My desire was also based upon teaching I remembered hearing at the little Cheney Mission Church and had heard my parents discussing. Evidently the Lord honored my sincerity as I prayed for that experience of sanctification as a definite work of grace in my life because I felt a witness in my spirit that it was, "Petition granted!"

Next, I fixed my spiritual focus upon that marvelous experience of the Baptism of the Holy Spirit. I was fully determined not to get up out of my seat until I had received the experience, even if

I were still there the next morning! And, again, my gracious Lord saw the sincerity of my heart and my intense hunger for that experience for soon I was no longer speaking English, but was clearly speaking fluently in a heavenly language, worshipping and glorifying the God of my salvation!

I am told by those who gathered around me that evening to lay hands on me, praying and agreeing with me that I might receive the experience I had come seeking, that my face shone with a radiance that was extraordinary. In just a few minutes I was completely lost in the Spirit and for the space of more than an hour I continued to glorify and magnify the Lord in the Spirit realm.

When I finally came "down out of the glory clouds," it seemed like I was walking on air. But each time I tried to speak in English I kept going back into that heavenly language. Truly, this was an awesome experience that I will never forget nor shall any skeptic ever be able to convince me that it was not a valid, biblical experience! I left the church that night quite late, feeling "endued with power," even as Jesus had promised it would be. I would add, emphatically, that this endowment has remained in full force throughout the subsequent years. That "endowment of power" has been the key to any success I have enjoyed in now more than fifty years of full-time ministry.

After that wonderful Sunday night service finally concluded, I was asked to "preach" in a service the next night at a Masonic retirement home in Zenith, Washington. The young people of the church had been conducting a Monday night service at that home for a number of years and were looking for a volunteer to share the Word with the group that evening. They invited me.

I could have said, "Oh no; it's too soon. I'm still a babe in Christ." But, knowing that God had called me to ministry and that I had wasted too many years already, I said, "Yes, I'll give it a try, and if God will help me, I'll make it through!"

And so on that Monday evening of February 11, 1952, I made my second attempt at preaching (my first attempt was at age fourteen in Kansas). My topic was "Reading and Studying the Bible,

God's Word." It was something I had been doing for one full week already and so it occurred to me that I could now "speak out of experience." I remember emphasizing the need to ask the Holy Spirit to reveal "nuggets of truth" as we read and studied God's Word and believe that He did.

That speaking engagement was the beginning, for me, of over fifty years of preaching the Gospel of the Lord Jesus Christ. In those early days, I made a vow to God that I would walk through every door opened to me for preaching His Word. I further promised the Lord that I would turn down no invitation to preach His Word unless the Holy Spirit should forbid me to go there. Only once in fifty years have I turned down an invitation to preach in a certain place because I felt a definite "check" about going there.

Because of that vow early in my walk with the Lord, I have preached in almost every conceivable place and situation—in churches, nursing and retirement homes, in jails and prisons, in schools and colleges, on street corners, on "skid row," in tents, brush arbors, stadiums, open air, in homes, and in hospitals. You name it and I've probably preached there! Why? Because of the vow I made to God. And, I can truly testify, to His glory, that He has faithfully confirmed His Word as I've preached it all over the U.S.A. and throughout the world, with signs following.

His Visitation

It was Wednesday, February 20, 1952, when I accompanied my brother Louie and Brother Grasley to a special service at a church in Renton, Washington. Louie drove and Brother Grasley sat in the front passenger seat. Brother Grasley was to be the guest speaker. I sat in the back seat of Louie's car for that short trip of a few miles. While Louie and Brother Grasley conversed in the front seat as we traveled along, I suddenly seemed to be in a trance, overshadowed by the Holy Spirit. I'm uncertain of the duration of that experience, but I was definitely aware of the presence of the Holy Spirit and knew that a message was being conveyed to my heart at that time. For those few moments I became oblivious to the conversation between Louie and Brother Grasley.

I did not hear an audible voice, nor did I see a vision, but I did receive an intelligible and indelible impression (a message) from the Lord that was crystal clear. In essence, the Lord assured me of His call upon my life to preach His gospel and then He revealed to me (or made me to know) truths from His Word that I should concentrate on proclaiming. These concerned: 1) *faith* to believe for the miraculous because His Son, Jesus Christ, is the same yesterday, today, and forever (Hebrews 12:8), and, 2) the *immanent return* of the Lord Jesus Christ to the earth. Not that these were to be the *only* truths that I was to proclaim, but I was to be faithful to proclaim these truths and not to neglect them. I also was shown things to come in the last days before Christ's second coming that I would either experience or witness. These were: 1) miraculous, divine *healings* of sickness, disease, deformity, infirmity, etc., 2) reoccurrence of *angelic visitations*, 3) incidents of *miraculous transportation*, and (4) *the dead raised* to life again.

Being only seventeen days old in the Lord, that revelation brought the fear of God into my heart in a new dimension. I certainly did not want to be guilty of doubting these things revealed to me, right there in the back seat of Louie's car that night and, by the same token, I knew this was not an experience to publicize, at least not at that time. So, I kept these things in my heart, resting assured that in due time I would realize the fulfillment of all those things shown to me in the Spirit on that day.

As the days and weeks went by, I continued to read and study the Word of God and to seek the Lord in prayer with great intensity. I was beginning to receive numerous invitations to preach in youth services, at rest homes, at skid row missions, etc. Original friendships began to fade and new ones to develop.

Within two months of my conversion it became apparent that the Lord was drawing the young man, Art Morlin, four months my junior, and me together. We began meeting together, sharing our vision of ministry (as Art also felt a definite call to the ministry), discussing possible plans for the near future, studying the scriptures together, and seeking God together in prayer. In a short while camaraderie between Art and I developed like unto that between David and Jonathan of Old Testament times—one which is still intact half a century later! Our hearts became "knit together" until it seemed that we were inseparable.

Oft times when Art and I would withdraw to some quiet place we would discuss our hearts' convictions, the call of God on our lives, and other spiritual concerns and thoughts. Never once did we argue or disagree concerning our views, aims, and purposes. Art was perhaps the only person with whom I shared the revelation I received in the back seat of Louie's car on that night of February 20. He told me that he, too, had received similar revelations from the Lord.

Oft times on Saturdays, when other young people were out finding ways to have fun (playing games, snow-skiing, going swimming, etc.) Art and I would go out on a hillside somewhere or to some other secluded place and there spend hours seeking God in prayer, beseeching Him for His direction and blessing on our lives. We attended many revival services and special services at other churches in the Seattle area, especially the Bethel Temple Church in downtown Seattle. Of course, we were always in our own church at the appointed time, realizing the scriptural injunction that as stewards of the manifold grace of God, we were to be found faithful.

As the weeks went by we realized that we were truly growing rapidly in the grace and knowledge of the Lord and that we were becoming increasingly stronger in the Lord and in the power of His Might.

It wasn't long before Art and I began making plans to attend a Bible school as we were now becoming anxious to answer the call of God on our lives to the ministry. Since I had known of a Bible school in Baxter Springs, Kansas (my dad had attended there a semester or two in the late 1940s or early 1950s), we reached the decision that we would at least pursue the possibility of attending there in the fall of 1952.

This was a Bible school with a unique philosophy that especially appealed to Art and me. For one thing, it was a school with the Bible as its only (or at least "*main*") textbook. The fact that it was a "faith" operation and no tuition was charged—one that relied on the freewill love offerings of Christian people of like faith and convictions—appealed to us most. If the dean and faculty of that school perceived that someone had a definite call of God to the ministry and was desirous of attending that Bible school as a means of preparing to answer that call, they could attend without charge. Too, the school had only about four months of classroom teaching; then the ministerial students would go out "into the field" to put to practice what they had learned.

Prayer, everyone seeking God for the unfolding of His Will for each individual life, was also an integral part of the school's philosophy. Thus, it was strictly a Bible school. No accreditation was offered, just intense study of the Bible and ministerial philosophy to prepare students for the preaching of the Gospel. All of this appealed to Art and me, as did the fact that it was a relatively small school with opportunity to really know others and be personally discipled.

Christian farmers and lay people would donate food (beef, pork, chickens, eggs, canned foods, etc.) for the students and faculty, thus the whole concept of the school was that of a *faith operation* in which God was trusted to provide all that was needed.

Remembering that my father had attended the Apostolic Faith Bible School a few years earlier, I wrote to him relating Art's and my desire to attend there in the fall. I asked him if he could send us some information about who to contact, phone numbers, addresses, etc., so that we could begin the process of enrolling in the school.

While waiting for an answer from Dad concerning that Bible school, Art and I had attended a camp meeting service at Bethel Park in Federal Way, Washington. It was a very inspiring, challenging service, charged with the Presence of the Lord! On our way home after that "super service," the Presence of the Holy Spirit suddenly descended upon Art and me. It was so powerful and so awesome that we found ourselves worshiping and praising God as tears of joy streamed down our cheeks. I finally told Art, "I've got to pull off the road. This is too glorious to drive this car in!" So, as soon as I saw a wide place along the road, I pulled over and parked.

We found ourselves engulfed in a "cloud of glory" as we just sat there, weeping and worshipping our Blessed Redeemer. Then, suddenly, a somewhat fearful (godly fear—not dread) challenge began to pour into my soul and spirit, and this was the clear message I received: "Say not there are yet four months and then comes the harvest; lift up your eyes and look at the fields, for they are white already to harvest." I at once recognized this as a portion of John 4:35. I then began to reason with the Lord saying, "But, Lord, I haven't been to Bible school yet. I have no formal training for the ministry. How can I go out into full-time ministry without first attending Bible school?"

I thought to myself later that my words sounded something like Moses when the angel of the Lord appeared to him in the midst of the burning bush near Horeb in the Midian Desert. "They will not believe me nor hearken to my voice . . .," he said (Exodus 4:1). He felt inadequate and ill-prepared to do the stupendous thing God was calling him to do. Likewise, I was pleading my cause to the Lord (of course, on an immensely smaller scale), telling Him that, "I just don't have what it takes!"

While I was thus reasoning, another powerful impression in the form of a challenge came pouring into my spirit. Again, it was directly from the scriptures and this is what the Lord dropped into my heart: 1) "But the Comforter, which is the Holy Ghost, whom The Father will send in my name, He shall *teach you all things* and bring all things to your remembrance, whatsoever I have said unto you." (John 14:26); 2) "If any man lack *wisdom*, let him ask of God, that giveth to all men liberally, and upbraideth not; and it shall be given him." (James 1:5); 3) "But *the anointing* which ye have received of Him, abideth in you, and you need not that any man teach you; but as that same anointing *teacheth* you all things, and is truth, and is no lie, and even as *it hath taught you*, ye shall abide in Him" (I John 2:27).

All of this seemed overwhelming to me at the time as these scriptural challenges were dropped into my heart in rapid succession, but I determined not to second-guess or doubt what God was challenging me with, but that I would rather trust Him with all of my heart—*with every fiber of my being!* As I related these things to Art, he concurred.

"This *must* be the path God desires to lead us in," he responded.

I was beginning to realize, little by little, that God had a plan for this Kansas farm boy that was altogether unique and fearfully wonderful!

Comrades in Christ

When Dad's letter arrived I eagerly opened it—only to find that he was advising us to put our plans to attend the Apostolic Faith Bible School on hold. I had previously advised my parents that Art and I were planning to drive down to Kansas the last part of July, hence Dad suggested in his letter that we wait until we arrived there before he explained why he was suggesting we put our plans to attend the Bible school in Baxter Springs on hold.

It was interesting for Art and me to note that the first scripture verse that was dropped into my heart that night as we drove home from the camp meeting service included the words, "Say not, there are yet four months . . .," because four months was the approximate space of time from that date until the start of the fall session of Bible school. Four months was also the approximate duration of a semester of training at the Apostolic Faith Bible School there in Baxter Springs, Kansas.

After much prayer, heart-searching, and discussion, Art and I came to the conclusion that it was time for us to "spread our wings" and launch out into full-time ministry. Based on that decision, we thought it both wise and appropriate to go to our dear pastor, the late Rev. Frank McAllister, whom we held in high esteem, to inform him of our plans to go out into full-time ministry.

"I am not surprised," he told us. "I knew it would be just a matter of time," he went on to say. However, he expressed reservations about our launching out into the somewhat "unknown" territory of evangelic ministry without some formal training. Nevertheless, seeing he could not persuade us otherwise, he charged us to "make full proof" of our ministries and then bade us Godspeed!

Art and I both submitted termination notices at our respective places of employment in preparation to depart for the Midwest, where we hoped to begin a lifetime of service to the Lord and His Church. We spent a lot of time in earnest, fervent, prayer during those final days prior to our departure, seeking God for His guidance and blessing as we made the necessary preparations for the big trip ahead. We were both thrilled and excited about this new venture we were about to embark upon. As we prayed for guidance, we always seemed to receive the very same answer, or impression. Never once did we have a disagreement or contradiction, which was in itself amazing to us. We regarded that as a sign that we were moving within the Will of God for our lives at that time.

Shortly before we were to leave for Kansas, my brother Louie helped me "swing a deal" for a newer and better automobile—a 1949 Oldsmobile "Rocket 88." After advertising my Plymouth convertible in a newspaper, I sold my car to the very first person who called about it—a distinct blessing, especially considering the timing.

Because Louie had gone into business for himself, he decided to make the trip to Kansas with Art and me, a decision we both welcomed as he had been such an enormous blessing to both of us. Our plan was to drive "straight through" without any overnight stays, so an extra driver was a welcome advantage.

We left Seattle late on the afternoon of Tuesday, July 29, driving south to go by way of San Francisco in hopes of seeing our brother Lloyd before he shipped out for Korea on a troop ship. Unfortunately, we were a few hours too late. The ship had departed before we arrived in the Bay area about midday, so we turned eastward for the next leg of our journey.

Our only stop, with the exception of a few "pit stops," was in Yosemite National Park to see the great spectacle of "falling fire," a summertime night event in the park. The nearer we got to south-central Kansas, the more excited we were. The family there was also excited as they anticipated our arrival.

At long last we arrived at my parents' home on Friday, August 1. What a reunion that was for me! I had left there less than a year earlier—a backslider, hooked on tobacco and far from God. Now I was there to begin a brand new era of my life—entering into full-time ministry.

It was also an exciting time for my friend and colleague, Art, as he had never been to the Midwest before. He had met my parents the previous summer in Seattle when they were visiting Louie and his family, which included attending church services at the Church by the Side of the Road—Art's home church. Art was now the newest member of the Ott family, as my parents' home would become our "headquarters" when stepping out into the ministry.

On Saturday, August 2, Dad drove us to Cheney to meet Pastor Earl Neilson and his family. We were also there to help plan the very special occasion the next day: Sunday, August 3; an ordination service for Art and me. Everybody was up early at the Ott residence south of Cheney on Sunday morning, getting ready for the events of the day. First it was Sunday school, and then Sunday morning worship service, followed by "dinner on the grounds."

At 3:00 P.M. everybody gathered at the Cheney Mission (Apostolic Faith Church) for the big event—the ordination service for Art and me. In those days, people entering the ministry were usually not ordained to begin with. The credentialing process normally began with some type of certificate or ministerial license. Then, after making proof of one's ministry, ordination would be the next consideration. But even the licensing process generally follows some degree of formal training (college, Bible school, etc.).

Of course, Art and I would have been happy to have simply been licensed to preach the gospel. We had no ambition of "starting at the top of the ladder" or any such thing. Our plan had been to enroll in the Apostolic Faith Bible School in Baxter Springs when the fall session began. But, upon arriving there in Cheney, my Dad and Pastor Earl Neilson suggested that we reconsider that plan. There had been a "split" in the movement that operated the Bible school and things were in somewhat of an upheaval. Of course, this came as a complete shock to us; we were not aware of that having happened.

Upon learning about this "split" in the movement that operated the Bible school, the experience we had had while driving home from the camp meeting service at Bethel Park in Federal Way, Washington, began to come into focus. Those words, "Say not there are yet four months . . .," were beginning to have new meaning to me with reference to Divine Guidance about the full gospel ministry that I, along with my friend, Art, were about to be ordained to and set apart for.

Based on what Dad had shared with Pastor Earl Neilson concerning my somewhat accelerated spiritual growth up to that point, my being raised up from the "death bed" at age fifteen, and having had the call of God on my life since age five, Pastor Earl concluded that this should be—that it was the Will of God that I, along with my friend, Art, should be ordained. Thus, even though it would be "an exception to the rule," this special ordination service for Art and me was set for 3:00 P.M., Sunday, August 3, 1952.

Ordained

My Uncle Paul Bailey (Mother's brother) was pastor of the New York Tabernacle Church in Wichita, Kansas at that time. Of course, he was invited to take part in this very special occasion and did. A feeling of deep humility and gratitude pervaded my whole being on that Sunday afternoon. That these men of God had confidence and trust in me was indeed humbling. I also felt somewhat awed about the whole matter. It was as if I almost had to pinch myself a few times to see if this was for real, especially when these good men were willing to include my dear friend and colleague, Art Morlin, in the process even though they knew him only as that.

Another striking thought about my ordination service was the fact that it was set to take place on August 3, 1952—exactly six months to the day, February 3, after I had bowed my knee in complete surrender to God in that glorious service at the Church by the Side of the Road in Seattle. Could this really be possible? Yes, it could—and indeed was!

Sunday morning service at the Cheney Mission Church seemed charged with enthusiasm, anticipation, and great joy. The "Prodigal Son" had come home and would soon be set apart for full-time ministry through this special ordination service! For that little church, and especially for my family members—who were prominent members of the congregation—it was somewhat of a celebration.

Pastor Neilson announced that there would also be a water baptism service along the Ninnescah River south of town following the ordination service. My Dad, a lay minister, would assist in both services. I don't suppose Dad was so proud in all of his life as he was on that Sunday to witness and *be a part of* something as grand and glorious as what was happening to his number four son—the one who had been given less than a chance in a thousand to survive a grave illness five years previous to this!

Mother was also overflowing with joy and great peace that day. Four of my younger siblings were present for this monumental event, as well as my beloved older brother, Louie, who had been so very instrumental in helping me get grounded in the things of the Lord after my surrender to God at an altar of prayer just six months earlier. Indeed, it was a "day of days" to be remembered, especially by the Ott family.

Although I cannot recall the details of that ordination service fifty years ago now, I do remember being caught up, as it were, in rapturous excitement and exhilarating joy. It was indeed a most sacred and monumental milestone in my life. I scarcely could take it all in. Many tears of joy were shed in that little church on that afternoon, not only by Art and me, but also by my own family, as well as all the members of the church family.

Even though Art and I both had been previously baptized in water (myself in that same river at age fourteen), we felt the need to be re-baptized, thus this addendum to the ordination service. Many of the saints from the Cheney Mission gathered there at the river that afternoon, singing, worshipping, and praising God while Dad and Pastor Neilson officiated in baptizing the two of us. As we came up out of those waters to walk in newness of life before our Lord and King of our lives, somehow a feeling of deep satisfaction and fulfillment came over Art and me.

Pastor Neilson had announced that I would be preaching in the 7:00 P.M. service that Sunday. Of course, I had already preached on numerous occasions in the Seattle area, but my friends and relatives at home had not yet heard me do so, so there was eager anticipation on their part and a bit of anxiety on my own. Admittedly, I was a little nervous about that speaking engagement, yet I felt "strong in faith," which provided me with the needed confidence.

When Art and I arrived at the church in Cheney that Sunday evening, we immediately sensed the excitement and anticipation of the people, as well as the Presence of the Lord. It was awesome! By the time the service was to begin, the sanctuary was completely full and, understandably I suppose, all eyes were upon these two twenty-year-old, newly ordained preachers. Having observed earlier that there was a small room on either side of the platform, I had requested permission of Pastor Neilson to wait in one of those rooms until it was time for me to preach. We'd agreed on a signal to let me know when the time came: Art would lead the congregation in singing the chorus of *Only Believe*.

My reasons for wanting to wait aside in that small room were twofold. First, I wanted to hold the "jitters" to a minimum, and, secondly, in order to seek the Lord in earnest prayer for a special anointing to minister in the power of the Holy Spirit.

While I was fervently praying in the small room, I suddenly experienced a sharp pain on the right side of my abdomen. The pain went away and then came back again, several times. It was then that I realized that the Holy Spirit was imparting a "word of knowledge" to me. That "word" was that someone in the congregation that night had been suffering with severe pain in that part of their body.

"You are to call for that person to come forward to the altar for believing prayer," was the instruction I received. So, when it came time for me to preach, without a word of greeting, I immediately said, "Every head bowed, please!" This was a strange way to begin my first preaching engagement after being ordained earlier in the day, I know. But I was certain I had heard the Holy Spirit speak this into my spirit and I certainly did not want to grieve Him by not obeying. I started with these words: "The Holy Spirit revealed to me while I was in this side room praying that there is someone here tonight who has been experiencing severe pain in the right side of your abdomen. If you will get up and come forward now, God will heal you!"

To my surprise, even shock, no one responded—at first. So, I reiterated that I was very positive that the Holy Spirit had dropped this knowledge into my spirit, thus I urged.

"Whoever it is, please be obedient to the Lord and you will receive healing from Him. I'm sure of that!" Still no one came forward. Finally, feeling somewhat defeated momentarily, I started to say, "Alright, if whoever it is that needs this healing won't respond . . ."

Just then my fourteen-year-old sister, Beulah ("Boots") stood to her feet weeping and interrupted me, confessing that it was her who had been experiencing the pain that I had described. She had been in pain for several days and was beginning to feel quite discouraged because she had sought the Lord numerous times for healing, but no healing had come.

Oh, no! I thought inwardly. *This has the appearance of a "staged incident." What will these people think now?*

But since no one else had responded, I called for my sister to come forward. I went down off of the platform, calling for my friend Art and Pastor Neilson to join me for believing prayer over my sister. As we prayed, Boots immediately began weeping, shouting, "It's gone! It's gone!" She was healed instantly and never experienced that pain again!

My message that night was on faith to believe God for the miraculous. It was very well received. Having my beloved brother Louie present for the events of that unforgettable Sunday was the "icing on the cake" for us. God was so good to allow this.

Camp Meeting

On the following Wednesday, August 6, Louie boarded a bus to return to Seattle while Art and I drove to Joplin, Missouri, to attend the National Fellowship Camp Meeting there. Although we had missed the first two days of the meeting, Art and I attended youth services each evening prior to the main services. A contest was in progress with the memorization of Scripture its main thrust. Rev. Calvin Cook and his wife, Steryl, were conducting these youth services and were offering a nice Bible dictionary to the winner of the contest, the one who memorized and then quoted the most scripture verses flawlessly. What a distinct blessing that turned out to be for me, not only because I was the winner of the contest, but also because of the "hiding of God's Word" in my heart. I memorized and quoted twenty chapters during those eight days, as well as dozens of single scripture verses.

Over fifty years later I still have that Bible dictionary, although it is well-worn from much use. On the back of the front cover, inscribed in magnificent handwriting, are these words: "Presented to Gail Ott for Excellence at the National Fellowship Camp Meeting in Joplin, Missouri, August 4–13, 1952," and signed, "Rev. Calvin Cook."

Two other events of significance happened at that camp meeting while Art and I were in attendance. First, Pastor Earl Neilson had met with the elected officials of the newly formed Ministerial and Missionary Alliance, a spin-off from the split in the Apostolic Faith Movement, to discuss their acceptance of Art and myself as ordained ministers. Pastor Neilson informed them of the special ordination service that had been held for us the previous Sunday in Cheney, Kansas, and, in turn, recommended to the credentialing committee that, as such, we be accepted into that alliance. Since Art and I were not in attendance at that meeting, this entire decision rested with the officials of the organization and Pastor Neilson.

When the first opinion was rendered (a negative), Pastor Neilson responded.

"Very well, but if that is your final decision, then please remove my name from the roster. That is how much I am convinced that God's hand and blessing is upon these two young men."

At that declaration, the committee discussed the matter further and reconsidered, fully agreeing to accept both of us as ordained ministers and extending to us "the right hand of fellowship," as well as the full privileges of membership. Of course, all of this was a consideration and a blessing that we had neither expected nor anticipated, thus we felt both humbled and honored by the decision. What a tremendous blessing it was to two young men just entering full-time ministry to have a friend like Pastor Earl Neilson!

The other significant happening while we were in attendance of at camp meeting was a magnificent dream or "night vision" that I received from the Lord. It happened like this: While sleeping on an army cot in a small tent there on the campgrounds, I was suddenly alerted by a magnificent vision of Jesus coming toward the earth in a white cloud. In that vision I was standing under a mulberry tree near the northwest corner of my parents' house when suddenly I looked up and saw the Lord coming down toward me. Just then in the vision, I left the ground, rising rapidly toward the Lord Jesus. As I ascended upward, I went right through that mulberry tree, yet never broke a branch or felt any sensation of pain or resistance as I rose upward, going toward the Lord!

It is impossible for me to fully describe the awesomeness of holy exhilaration that surged through my whole being at that exact instant. It was indeed a "joy unspeakable!" To this day, a half century later, I still get "spiritual goose bumps" when I think about that blessed experience.

But, just as quickly as I saw myself going up to meet the Lord in the air, the scene suddenly changed, just as if I were looking at a full-sized motion picture screen.

In the second scene of this splendid vision, I was inside my parents' house, standing in the dining room and looking into the living room. Seated there on a couch against the south wall of the room, directly in front of me, were two of my brothers, Lester and Dwane. At that time, they were the only remaining members of my family who were not saved. My oldest sister, Pauline, had once been gloriously saved, but at that time was not walking with the Lord. She was not included in this vision, however.

As I stood looking at Lester and Dwane not a word was spoken, yet a dire sense of need was impressed upon my spirit. Then, just as suddenly as they had appeared before me, my two brothers were gone. It was as if having seen them on the last page of a large pictorial book when suddenly the book was closed.

When the vision ended, I immediately jumped up off of my cot and then fell upon my knees in prayer. There was no doubt in my mind that God had given me this vision and that the vision had a significant meaning. Therefore I entreated the Lord in fervent prayer that He might reveal to me its meaning. How long I stayed on my knees in prayer I don't know, perhaps only fifteen to twenty minutes, but I distinctly remember receiving a crystal clear, concise interpretation from the Lord. Once again, I did not hear an audible voice, nor did I see words written across the sky, but I did hear from the Lord. Of that I am certain. The words were clear and to the point: "I am coming back to earth again and your two brothers are not saved!" The answer was so clear that I knew the Lord was giving me a burden to pray and believe for Lester and Dwane to be saved.

From that time on, and for the next nine months, I prayed often and earnestly for the salvation of my two brothers. At the time God gave me the vision, Lester was in Germany serving in the United States Army and Dwane was somewhere in Kingman County, Kansas, working for a farmer. He had fallen in love with a Catholic girl in Kingman and was planning to be married to her. He had also been drinking alcoholic beverages quite frequently and was fast becoming an alcoholic at the age of eighteen. The subsequent results of this vision and the succeeding nine months of fervent prayer for Lester and Dwane will be covered in a later chapter . . .

Stranger in the Storm

After returning to Cheney from the camp meeting, Art and I began to seek God again in earnest prayer, requesting Divine Guidance for our lives and ministry. It was mid-afternoon, Monday, August 18, that we made the decision to get into our car and take off for somewhere, not knowing for sure where, but fully trusting the Lord to give us guidance. We drove northeast toward Kansas City, Missouri, arriving there around 9 P.M. that night. Without understanding why, we both felt impressed to turn northward on U.S. Highway 69, heading north toward Iowa.

After driving about an hour from Kansas City, a rainstorm descended upon the area we were driving through. The rain fell lightly at first, but quickly turned into a torrential downpour. In a short while the visibility had been reduced to near zero. We could hardly see the hood of the car through the blinding rain and thus were made to realize that it was dangerous to be on the highway. We agreed to pull off the road as soon as we could find a place to do so. A few miles ahead we noticed a traveler's "turn out" along the highway, so we pulled off of the road there to wait for the storm to break.

Since the trunk of our car was filled with the small tent and cots we had used at the camp meeting, along with other camping paraphernalia and our sound system and musical instruments filled the back seat, we concluded that we would just try to get as comfortable as possible on the front seats for the duration. I was seated at the steering wheel and Art was on the passenger's side.

With those huge raindrops beating relentlessly upon our car while lightning flashed across the sky periodically, followed by loud claps of thunder, we sat there wondering if we had somehow missed the guidance we had sought from the Lord. We were carefully trying to be very sensitive to the Holy Spirit and certainly did not want to grieve Him by getting out of God's Will for us at that time.

After we had discussed the matter for a short while we decided to just stay put right there where we were until daybreak. After reading a chapter from the Bible by the dome light and joining in another session of prayer, we tried to settle down and go to sleep. For some reason, I said to Art, "Maybe we should lock our car doors while we sleep." Art agreed, so we both locked the door on our respective sides of the car.

About fifteen minutes after we locked our doors a big, flatbed semi truck pulled in and parked behind our car. His headlights were very bright and somewhat annoying until the driver finally turned them off. Apparently the truck driver felt as unsafe as we did to be on the road in such a severe storm. Considerable time had passed since the truck parked behind us and I was still awake. Many thoughts were crossing my mind while I sat there listening to the rain beating upon our car. Finally I spoke to Art, who was almost asleep by then.

"Did you lock your door?" He answered in the affirmative that he indeed had locked it. "Why don't you check it again," I said back to him, to which he replied, "Hey man, what's up with you? Are you afraid of something?"

"Well, Art," I said, "we don't know anything about that truck driver back there behind us, so I'll sleep better if I know for sure that the car doors are locked so I just thought it might be good to double-check to see that they are locked! OK?"

Art double-checked his door and assured me that it was locked. After awhile we both were sound asleep while the rain continued to pour down. How long the rainstorm continued, I don't know, but it did stop sometime after we fell asleep.

Early the next morning (Tuesday, August 19), just as daylight was beginning to break through the darkness, while all was quiet,

I was suddenly startled and awakened and very much astonished at the scene that was before my eyes. The right car door was open and there stood a man between the open door and Art who was still sound asleep. All that I recall seeing of this man was his head and shoulders. I did not see his hands, legs, or feet. My immediate impression was that he had somehow gotten the car door open and was attempting to rob Art of his wallet. Without giving a second thought as to what I should do, I at once doubled up my left fist and started to punch this man in the face, but, to my utter amazement, just as I started to move my fist toward his face he literally vanished right before my eyes.

The only way I know how to illustrate what I saw is to liken this stranger's sudden disappearance to the activity of a light bulb. When the light switch is flipped to the *off* position, the light around it seems to be swallowed up by the bulb. It doesn't take off into space— *it simply disappears*. When this stranger vanished out of my sight in an instant of time, changing from visible to invisible, I suddenly felt the hair stand up on the back of my neck. I also noticed the hair standing up on my left forearm, as the arm suddenly seemed frozen right before my face, clenched fist and all! My heart was also pounding and it seemed that I was momentary breathless.

Within a few seconds many thoughts raced through my mind. Was this just a bad dream that I'd had? Was there really a man standing there in that open door? Was the car door actually open? Yet I knew it was not just a bad dream or a hallucination. I knew for certain that I had looked into the eyes and upon the face of a man!

Suddenly then, I looked back in the direction of the right door. This time the door was closed, but not tight. It was only to the first catch and now I could see daylight through the space at the top of the door. Then I looked at the lock button on the right door. It was now in the unlocked position. I distinctly remembered asking Art to double-check that his door was locked, which he checked and confirmed that it indeed was before we went to sleep.

For the space of twenty to thirty minutes I just sat there spellbound, taxing my mental faculties to come up with a suitable explanation of what I had just experienced and what the meaning of it might be while Art continued to sleep soundly.

I thought about the man's face I had just seen. It was a picture of plight. The look on his face seemed to be a sorrowful one. But, the description of that look that I could never forget seems most accurate to me as a look of *entreaty*, like the man was seeking help of some sort.

While I reasoned thus, I was suddenly struck with a sense of shame. *Why was it that I wanted to hit this man in the face with my fist? Wasn't that sorrowful look on his face also a kind look?* By thus reasoning I concluded that my reaction to being startled and awakened was instinctive, not vindictive.

Another thought that came to my mind during those moments was the fact that in the Bible, in Isaiah 53:3, the promised Messiah was depicted as "a man of sorrow, acquainted with grief." *Maybe that was Jesus*, I reasoned. Yet nothing I could think of seemed to satisfy my quest for an explanation of what I had just experienced. At last I decided I would awaken Art—however, I would not tell him of what I had just experienced, but would rather ask him some questions. "Did you have some kind of dream while you were sleeping?"

"Yes, I did," he replied. "*Why?*"

"Tell me what you dreamed," I urged him.

"Well," he replied, "I dreamed that you and I were running across a large field, ripe for harvest, with each of us accompanied by a young woman. We were holding hands as we ran carefree and happy across that beautiful harvest field."

"But you didn't see a man with a dark complexion and black hair?" I probed.

"No. Why?" Art asked. It was then that I began relating to him what I had experienced earlier that morning while he was still sleeping. I first drew his attention to the position of the door on his side of the car, which remained open to the first catch, the lock button still in the *unlocked* position. I also reminded Art of the fact that I had asked him to double-check that his door was locked before we both fell asleep.

Then as I was about to tell him of the man whom I had seen standing beside him with the car door open, suddenly an awesome cloud of heavenly Glory descended upon us. All the inside of our car seemed to be suddenly charged with a sacred, glorious Presence that was so awesome and powerful that I literally felt as if I'd either die or be raptured up to heaven! We were both speechless for the next two-and-a-half to three hours with the exception of breathing out words of praise. All we could do was just to praise and glorify the Lord. When that cloud of Glory would seem to lift just a little bit and we attempted to speak again, another wave of Glory would sweep over us in great billows.

This continued for at least two hours, and during that time we were totally oblivious to any traffic that might have been on the highway. Apparently the big truck that had been parked behind us had also returned to the highway, although we were not cognizant of its moving. We were so totally engrossed in what we were experiencing that our total attention was riveted to just one thing: God's Presence. It was too wonderful and glorious to risk having it lift from us because we did not stay focused.

When the Glory finally subsided and we began to feel that we were coming down out of that cloud, I finally was able to relate to Art the full account of seeing the dark-skinned, black-haired stranger standing beside him with the car door open. Yet even while relating this story to Art there were interruptions of weeping and praise that I was unable to hold back. We had already shed so many tears of joy until I didn't think there could be any more!

At last I started the engine and we proceeded on northward toward Iowa. But even as we drove along the way we continued in a mode of weeping and praising God. By the time we reached the small town of Leon, Iowa, we had pretty much returned to normal; at least enough to stop at a service station to refuel the car.

From the town of Leon we continued on a northward course until we reached Meriden, Minnesota. There we turned eastward on U.S. Highway 14 and drove until we came to a small state park a few miles west of the small town of Camp Douglas, Wisconsin. For some reason we both felt strongly impressed to turn into that small park, which we did. There was no park ranger there, so we set up our small tent and then agreed that we would stay there for a while to seek God in prayer and fasting. We also agreed that we would neither eat nor drink any liquid until we had heard from God.

Now to some people this might seem like a very foolish decision to make. I certainly would not recommend anyone else do the same thing *unless* they were absolutely certain that the Lord had led them to do so, as was the conviction of our hearts at that point in time. We had both decided conclusively that we wanted to have God's favor and to understand His will for our lives even more than life itself!

During our stay in that small park, in between our times of Bible study and sessions of prayer, we would discuss the experience I had had on the previous Tuesday morning when I saw the man that appeared on the inside of the right car door.

"What did he look like?" Art asked me. "Did he resemble anybody we know?" As I thought about his questions, I could not think of a single human being I had ever met that he resembled, but I could never forget that look on his face. It was a somewhat somber, sorrowful, look that has haunted me ever since I saw this stranger that morning. We discussed Isaiah 53:3 and suggested that maybe it was Jesus, but somehow that was not a satisfactory answer.

We also postulated that it might have been an angel, for God's Word tells us that angels sometimes appear in the guise of men. Yet for some reason every conceivable interpretation we came up with always left me wondering. For sure, however, I was absolutely positive that this experience had a definite, significant meaning. I would simply have to wait for God's timing to receive the interpretation. And, nine months later, I did, indeed, receive an interpretation—in almost as glorious a manner as was the experience itself! Indeed, this was *my* "Macedonian Call!"

Chapter 9

THE "SAWDUST TRAIL"

Afterseveral days of intense, earnest, and fervent prayer and
heart-searching, totally resolved not to move on until we
had heard from Heaven, our request for guidance did eventually come. We did not see a great light, nor did we hear an audible voice, but on the morning that our answer came we were
made to realize that God had heard the cries of our hearts and the
groanings of our spirits (and, undoubtedly, overlooked our igno-
rance). The answer was clear and simple, but compelling and satisfying to us.

"Continue to walk close to Me and hearken to the leadings of
My Spirit, and surely I will open doors before you and will show
you the path I would have you take."

To this day, I still do not understand why the Lord allowed us
to go so far away simply to fast and pray for divine guidance and
favor. But, I do know that we were carefully and sincerely looking
to Him for His guidance every mile of the way and it was not until
we came upon that small state park that we felt "this is the place to
turn aside and seek God in earnest, fervent prayer with fasting for
His direction for our lives at this point in time."

Another amazing feature about our stop and stay at that small
Wisconsin state park was that during the entire duration of our time

there we were never interrupted by anyone. Our only visitors were the large, hungry mosquitoes that converged upon us at nighttime.

After dismantling our small camping tent and loading all of our belongings back into the car, we drove into the town of Camp Douglas where we filled the gas tank, bought a few groceries with which to break our fast, gave thanks to God, ate, drank some orange juice, and then turned southward.

We arrived in the city of Burlington, Iowa, by mid-afternoon that day. Realizing that our funds were dwindling fast, we decided to seek some kind of temporary employment there, but our efforts went without success. So, we found a city park and decided to camp out overnight. It was a clear, starlit night, so we decided just to sleep on our cots out in the open.

This was fine until around midnight when we were rather rudely awakened by two city police officers who told us it was not permissible for us to camp, so we had to fold up our cots, get into the car, and drive to a different location. We parked and spent the rest of the night in the car. After a time of prayer, seeking God for further guidance the next morning, we decided to drive on south to the city of Fort Madison, Iowa—twenty-eight miles south of Burlington.

Upon arriving in Fort Madison that morning we went to an employment office to inquire about job opportunities. The receptionist there told us that the Burlington Northern Railroad needed workers, so we went to the company's personnel office immediately. Upon being interviewed for the jobs with Burlington, we told the agent that we were ministers and were seeking only temporary employment.

"I'm afraid I can't hire you for the openings we have at this time," he said. "We are looking to hire permanent employees. However," he went on to say, "I noticed an ad in the morning paper that Benbow Coal Company is in need of two able-bodied men. Perhaps you can land a job there." He gave us directions to the coal company office and said, "Good luck, fellows!"

We thanked him and then drove across town to that business establishment. Upon arriving there we were met by Mr. Benbow, the owner, a very pleasant gentleman probably in his early sixties. We told him we were in need of work for a week or two but were not seeking permanent employment.

"Too bad, guys," he told us. "I just hired a couple of guys from Arkansas this morning and sent them out on the job."

"Well, thank you just the same," I told him, as Art and I turned to go back to our car.

"Just a minute, guys," Mr. Benbow called out. "I'm not sure I'm going to be happy with these two guys I hired this morning. I'm a pretty good judge of character and I'm sure that by evening I'll know whether or not I'll want to keep them on. Here's my home phone number," he said, handing me one of his business cards. "Give me a call around six this evening if you haven't found jobs by then. OK?"

To that we agreed, thanked him, shook hands with him, and then drove away to look further for some kind of temporary employment. We went to perhaps a dozen or more business establishments in Fort Madison that day, hoping to find a way to earn enough money to get us back to my parents' home in Kansas, but without success. We even walked around in several residential areas, ringing doorbells, trying to find a lawn to mow or some yard work to do, but again our search was unsuccessful.

At about two that afternoon we had parked our car on a street in the industrial area of Fort Madison, taking a little time out to eat the last bit of food that we had left (three or four slices of bread and a small amount of oleomargarine. Since we always took time to thank God for any food we would eat (even an ice cream cone), we paused to do so now. It happened to be "my turn" to offer thanks for the food that we were about to eat, so I prayed. But at the conclusion of my prayer, I felt inspired to "tack on" an addendum to that prayer of thanksgiving, which went something like this: "And, Lord, we also thank You, by faith, for our next meal, even though we do not know where it will come from, because we have complete confidence that You will provide for our needs. We, therefore, thank You in advance in the Wonderful Name of our Blessed Redeemer and Lord, Jesus Christ. Amen!"

Little did we realize or even suspect the wonderful miracle of provision that the Lord had in store for us. After a totally unfruitful effort to find a job of any kind the rest of the afternoon, we decided to give Mr. Benbow (the owner of the coal company) a call, so we stopped at a hotel to use a pay phone in the lobby. By this time it was a little past six o'clock. We had exactly one nickel left to our names—just enough to make the phone call to Mr. Benbow. That was what a local call cost from a pay phone in that era of time.

Something went wrong when I was dialing Mr. Benbow's number and my nickel was gone. I then turned to Art and spoke.

"Since we don't have another nickel to try the call again, let's just drive over to this man's house." Art agreed, so we looked up his address in the phone book and got back into our car to drive to his house. By now we were faced with another dilemma—our car was very nearly out of gas and the gauge was very accurate. When it said "empty," that meant it was empty! We had learned this by experience. So, we paused to ask the Lord to multiply what little fuel we still had—mostly fumes! We had agreed that if we did run out of gas before we got to Mr. Benbow's house we would walk the rest of the way.

After praying for God to be with us and to multiply the gasoline in our car, we started the engine and drove to the Benbows' home, which was in the "upper crust" area of the city. When we rang the doorbell at the Benbows' home, we were expecting to see a surprised (or even shocked) look on Mr. Benbow's face when he opened the door. We were the ones who were surprised, however, when he spoke.

"Welcome, fellows, come right on in. We've been expecting you!" Art and I looked at each other in wonderment at this surprise welcome.

"Oh, no," I said, "We don't need to come in. We had a little problem trying to call you at a pay phone, so we just decided to come by your house to inquire about a job with you."

"Oh, but you must come in, gentlemen," he replied. "My wife has fixed supper for you and she'd have her feelings hurt if you were to leave now." We reluctantly consented to do so, since he insisted so adamantly.

Mr. Benbow then closed the door behind us and said, "Follow me," as he crossed the living room and entered a large hallway that took us to a dinette room adjacent to the kitchen. There in the middle of this dinette room was a table, fully set with beautiful dinnerware, silverware, cloth table covering, cloth napkins, plus a magnificent array of food. It was a setting fit for a king!

Still, as we immediately observed that there were only two place settings, I ventured to suggest that Mrs. Benbow had prepared that lovely meal for the two of them, not for two strangers.

"Thank you for your kindness," I said to them, "but we can't sit down here and eat your supper. We weren't even supposed to come here to your house. You only asked us to call you by phone."

"You don't understand, fellows," he insisted. "We've already eaten our supper. My wife prepared this meal for you two young guys, so please be seated and eat it before everything gets cold," he insisted. It was at that point that Art and I realized that we were experiencing a beautiful miracle of provision, so we thanked them for their kindness and hospitality and sat down at the table spread with a truly delicious meal that included beverages and dessert!

Art asked the Benbows if they would mind if we offered a prayer of thanks before we started eating, to which they responded, "Not at all!" In his prayer, Art not only thanked the Lord for the lovely meal that we were about to partake of, but also prayed that God would especially bless these gracious people for their kindness, generosity, and for the hospitality shown to us. While we ate and enjoyed the fabulous meal, the Benbows sat across the room from us, conversing with us, demonstrating sincere interest in our resolve to answer God's call to the ministry.

After we had eaten the meal these lovely people had provided for us, they then offered to give us a room for the night. But to that, we insisted that we would be just fine sleeping on army cots in our small tent.

"There's just the two of us in this big house," Mr. Benbow stated. "You fellows wouldn't be any bother." Again thanking them kindly for all of their hospitality and for their gracious offer to stay with them that night, we insisted that we'd be just fine spending the night in the city park.

"Well," Mr. Benbow said, "If you insist on sleeping outside tonight, don't go to the park. You'll get woke up over and over again because there's a lot of activity there these warm summer nights. We've got a vacant lot up on the bluff on the north side of town. I'll drive up there and you men can follow me in your car. OK?"

We agreed, thanking Mrs. Benbow again for the delicious meal, and then got into our car to follow him to that vacant lot. Of course, we were aware that the gas gauge in our car was now on "empty," but we didn't want to tell Mr. Benbow about that, so we were earnestly praying for another miracle of multiplication as we drove behind him. Most of the road to that vacant lot was uphill, and there was even some rather steep grade the last half-mile or so. Indeed, the Lord answered our prayers once again.

When we arrived at the vacant lot, Mr. Benbow parked his Buick with the headlights on "high beam" to show us where we could set up camp for the night. While we were getting our camping gear out of the trunk, Mr. Benbow went to the house next door to inform the neighbor that we were his guests and that he had given us permission to camp there overnight. The neighbor happened to be a Mr. Schaeffer (one of the owners/founders of the Schaeffer Pen Company of Fort Madison), and the "house next door" seemed more like a palace than a home to Art and me. It was a huge, very elegant home.

Mr. Benbow came back out to where we were and spoke to us.

"Everything's OK. I told the Shaeffers that you guys are my new vice presidents of the company and they had nothing to fear about your camping out here for the night." Obviously, Mr. Benbow had a good sense of humor, which was a blessing to two young, itinerant evangelists as it made us feel at ease.

Before leaving to go back home, Mr. Benbow said, "By the way, fellows, I let those two 'Arkies' go this afternoon, so you guys have got a job for tomorrow and for as long as you need to work. Report at my place of business around eight in the morning and I'll get you lined up for your job. OK?"

"We'll be there," I assured him.

"You can count on us!" said Art. With that, he departed for home and we continued to ready our camping gear for a night's rest. Since it was a lovely, crystal clear evening and the view of the city from high upon the bluff where we were was simply magnificent, we decided not to set up our small tent. We would just sleep out under the stars on our cots. After a time of prayer, we turned in for the night.

As we were folding out our cots and putting our gear back into the car at 7 A.M. the next morning, just praising the Lord for His goodness to us, a gentleman emerged from the Shaeffer house carrying a large silver platter with a fabulous array of food on it (cereal, sliced fresh peaches, pure cream, orange juice, pastries, etc.).

"I'm Mr. Shaeffer, and my wife and I thought you fellows might like to have some breakfast before you go to work for Mr. Benbow this morning," he said to us.

Needless to say, we were nearly overwhelmed, as we had already agreed that the delicious meal we had eaten at the Benbow's home the night before would be more than sufficient for breakfast, too. Besides, we had no money to eat at a restaurant or to buy groceries at a store. *And, now this!*

After handing the platter of food to us, Mr. Shaeffer said, "If there is anything else you'd like, just let us know." We thanked this gracious gentleman for his kindness and generosity to strangers he'd never seen before and said, "This will be more than sufficient."

"OK," he said, "Enjoy your meal," as he walked back to his house. After thanking the Lord for His bountiful, even miraculous provision for us, we ate the rich, tasty food that Mr. Shaeffer had brought out to us. While we feasted, we both spoke of our amazement concerning how God had used two, apparently wealthy men, to feed two "flat broke," humble upstart servants of His! To us, it was truly wonderful!

Art and I both walked over to the Shaeffer's house to return the silver platter, plates, bowls, silverware, etc.—once again expressing our gratitude to those gracious people for their deed of kindness toward us.

Next it was off to work at the Benbow Coal Company—but not until we bowed our heads and prayed for yet another miracle—that of once again multiplying the fuel in our gas tank so that we could make it to our new job on time. And, again, God indeed answered our prayers for we made it there just fine! Of course, I did my part in helping with this "miracle of multiplication" by shifting the transmission into neutral and shutting off the ignition since most of the way back to town was *downhill*.

Arriving at the coal company, Mr. Benbow met us and said, "Look fellows, you're going to need a place to stay while you are working for me, so before you begin your job, I'm going to take you over here to a hotel where you can get a room for a very reasonable rate. At the hotel, Mr. Benbow engaged in a bargaining session with the clerk for the room rate.

"They can have the room for two dollars," the clerk growled. "Is that by the week or by the month?" Mr. Benbow teased.

"It's the nightly rate, Sir," the clerk answered back.

As Art and I were signing the registration card, Mr. Benbow told the clerk, "These two guys are the new vice presidents of my company! So, I will guarantee payment for their room rent." When he told the clerk his name, she brightened up, for although she did not recognize his person, she at once knew that this was one of the wealthiest men in Fort Madison!

Next Mr. Benbow pointed out a very nice, clean, little café about half a block from the hotel, which he assured us served really good food for a very reasonable price. In addition to all that, he advanced us twenty dollars, which was an enormous blessing, as we certainly needed to gas up our car. We spent five dollars on gasoline, then kept the other fifteen to eat on for the week.

After getting settled in at the hotel, we went back to the coal company to begin our jobs, which consisted of shoveling coal into a truck, delivering it to residences there in Fort Madison, and then unloading the coal from the truck into the customers' basements.

It was probably about the hardest work either of us had ever done and also the dirtiest. Often the wind would blow coal dust back into our faces, which usually were moist with sweat because it was August and very hot weather! But we knew that God had provided for our needs and thus we enjoyed the work even though it was hard, dirty, and hot!

A trusted employee of Mr. Benbow's, his business manager for the coal company, told Art and me the interesting story of why this man keeps the coal company operating.

"You probably think he's a poor merchant eking out a living by selling coal to people. Well, let me tell you something—he is one of the wealthiest men in this city." He went on to tell us that Mr. Benbow owned the main bank in Fort Madison, a men's clothing store, and numerous other businesses in the city, besides two hundred or more houses that he had rented out or was selling to a buyer. He went on to say that the Benbows were planning to build a mansion up on the bluff north of the city.

"Up there where one of the Shaeffer brothers lives, one of the owners of the Shaeffer Pen Company, a world-renowned factory!" And, of course, he was referring to the large lot that Art and I had camped out at overnight.

He proceeded to tell us that the reason why Mr. Benbow operated the coal business was because of the fact that his father had established the business there in the mid-1800s and that it was the very first business establishment in Fort Madison. For that reason, Mr. Benbow chose to keep it alive as a business, certainly not because he needed it to make a living for himself. In essence, he kept the business going for "sentimental reasons!" What an interesting and gracious man he was!

We worked for Mr. Benbow for about ten days and then moved on. After we paid our hotel bill, Art and I had ninety dollars left to help us on our journey back to Kansas and beyond.

It didn't seem like we actually accomplished much on this excursion to Wisconsin and eastern Iowa, but we'd learned some invaluable lessons of faith and trust in God and also experienced firsthand God's miraculous provision when we had depleted our meager resources. Too, the experience in northern Missouri on that morning of August 19, 1952, (the "stranger" that appeared in our car) has, since that day, affected my life and ministry as perhaps no other experience in my seventy-plus years of existence here on God's planet earth!

By *Faith*, Not by Sight

Arriving back at my parents' place in Kansas, there were yet further lessons of trust and obedience for us to learn. It was now early September, 1952, and Art and I had found odd jobs in the area to earn a little more money, which we would need for our next excursion, wherever and whenever it would be.

Hearing that Art and I were back at our parents' home, my brother Dwane came to see us. While visiting with him, I told him about my time in Seattle and of what a beautiful area it was.

"You'd love it there, I'm sure," I told him. "Why don't you consider going out there," I went on to say. "Louie would be glad to have you come live with his family." Then, I made him an offer.

"If you should decide to go to Seattle, I'll buy you a bus ticket! How about it?" I asked.

"Oh, I don't know," he replied, "I'll have to think about it." Shortly after that conversation, Dwane left and did not give any indication when he'd be back. Much to my surprise, he returned within two hours and came to ask me a quick question.

"Does that offer still stand?" he said.

"Oh, yes," I said. "If you want to take me up on my offer, I'll buy you a bus ticket like I promised." Then, I asked him if he had any idea of how much the bus ticket might cost.

"Thirty-eight dollars," he answered. "I just went to the bus depot to check on it."

"You'll have to give me a couple of hours to come up with the money, I told him, to which he agreed. Shortly after that conversation I drove to Great Uncle George Allen's farm to ask if he needed any help with farm work. I told him I needed forty dollars and would work it out if he could advance it to me. Of course, I explained to him just what it was I needed the money for, so he quickly agreed and wrote me out a check. He stated that he needed to get his next wheat crop planted and would like for me to do that for him, to which I agreed. I'd had a lot of experience in that kind of work.

Driving back into the town of Cheney I was able to get the check cashed at a local business establishment. When I arrived back at my parents' home, Dwane was there waiting for me. He was ready for "a change of scenery," he said. So, much to the surprise of all of us, he was on the bus bound for Seattle the next day.

There was, of course, a "method to my madness" in persuading Dwane to make this change in his life by way of a change in location; namely because I was persuaded that he would no doubt continue to live in sin and make foolish decisions as long as he remained there in Kingman County, Kansas. Too, I had been praying earnestly for his salvation for about a month now (since the "night vision" I'd had at the camp meeting in August), so I was perhaps doing my part in helping to see those prayers answered. At least I was certain that the Lord knew my heart and understood my motives!

During the week that Dwane left for Seattle, there was a "revival meeting" in progress at the Cheney Mission Church with a Rev. William Kelly as the evangelist. Art and I were attending services each night, along with my family and many others. It was during those evangelistic meetings that we learned that a small boy had died. His parents were members of the church, thus there was a somber mood on the day of his death that was apparent in the service that night.

When Art and I came home to my parents' house that evening to get ready to go to the revival service, Mother broke the news to us about the lad's death. I distinctly recall my personal reaction to learning of this sadness. It caused me to have a sick feeling in the pit of my stomach. I also began to sense a feeling of intense anger toward the devil, whom Jesus said, "comes only to kill, steal, and destroy" (John 10:10). Art shared virtually the same feeling with me.

Arriving at the revival service in Cheney that evening it was at once apparent that a mood of sadness and even disbelief pervaded the spirits of those in attendance. Pastor Neilson opened the service with prayer, which included a sincere petition that God would comfort the family that had lost their son. He then invited the young people of the church to come to the choir loft during the time of congregational singing, insisting that Art and I come join them, which we did.

While the choir and congregation were singing a hymn, I found my thoughts being dominated with a deep sense of sympathy for the parents and family of this small boy, aged five, who had died that day. Heartfelt compassion welled up within my innermost being because of the grief and sorrow I knew these godly parents were experiencing at that moment.

I do not recall what hymns were being sung, but suddenly, about halfway through the second hymn, an extremely powerful and somewhat frightening impression came pouring into my spirit like a flood. It was not something that I had premeditated or pondered in my mind prior to that moment. All at once I ceased singing because I seemed to suddenly become consumed with an irresistible and incredible thought, which I knew was not a product of my intellect. I thought it would go away, so I hesitated. But go away, it would not. On the contrary, it continued to intensify until I felt like I would explode if it continued. I was made to realize that the

Holy Spirit was dropping this powerful impression into my spirit, though I did not understand it at that moment.

I hesitated momentarily, thinking to myself that this tremendous impression would soon go away, but again, it did not. At last I realized that the Lord God was trying to get my attention. It was at that point that I turned to Art.

"I'm sorry, but I've got to get out of here right away." To my surprise, he said, "Me, too." I was not aware that he was feeling virtually the same impression that I was. We laid down our hymnal and left the choir loft to exit the building. As we walked near Pastor Neilson, who was sitting in the pulpit pew, I leaned over and whispered to him.

"Please excuse Art and me. We've got to leave now." He nodded in agreement as we quickly and quietly exited the building.

It was not necessary for me to tell Art why I had left the service, nor did he need to tell me why he had left. We both had received from the Lord the same stupendous impression simultaneously, which was: "Go in My power and raise that boy from the dead!"

What an awesome thought for two twenty-year-old beginning preachers! Awesome, yes, but also frightening. Without doubt, this was to be the single greatest challenge of my entire life! It was unlike anything I had ever experienced before, nor have I ever experienced anything like it since that time. After getting into our car, before driving away, we shared our thoughts with each other and then concluded that we would drive to my parents' house out on the farm to seek God in prayer before doing anything else.

As we were driving there, I was filled with a tremendously powerful, godly fear. It was not a fear born of dread or cowardice, but rather a fear of failing God—of not obeying the prompting of the Holy Spirit. At any price, I knew that I must obey my Lord and my God!

Upon arriving at my parents' home, Art and I both literally threw the car doors open, jumped out of the car, and dashed into the house. My youngest brother, Gary, had stayed home from church that night because he had been late doing his chores (milking cows, etc.) He was sitting in the living room when Art and I came into the house, but all that we said to him was, "Corky (his nickname), we're going in there to pray."

As we entered my parents' bedroom, closed the door, dropped to our knees and began to cry out to God in anguish of soul, I think we must have scared Gary half to death because he told me later that just the tremendously intense look on our faces as we crossed the room in front of him told him that something unusual was going on with us.

For about the space of an hour, Art and I probably prayed more earnestly and fervently than we had ever prayed before or ever would again. That prayer time was truly a "Gethsemane" experience for both of us! We literally groaned in agony of soul as we cried out to God under the burden of the awesome challenge that had come to us.

At first our pleadings were, "Oh, God, please lift this burden from my heart; please take this feeling away before it crushes my soul. It's going to kill me, Lord," I said, "if You don't take it away. I don't know how I can endure it much longer."

But the feeling did not go away, it only intensified more and more. I know now, of course, that the Lord was bringing me to a place of submission and complete surrender to His Will. He was allowing Art's and my faith to be tried.

After some thirty or forty minutes of agonizing prayer in that manner, I found myself in a different mode. Now I was beginning to say, "Oh Lord, if You won't lift this burden and take away this crushing feeling, then would You please give me the courage and the spiritual power to do this thing which you have called on me to do? I won't go unless I have the absolute assurance that You will go with me!"

After we both prayed for twenty-five or thirty minutes in this mode, this powerful and somewhat frightening feeling began to change from one of a godly fear to one of assurance and confidence. As I found myself yielding to the Father's Will, the next mode or direction my prayers took was, "Lord, all I ask is that You show me that this is indeed You and not just a personal impulse, then I will go in the power of the Holy Spirit to do 'the impossible,' for You have told me in Your Word that 'all things are possible' If only I believe!"

"Oh Lord," I went on, "I know that with You nothing is impossible! So, Lord, I will do anything You want me to do no matter what men may think or say, for I'd rather have Your power and the anointing of the Blessed Holy Spirit than man's approval!"

After praying thus, my feeling began to change to one of incredible assurance and confidence. I sensed faith beginning to rise in my heart to a degree I had never before experienced. And, I am confident that it was at that point in my praying that the Holy Spirit supernaturally imparted to me the spiritual gift of faith, emptying me of all doubt concerning this "special assignment." This is the "God kind of faith" that causes one to *know that you know* as you go forth in His Name and according to His Will that He will surely be with you! And, "If God be with you, who [or what] can be against you?" (Romans 8:31).

A wonderful peace began to sweep over my entire being at that point and I suddenly realized that I no longer had that "fear of failure" or the "fear of man" bombarding my thoughts. The final moment of this hour-plus of intense prayer was somewhat of a dialogue between the Lord and myself. Art later related to me that he had experienced virtually the same sequence of emotions as he also earnestly prayed—godly fear bordering on fright and dread at first, then submission and surrender to God's Will, followed by tremendous assurance and fearlessness, and then strong faith arising in his heart, then finally this dialogue with the Lord.

Now when I assert that a dialogue ensued between me and the Lord, by no means do I intend to leave the impression that God was talking "out loud" to me. It was, however, at this stage of intense prayer that my voice silenced and I now had entered into a deep trance-like state of consciousness in which I was communing with the Lord in the Spirit realm. It has been my joy and blessed experience to enter into this realm of sacred communion with the

Lord on several occasions since that encounter. In moments like these, one becomes highly alert and acutely sensitive to the wooing of the Holy Spirit accompanied by a deep, settled peace and restful joyfulness.

In essence, here is how this dialogue between myself and the Lord unfolded: At first I reasoned in my heart.

But, Lord, what if the parents of this little boy who had died are unwilling to allow us to go to the mortuary in Kingman to carry out this 'venture of faith?' After all, it's already well into the night. We would have to contact the mortician, convince him to let us enter into the morgue, and then call for this child to come forth from the dead! Besides that, Lord, the child's body has undoubtedly been embalmed, so how are we going to deal with all of these factors, Lord?

What I heard the Lord say to me in the Spirit realm in answer to these questions was: "You will at once be met with disbelief and even unbelief. What I have called you to do will appear to these parents as something abstract and far out, a source of added grief and anguish to them. Indeed, they will be unwilling to go through with this that I have put upon your hearts to do. But, you must obey Me regardless of rejection and unbelief. I, the Lord, have put this thing into your hearts. Therefore, go . . . doubting nothing, and I will be with you and will strengthen you with my might."

But, Lord, I again reasoned, *What if the child's body has already been embalmed?* The answer to that question came immediately, and crystal clear: "Lord, by this time he stinketh; for he hath been dead for four days" (the disciples' words at the grave of Lazarus just before Jesus raised him from the dead, as recorded in John 11:39).

That was the catalyst that ended all of my "what if" wonderings. From that moment forward I knew that I had Divine assurance for, "With God, all things are possible!" And since I was going with Him and He was going with me, all the hesitations were settled! Getting up from our knees, Art and I got back into our car and proceeded toward the farm where this family lived, a few miles away. As we drove by the church in Cheney, folks were beginning to file out of the sanctuary. The revival service was over for that night

With a tremendous feeling of power and assurance, we drove straight out to the farm where these people lived. When we arrived there, it was at once evident that a number of friends and relatives had gathered at the home to express their sympathy and condolences to the family. This, of course, made our mission a little awkward, but by no means did it dampen our spirits.

Upon being invited into their home, acting as the spokesman, I first expressed to these grief-stricken parents our deepest sympathy in the loss of this son who had been so very precious to them. Then I proceeded, both carefully and deliberately, to relate to them our mission.

As long as I live, I'll never forget the look that came on that mother's face as I opened up my heart to her, explaining how God had spoken to us about this and of how we had spent an hour or more in intense, earnest prayer before coming there. I tried to be as compassionate as I possibly could, taking care not to come on too forcefully as I told the parents how God had spoken to Art and me simultaneously about coming here, by faith, to raise their son from the dead.

The look on that godly, devoted mother's face was one of mixed emotions. Undoubtedly, the thought of having her little son restored to life again excited hope in her heart, but there was also a distinct look of apprehension on her face. As for the father of this child, he seemed to be numb; stunned by the stark reality that his precious son was gone. It was understandably obvious that he was stricken with grief. One of the first responses to come from the mother was, "I don't think there would be any use in it now. They've probably embalmed his body by this time."

"Yes," I said. "That thought occurred to me also and when I asked the Lord about it, the answer He gave to me was John 11:39 ["... by this time he stinketh; for he hath been dead four days."] I was careful to assure these parents that Art and I were not there to pressure them into something that they were uncertain about or unwilling to give consent to, but rather to challenge them to believe God for a mighty miracle—the restoration of their son to life again and to simply cooperate with the Holy Spirit in that which He had told us so clearly and powerfully to do. We also assured them that we would definitely not go to that mortuary and attempt to raise this child from the dead without their consent and that God had shown us in advance that the decision to do that would have to be made by them.

While we were still conversing with these parents about this matter there came another knock at their door. When the door was opened, in walked Pastor Neilson and Evangelist William Kelly. With scarcely a word of greeting, Pastor Neilson (who had been there with the family earlier in the day) said to the parents, "If these boys are here to raise your son from the dead, please cooperate with them because God spoke to me when they left the revival service tonight that this was the reason why!" He then added that he had told Brother Kelly at the conclusion of the service that evening, "Those two young men who left the service this evening during congregational singing have gone to raise that little boy from the dead."

Surprisingly, Brother Kelly's response to Pastor Neilson was, "If they have, count me out; I don't have that kind of faith!"

"You will go with me out to their home, won't you?" Pastor Neilson asked Brother Kelly, to which he responded in the affirmative.

Pastor Neilson told everyone there in that living room and kitchen how that on the way out to their home, the power of God had come upon him so mightily that he had to pull his car off the road and park for a while. "It was so strong," he said, "until I felt as if I might be raptured!" He explained that they'd had to stay parked there along the highway until he finally regained his composure.

After Pastor Neilson compassionately urged these parents to cooperate with Art and me and to believe God for a mighty miracle, a moment of deathly silence seemed to come over both of them momentarily. It was as if they were weighing the matter in their minds. Then, finally, the silence broke with the mother responding.

"No, I don't think we want to go through with this. He's gone now and we've just got to accept it." Her husband agreed with that decision.

"That's alright," I told them. "And I pray that we haven't added to your grief and sorrow by coming here tonight. But I also hope that you might understand that we most assuredly felt that God had clearly spoken to us about this matter and that it was such a powerful impression until we simply could not ignore it. That is why we came."

"I understand," the mother sobbed, "and we appreciate your willingness to do what you feel God has led you to do. But, again, we don't feel like we can go through with it. He's gone now and we'll just have to face the reality that we don't have him any longer."

As soon as this mother had expressed that decision on their part as final, another awesome feeling of peace came over my spirit—a peace of satisfaction that, although it was an extremely difficult and awkward situation for Art and me, yet we had not been disobedient to the prompting of the Holy Spirit; hence we were at peace about their decision, even though there was a feeling of disappointment on our part.

Pastor Neilson, however, was not yet willing to call this matter off. To him, it was "an appointment with destiny," hence he continued to plead with these parents to reconsider their decision. "Because," he said, "I am convinced beyond the shadow of doubt that God has sent these two young men here to raise your son from the dead!"

Evidently the mental and emotional pressure of this ordeal had become too much for this devoted mother for, at the continued urging of Pastor Neilson to reconsider their decision, she began to weep, almost uncontrollably, almost screaming at times. It was, indeed, a heart-rending cry, which admittedly had a dampening effect upon our spirits.

So as not to bring additional strain upon these grieving parents, we all decided that we should leave and let them get some rest, which they were obviously in need of. It had been a long day for them. We prayed with them briefly and said, "God bless and comfort you, and may He give you rest tonight."

As we were departing, the mother said to us, "They are bringing his body in the casket here to our home tomorrow. If you still feel like God wants you to bring him to life again, please come back and we will see." Although out of courtesy and respect we agreed to her suggestion, yet in my heart of hearts, I knew that once that burden lifted and the intense feeling was gone, it would not return to us.

Driving back to my parents' home, I questioned thus: "Why would God speak to us so forcefully and powerfully to go there to that home to raise this child from the dead and then nothing come of it?" I was not asking that question in unbelief, nor was it arising from a concession of defeat, for I remained absolutely certain that God had indeed sent Art and me on this mission; this venture of faith, even though I did not, as yet, fully understand. My real concern was this: *Was God's purpose defeated or thwarted by the decision of these parents not to consent to our going to the mortuary in Kingman for the purpose of raising that little boy from the dead?*

It was not until sometime later, as I was pondering this matter in my mind and in my spirit, that God spoke to me very clearly, causing me to know that His primary purpose (for me, at least) was to test my obedience to Him. He reminded me of the story in the Book of Genesis in which He told Abraham, His friend, to take his son, Isaac, whom he dearly loved, to Mount Moriah and there offer him upon an altar as a burnt sacrifice to Him . . . and how He stopped Abraham from slaying Isaac at the last second (the knife had been raised in Abraham's hand to come down upon Isaac with the death blow). He then showed Abraham a ram caught in a thicket by its horns that he could use to sacrifice unto Him in the stead of Isaac, his son.

It was then that I was made to know that Art and I had been given a "test of obedience and of faith" in this ordeal with the boy that had died. God knew when He called Abraham to go to Mount Moriah to offer Isaac, his son, as a sacrifice to Him that He would not actually allow him to kill Isaac. Even so, God knew exactly what the outcome would be when He called Art and me to go raise the small boy from the dead on that September evening of 1952. Thus I recall the words of Samuel, the prophet, spoken to King Saul of Israel: "To obey is better than sacrifice . . ." (1 Samuel 15:2). Hence I refer to this experience as my "Mount Moriah Experience."

Canvas Cathedrals

It was shortly after the death of that small boy that a young evangelist whose name was Gilbert Cowart had erected a 40 x 60-foot gospel tent in the town of Norwich, Kansas, to conduct a revival crusade. Art and I drove over there to attend a couple of nights of the crusade services. Now it so happened that Rev. Cowart's wife was about to give birth to a child that week, thus he was in a dilemma. He wanted to be with his wife, but he had set up this tent and had gotten a ten-day crusade underway. So, he came to Art and me and asked if we'd consider taking over that tent crusade. There were five nights remaining of the ten-day crusade. Of course, we were delighted to be afforded the opportunity.

"We'd be glad to do that!" we told him. The gospel tent that Rev. Cowart had set up in Norwich belonged to the Ministerial and Missionary Alliance that Art and I had been accepted into while at the camp meeting in Joplin, Missouri, the previous August. The policy for using the tent (one of several) was that any member of the Alliance that desired to use one of the gospel tents for revival crusades could use it for as many as three crusades. After the third crusade, if another member of the Alliance desired to use that tent, it would be required that it be turned over to that minister. Of course, Art and I were not on the "waiting list" for the tent that Rev. Cowart had erected in Norwich, but we were blessed to be thrust into that position by virtue of Rev. Cowart's forfeiture of his use of it.

The remaining five nights of the crusade in Norwich, while not "earthshaking," were at least a start for Art and me. It was also a confirmation to us concerning the answer we had received from the Lord after our time of prayer and fasting in the small state park near Camp Douglas, Wisconsin, in which the Lord assured us that He would indeed open doors for us as we continued to walk with Him and obey the leadings of His Holy Spirit.

Actually, Art and I preached only one night each of the remaining five nights of the Norwich Crusade. We had asked my Uncle, Paul Bailey, to come out from Wichita (where he was pastoring a church at that time), and preach three of those five nights, which he did. Uncle Paul had lived in the vicinity of Norwich prior to his conversion and was quite well known there, especially by several men whom he had whipped back in those days!

My younger sisters, Janice, sixteen, and "Boots," fourteen, came to the nightly meetings to provide special music. Janice played an accordion for the congregational singing, as well as for duets that she and Boots sang. It was during the Norwich tent revival that a young schoolteacher lent me the book, *Healing the Sick and Casting Out Devils* by Rev. T.L. Osborn. I could hardly lay that book down until I had read it in its entirety. What a faith-builder that book was for me! After returning the book to the young lady who had lent it to me, I purchased a copy for myself. It's been a favorite of mine across the years. It is indeed a "classic" and soon became a study and a text book to me.

After the Norwich Crusade was concluded we dismantled the tent, taking care to diagram the layout of everything—the position and distance of the stakes, etc., which was most helpful the next time we would use the tent.

We used Dad's wheat truck to transport parts of the tent from Norwich to the farm where my parents lived. In order for us to transport the tent from Norwich to other places for crusade meetings we decided to build a two-wheeled trailer to pull behind our car, which we did with the help of my dad. It was quite attractive and we were happy to have it. We painted it green, as near to the color of our 1949 Oldsmobile as we could get. Across the tailgate of the trailer we carefully painted the words "Christ for Victory" in a bright silver color. We also designed and had two hundred copies of a *Revival Song Book* with "Souvenir Copy of Morlin-Ott Evangelistic Association" printed on the front cover. It also had a globe with a cross in the center of it that displayed the words "Christ For Victory" printed across the globe. They were printed by Gospel Publishing House in Springfield, Missouri, and made available to audiences for the price of fifty cents.

Once our trailer was finished and we had received our new songbooks, we were ready to launch out into the tent revival arena, which was quite popular in the early '50s, especially in the "Bible Belt" where we were. Since it was now into October and we had nowhere in particular to go with our tent, songbooks, guitar, and sound equipment, we again took on a week or so of employment to earn some funds for our next excursion.

When "the moment of truth" came for us, we decided to take off for *somewhere* with the tent in hopes that *some* pastor in *some* town might be interested in having us conduct a tent crusade in his area. It was often possible to draw people to a tent meeting where they would not attend a church (at least not until they were converted).

After a time of seeking God in prayer, we bade our family farewell and took off for the Oklahoma Panhandle. We knew that a Rev. Tabor was pastoring a church in Guyman, Oklahoma, so decided to go there and look him up to discuss the possibility of a tent crusade in his town. Although Rev. Tabor was very friendly and hospitable to us, he said that he did not think it was a good time for a tent meeting in Guyman.

"The weather is beginning to turn cooler," he said, "and you'd have a hard time getting people to come out to a tent meeting this late in the fall." Then he made a suggestion to us.

"Why don't you boys go down to the Houston area? The weather there would still be good for this type of revival crusade. There is a Sister Pauline Parham who is the pastor of the Knox Street Full Gospel Church there. She could give you assistance and guidance as to what areas you might be able to set up your tent in."

Rev. Tabor bade us Godspeed as we drove away, enroute to Houston. We drove from Guyman to San Antonio and then east to Houston. We arrived on the Westside "outskirts" of the big city late in the evening on a Saturday night, so decided to stop at the first motel we came to for an overnight stay, which happened to be "The Alamo Courts," a small facility that consisted of several cottages with a carport for each room. The price was reasonable and the room was satisfactory, so we lodged there for the night.

Since neither Art nor I had ever been in Houston previously and thus were not at all acquainted with the area, we did not have a clue where we were with reference to the Knox Street Full Gospel Church. We agreed that we should get up early the next morning so as to allow ample travel time from our location to that church, taking into consideration that it could be on the complete opposite side of the city.

Early Sunday morning I went out into the courtyard, where there was a pay phone booth, to call Mrs. Parham. After she answered her phone, I identified myself and then told her that Art and I were there in Houston and that we were planning to attend the morning worship service at her church.

"Where are you now?" she asked.

"Well, we are at a small motel along U.S. Highway 90. It's called "The Alamo Courts," I responded.

"You don't mean it!" she exclaimed, "Then you are just across the street from the parsonage and the church is next door." Sure enough, as I turned and looked in the direction she had told me to, there it was, the Knox Street Full Gospel Church! What an amazing coincidence—*or was it?* Strangely enough, neither Art nor I had noticed that the cross street next to the motel that faced U.S. Highway 90 was Knox Street. For sure, we never dreamed that where we would stop for a night's lodging was next door to the church where we intended to attend the Sunday worship service!

"Sister Parham," as she was known to everyone there, had remembered seeing Art and me at the National Fellowship Camp meeting in Joplin, Missouri, the previous August. We also remembered seeing her there, although we had not gotten acquainted with her at that time. Incidentally, Pauline happened to be the widow of the late Rev. Robert Parham, the minister I had heard preach at the Cheney Mission Church some eight years previous, shortly before his untimely death in 1944.

"You will be preaching for me this morning, won't you?" she insisted.

"Oh no," I replied, "We're not here to minister. We were just hoping to attend your morning worship service."

"Nonsense," she retorted, "I want you to preach here this morning and then your friend Art can preach in our evening service, so get fired up and come on over!"

"Well, if you insist," I said back to her. "We'll do our very best."

"That's good enough for me," she said. "You are both 'on' for today! And why don't you come on over to the parsonage in about forty-five minutes and have some breakfast with Mother, Charles (her fourteen-year-old son), and me!" I reluctantly agreed, hung up the phone, and went back to our room.

"Art, you're not going to believe this!" I told him, rather enthusiastically.

"What's wrong?" he asked. "Is the church on the far side of town?"

"Nope!" I replied as I took him by the hand and led him over to the window of our room.

"Look across the street," I instructed him. "What do you see?"

"Well, I see a house," he replied.

"Now, look a little farther, around to the left," I said.

"There's a church there!" he exclaimed. "Do you mean to tell me that that is Sister Parham's church?" he asked rather excitedly.

"It sure enough is," I answered him. "And the house directly across the street is the parsonage—and we're invited to go over there to eat breakfast with them after while. And that's not all," I went on to say. "She insists that we preach in both services at her church today—me this morning and you this evening. How about that?"

All Art could say at that moment was, "Oh, thank You, Jesus! Praise God for being so gracious and kind to Gail and me! What a blessing. What a miracle that You allowed us to stop at this humble little motel to spend the night right across the street from the church that we wanted to find. Even though we didn't have a clue where the church might be, You knew where it was, and have blessed us abundantly! Praise Your Wonderful Name!"

We made haste to get dressed for church after a time of earnest prayer for inspiration and the anointing to preach God's Word. It was a most joyous moment for Art and me to meet Sister Parham, her mother, and her son, Charles, as we arrived at the parsonage for breakfast. We assured her that we certainly never dreamed of being met with such gracious hospitality and generosity.

Pauline's mother, Sister Fowler, was a godly, gracious lady with a true servant's heart. She, too, was a widow and had lived with Pauline, her only child, since the death of her son-in-law. She prepared a very delicious breakfast for all of us and we enjoyed it greatly, as well as our time of "get acquainted" fellowship around the breakfast table.

Sister Parham's fourteen-year-old son, Charles, was a gracious young man and very handsome, too. Art and I were very impressed with his mannerly and respectful demeanor. We bonded with him from the minute we met him, and the association became a friendship that remained intact until the time of his untimely death at age nineteen.

After a breakfast "fit for a king," Art and I returned to our room for some serious preparation and prayer for our preaching engagements of the day. With godly fear, coupled with holy boldness, we both preached our hearts out in the two services that day at Knox Street Full Gospel Church, concluding both services with an altar call and a time of prayer for the sick.

Sister Parham and all of her constituents seemed to be blessed to have two young itinerant evangelists as guest speakers at their church on that Sunday morning of October 26, 1952. A very generous offering was received for Art and me at the conclusion of the evening service, which was a distinct blessing since ours was strictly a "faith ministry."

Following the Sunday night service, Art and I met with Sister Parham and a few of the men of the church to discuss the possibility of a tent revival crusade in the area. After a somewhat extensive dialogue concerning this matter it was concluded that this would not be a good place for a tent meeting since vacant lots suitable for erecting a gospel tent were virtually nonexistent. We all agreed to pray about the matter, and then the meeting was dismissed.

Art and I were invited to the parsonage for breakfast again on Monday morning. As we settled down to eggs, bacon, and toast, Sister Parham spoke to us.

"Gentlemen, I believe I have a Word from the Lord for you with reference to your desire to conduct a tent crusade somewhere." She went on.

"Why don't you go to Mississippi and look up Brother Billy Sparks? He and his wife, Patsy, are pastoring the Cedar Creek Full Gospel Church there in the vicinity of the town of Crandall. I'm sure they would welcome you to that very needy area and I'm certain that you could have a really good tent crusade there."

As soon as Sister Parham communicated this "Word from the Lord," Art and I both sensed "the witness of the Holy Spirit" in our own spirits that this was the will of God for us at that time. As on other occasions, once that "witness" was realized, a peace and sense of satisfaction came over us—a quiet sense of restfulness, along with a surge of strong faith, began to pervade our entire beings and we knew we'd soon be headed east, Mississippi bound.

"But, why don't you stay around Houston for a couple of days," Sister Parham suggested. "There will be a fellowship meeting at the Full Gospel Church in Waller (Texas) on Tuesday. I have been asked to be the special guest speaker for that meeting and I'd feel honored to have you fellows come go along with Mother and me if you would care to. I believe you'd enjoy it and, too, you could get acquainted with other local pastors and evangelists there. How about it?" she asked.

Art and I both agreed that this was an excellent suggestion. We stayed over two extra days and were richly blessed by the inspiring and uplifting afternoon and evening services held in Waller.

Becoming acquainted with Sister Parham was, for me, the beginning of a long and most meaningful fellowship. She would later become pastor of the Cheney Mission Church in my hometown, where she served with dignity and sincerity for several years. It was on Friday, December 13, 1957, that her beloved son, Charles Parham, was killed in a traffic accident on the streets in Wichita, Kansas. My dad and I happened to be in Wichita that Friday morning and by coincidence (or perhaps by divine providence) learned of this tragedy and thus went immediately to Wesley Hospital where the boy had been taken. By God's grace, in some small way we were able to lend some moral and spiritual support to this dear, grief-stricken mother and servant of the Lord.

Some time later, although she was no longer pastor of the Cheney Mission Church in 1965, she was the unanimous choice of my family to officiate at the memorial service for my beloved mother on May 15, 1965, who was promoted to her eternal reward at the age of sixty-three.

Early Wednesday morning, October 29, 1952, Art and I left Houston bound for Mississippi. Sister Parham had given us general but sufficient directions to the Cedar Creek community of eastern Mississippi, which was about thirty miles south of the city of Meridian.

We arrived in the Cedar Creek area around four that Wednesday afternoon. Earlier that day, we had stopped at a small general mercantile store to ask directions to the Anderson Sawmill because Sister Parham had told us that the Sparkses lived directly across the road from the mill.

"You go a 'fer piece' up this here road," the clerk who gave us directions to the sawmill said, "and when you come to a 'Y' in the road, you'll be just a hop and a jump from that sawmill. You can't miss it."

We thanked him and drove on. However, when we came to the "Y" in the road, since we could not yet see the sawmill (it was actually down in a ravine out of sight from the "Y" in the road), we turned to the right, whereas we *should* have gone to the left. In a short while we realized our mistake, so started looking for a place where we could turn around and head back in the direction we were coming from.

Now, the roads in that area were all dirt (red dirt) and when the weather was warm and dry a car traveling thirty miles per hour or faster would create a "rooster tail" cloud of dust in its wake. While watching carefully for a suitable place to turn around (with both the car and trailer), I inadvertently allowed the car to drift over to the left until it was straddling the center of the road. At that point, we were nearing the crest of a slight hill when we met a big black De Soto sedan approaching us at a considerably high rate of speed. The driver of the big black De Soto sedan was also using "his half of the middle" of the road, thus we narrowly missed a head-on collision.

We both recognized the driver of that big black De Soto sedan as Brother Billy Sparks. We had seen him at the camp meeting in Joplin, Missouri, and also recognized the car, with Texas license plates on it. There could be no mistake! That was Brother Sparks! And, he was leaving a giant rooster-tail cloud of red dust as he sped along on this dirt road.

At the last instant, Brother Sparks swerved to the right, went down into the bar ditch, and then somehow got his car back up onto the road without losing control of it. He accelerated and continued on, lifting another red dust rooster tail behind him.

Art and I both breathed a sign of relief and immediately started praising the Lord, realizing that we had just encountered a close call. When we found a convenient place to turn around, we stopped for a few minutes to think the situation over.

"I guess I really blew it by running him off the road," I said to Art. "Maybe it made him pretty mad. I hope not! He's a big, burley guy. He might be mad enough to whip us. At any rate, he'd probably be in no mood to help us with a tent meeting after this close encounter," I said.

"Do you suppose we ought to keep going?" I asked Art.

"I don't know," he replied. Together we finally decided to "face the music." After all, we had driven all the way there from Houston, Texas, to find the Sparkses, so why not take the chance? Thus, after turning around, we continued back down the road until we reached the "Y" again. As we followed around to the right, sure enough there was a small house with a barn behind it and the big black De Soto sedan parked alongside the house. Approaching the house we could see the sawmill to our right.

Brother Sparks had been home only a few minutes when he looked out the kitchen window and saw Art and me approaching the driveway.

"Oh my Lord, Patsy," he exclaimed, "I just ran these guys off and now they've come to get me!"

"Oh, don't be so silly," she said back to him as they looked out the window together. "They're just a couple of young men," By this time we had parked and I was knocking at their door. Sister Patsy came to the door and spoke to us.

"Hello, fellows! Are you lost? What can I do for you? Are you looking for someone in this area?"

It was then that I divulged our identity and stated our purpose for being there.

"But, the first thing I want to do," I said rather sheepishly, "is apologize to your husband for running him off of the road a few minutes ago." Upon hearing me say that, Brother Billy came out of the kitchen and started apologizing to us.

"I'm the guilty one," he said. "I was driving much too fast on a dirt road and I almost hit you guys head-on, so I want to apologize to you for that," he added.

"Oh, no," I said, "It was the other way around. I was driving in the middle of the road, not paying enough attention to what I was doing, so I want to apologize to *you!*" We both breathed a sign of relief and sat down for a nice visit. That was the beginning of a lifetime friendship with Billy and Patsy Sparks and their family. At that time, Brenda was their only child. Linda and Marlon would join her a few years later.

The Sparkses invited Art and me to stay with them in their humble little two-bedroom parsonage, which we did for over a month. We were made to feel perfectly welcome by these gracious, hospitable servants of the Lord. We were soon both invited to preach at the Sunday services at the Cedar Creek Full Gospel Church.

In the meantime, Brother Sparks helped us find a suitable location to set up our gospel tent for a crusade. It was on the campus of an abandoned rural elementary school in the "Bright Water" community of Choctaw County Alabama, just across the Mississippi-Alabama state line.

With the help of Brother Sparks, we went right to work on Monday morning, securing permission to set up the tent there on the school grounds, hauling sawdust from the Anderson Sawmill to cover the ground area inside the tent, finding chairs, building a platform, etc., in preparation for the crusade, which was to begin on Thursday night, November 6. We publicized the crusade in and around the area, mostly by personal contact, calling on neighbors and personally inviting as many people as possible to attend the crusade.

During this Bright Water Alabama Crusade, which continued through Sunday night, November 30, many interesting things happened. Most of the time Art was the song leader and I was his accompanist on a guitar. Our own, personalized crusade songbooks would be used for the first time and consisted of sixty-five well-known and best-loved gospel hymns. Art and I always had to "compare notes" before each service since I could not play the guitar in every key. On the nights when the Sparkses accompanied us to the tent, Sister Patsy would bring her accordion and play for the song service, a welcome reprieve, at least for me!

We also persuaded Brother Billy to preach three nights of the crusade. He was a very dynamic and inspirational preacher, with considerably more experience than either of us, so this was like a "shot in the arm" for the crusade.

Several young men from both the Cedar Creek and Bright Water areas "bonded" with Art and me and were there for every service—a total of twenty-five nights. They became our "helpers" with the services and the equipment (P.A. system, microphones, guitar, etc.). They also served as ushers for the crusade. We did pass offering plates to those in attendance each night as there were expenses incurred in getting set up (electric power pole, sawdust, materials for the platform, etc.) and this was an interesting observation: There was never a single piece of money in any of the offerings we received bigger than a 50-cent piece. The largest single night's offering was $16.70—the smallest offering was fifty cents! The total offerings for the crusade were $101.73! But, we were blessed. We were not in the Lord's work for money. Our single greatest quest was to win souls to the Lord Jesus Christ. Everything else was secondary, and, thanks be to God, several souls were saved during the crusade. There were also a number of notable healings as we prayed for the sick each night.

On Fire for God!

Even though we were in the Deep South, it was now mid-November and the evenings were quite cool, so we kept the side canvas curtains lowered in an effort to keep it as warm as possible inside. But when the temperature dropped down into the mid-thirties after the sun went down in the evenings, we concluded that we would have to find a way to heat the interior up if we hoped to have the people come back each evening.

After discussing this dilemma with some of the local people, someone suggested that charcoal burning "smudge-pots" (also called "salamanders") would solve the problem. So, Art and I, along with Brother Sparks and one of the young men who had been helping us each night, drove into Meridian, Mississippi, to buy some of these amazing little heaters. We located a hardware store there in

Meridian that carried them. We decided to purchase six of these quaint little pots (small buckets lined with approximately one inch of clay with a number of one-inch holes around the side for air intake). They cost us $3.95 each. We also purchased about twenty bags of charcoal briquettes for fuel to burn in these *smudge pots*. The sales clerk advised us that if we would take them outside in the open air and let them burn for a few minutes they would burn smoke-free, which we found to be true.

Now since Art and I rotated nights preaching, we agreed that the man *not* preaching would attend to all the preparations for the service that night, which among other duties included getting the smudge-pots lighted and burning on the outside of the tent before carrying them inside. The one whose night it was to do the preaching would be free of those duties so that he could go into the "power room" (prayer room) to seek God for the anointing and inspiration to preach the Word that night. This prayer room consisted of a canvas curtain in the front left side of the tent, just next to the platform, that provided some privacy for the one praying and preparing there each night.

On one of the evenings when it was my turn to preach, Art and several of the young men who were our helpers had taken the pots outside the tent to get the charcoal briquettes burning. Apparently one of the young men came up with a bright idea.

"Why don't we siphon some gasoline out of your car," he suggested to Art. "That will get the charcoal burning real fast," he assured him.

"Sounds like a winner to me," Art responded. "Let's do it!" So the young man hurried over to his car and took out a small rubber hose. Someone had also found a quart glass jar, so the young man siphoned about one and a half pints of gasoline out of our gas tank into the jar and handed it to Art. Not thinking his decision through, Art lit a match, threw it into the smudge pot, and then proceeded to pour gasoline onto the charcoal. To his amazement, surprise, and shock, the fire quickly climbed right up the stream of gasoline, frightening Art so much that he jumped backwards. As he jumped, he inadvertently doused his jacket with gasoline and was at once "on fire." Frightened, he dropped the quart jar and took off running—full speed! As he ran past the corner of the tent where I was praying; I could hear the commotion.

The first sound was like a burning "blow torch" as the flames of burning gasoline on his jacket were being fanned by the wind of his swift movement. The secondary noise that caused me to run out of the tent was the voices of the young men, as well as their pounding footsteps, running after Art crying out.

"Stop! *Stop!*" Art just kept running all the while, struggling to get his navy blue blazer unbuttoned so that he could shed it from his body. In his struggle to get the jacket unbuttoned he finally popped the button off, then quickly dropped the burning coat. The young men who were chasing Art, intending to tackle him so they could extinguish the fire, were about thirty or forty feet behind him, thus when they reached the burning jacket one of them trampled the garment until the flame was extinguished. It took Art about fifty or sixty yards before he pulled up and stopped running. By the time he returned to the place where he had shed his jacket the young men had extinguished the fire and now were shaking dirt and dead grass off of it.

Indeed, the Lord had protected Art in this whole ordeal. Like the three Hebrews whom King Nebuchadnezzar had thrown into the midst of a burning fiery furnace, ". . . the fire had no power upon their bodies [no burns, no blisters] nor was a hair on their head singed; neither were their coats changed [burned, scorched], nor was the smell of fire on them (Daniel 3:27). So it was with my friend and colleague, Art Morlin.

One of the young men who picked up Art's jacket after they had extinguished the gasoline flames handed it to my stunned but happy buddy. Art's face was white and for a moment he was stunned, realizing that he was not burned at all by those flames; not a hair was singed nor was a fiber of his jacket burned! All that had burned was the gasoline Art had inadvertently splashed on his jacket. Undoubtedly within a few more seconds the fibers of his jacket would have ignited and the jacket would have burst into flames. But God's hand was upon him. Indeed, this was a miracle of divine protection! And, oh yes, one of the young men, walking back over the path Art had taken in his flight, even found the button he had popped off in shedding his jacket. *How amazing!* It was an incident that would never be forgotten, especially by Art himself.

Really, in the final analysis, all that the fire had done was burn out all of the gasoline Art had splashed onto his jacket, so much so that there was no smell of gasoline on it any longer. But it also burned just long enough, and no longer, that there was no smell of smoke on the jacket, either. About the only thing that was different about Art's jacket was that he needed to get the button sewed back on, which Sister Patsy did for him the next day. Needless to say, Art and our friends would be much wiser from "firing up" the smudge pots after this incident.

The smudge pots themselves worked great, making the inside of the tent "warm as toast"—that is, until one night a couple of small boys started throwing sawdust on top of the burning briquettes. That resulted in a near-evacuation exercise! But with the help of several men, the side canvas curtains were raised to allow a draft to blow across the interior of the tent. The smudge pots had to then be carried outside and away from the tent. This, of course, caused the temperature inside the tent to drop considerably, but the audience stayed with us until the conclusion of the service that night. From then on, through the conclusion of the crusade, "sentinels" were stationed alongside the six smudge pots to prevent any more "smoke outs."

"Cops and Robbers"

The Bright Water Tent Revival Crusade was indeed an enriching and satisfying experience for Art and me, and to some extent a maturing one. Sunday night, November 30, was the concluding service of the twenty-five-night crusade. We even had a service on Thanksgiving night, with a fairly good turnout. We had been invited to the home of a pastor in a nearby community (along with the Sparkses) for a wonderful Thanksgiving dinner. It was a great time of fellowship, as well as an opportunity to make new friendships with Rev. and Mrs. Earl Morgan, our hosts that day.

One final observation concerning the Bright Water Tent Revival Crusade: A godly Christian lady from the town of Toxy, Alabama, who had attended most of the revival services there in the Bright Water community, made a suggestion to Art and me.

"Why don't you brothers consider coming back in the springtime and conducting a tent revival meeting in *our town*? We sure need a revival there."

Somehow that suggestion seemed good to us and as we prayed about it that night we concluded that it seemed good to the Lord, also. We decided to give it some serious consideration. Of course, we would need to gain the backing and blessing of some local pastors there if we were to come. We would also need to secure the permission of the executive officers of the Alliance in order to plan the meeting. Early Monday morning, December 1, we contacted the president of the organization, explained to him our desire to continue using the tent in the spring of 1953 for a tent meeting in the town of Toxy, requesting permission to store the tent in a farmer's barn there for the winter. Permission was granted, thus the next move was to dismantle the tent, return all of the borrowed chairs, clean up the school grounds, and notify the power company that the power pole could be removed, along with numerous other details.

Once all of these details were attended to, we drove to the farmer's place, parked the trailer inside his barn, and then suspended the large canvas bags (five of them) from the rafters in the barn so as to prevent rats and mice from nesting inside them. The tent poles and stakes were left in the trailer and thus everything was stored in preparation for the Toxy Crusade that coming spring.

While dismantling the tent, Art and I talked about taking a day off before driving back to Kansas. After looking at a map of the region we were in, we decided to drive down to Pensacola, Florida, for a day of sightseeing and fun. One of the young men helping us that day, "Pub" Roberts, asked if we'd mind if he joined in going to Pensacola.

"Why not," we both agreed. We had also invited the Sparkses to go with us, but they declined because of other commitments that day.

So, early Tuesday morning we went by his home to pick up Pub, then were on our way. Since our drive to Pensacola that morning would take us through Mobile, Alabama, Pub asked if we'd mind stopping at a mortuary in Mobile where his older brother worked so he could run and say "hello" to him. His younger sister, Joyce, had moved to Mobile in search of employment a few weeks prior to our stop there.

When Pub emerged from the mortuary he told us that his sister had just gotten a job as a waitress in a restaurant in downtown Mobile.

"Why don't we stop and have some breakfast," he hinted. "We haven't eaten yet," he went on to say, "so this would be a good time to do that, and then I could see Joyce for a few minutes, too."

"Oh, sure, why not," we responded. The restaurant was easy to find and there was a parking spot on the street directly in front of the restaurant, so we parked there and went in to eat a meal.

When Joyce saw her brother she exclaimed, "Pub, what are you doing here?" He then introduced Art and me to Joyce and told her what we were up to.

"But, how did you know I worked here? I just started working yesterday morning!" He told her we had stopped at the mortuary to see their older brother who had, in turn, told him that she was now working at the restaurant. We all ordered a meal, which was served to us in fine fashion by Joyce. Then, since the restaurant did not have many customers, Joyce sat down in the booth beside her brother.

In the course of a brief conversation with her, Pub suggested that Joyce ask her boss if she could take the rest of the day off and go to Pensacola with us.

"You guys won't mind, will you?" he asked. Again, Art and I agreed to Pub's suggestion and so Joyce went, rather meekly, to her new boss to ask a "big favor" of him.

"My brother and two minister friends are here and they want me to go to Pensacola with them for the day."

"Sure, you go ahead and go with them," her boss said. "We're not that busy today anyhow, so we'll manage without you. It would be nice for you to spend the day with your brother and his friends."

Joyce was elated and so was Pub. Apparently they were from a very close family. But their joy would turn sour much quicker than any of us would ever have suspected.

After we finished eating our meal and paid the bill, the four of us emerged from the restaurant and got into our car with Pub and Joyce in the back seat, Art in the front passenger seat, and me at the steering wheel. Just as I was about to start the engine, there came a knock on my window. When I turned my head to see who it was, there stood a big, burley police officer. When I rolled the window down, he immediately spoke.

"You are all under arrest!"

"Under arrest!" I exclaimed. "For what?"

"You know for what, mister," he answered me back. "The four of you just robbed a grocery store." By this time there were several other police officers surrounding our car with revolvers on their hips. They were certain that they had caught the thieves who, about an hour earlier, had robbed a small grocery store.

"There must be some mistake, officer," I said to him. "Art and I are ministers."

"Aren't they all?" he snapped back at me. I had my big Thompson Chain Reference Bible in the front seat, right there between Art and me. I picked it up and pulled my ordination certificate out of the pages and handed it to him. He glanced at it for a moment and then growled.

"What dime store did you buy this at?" he said, handing it right back to me.

"I'm afraid we're going to have to take you to police headquarters for interrogation," he told us. Then he gave me strict orders not to try *anything funny* because I would be flanked on both sides and from behind with armed motorcycle officers who would shoot out the tires on our car if I attempted to escape.

"You follow that patrol car," he said, pointing to a vehicle that had stopped on the street in front of us, its red lights flashing. Then the officer went across the street and got into the unmarked police car from which he had "staked us out."

With red lights flashing and sirens screaming, we found ourselves *smack dab* in the middle of a police motorcade as we sped to the Mobile Police Headquarters. The patrol car in front of us pulled into a basement parking garage beneath the police headquarters offices and we pulled in right behind it. We figured we would be released in just a short while, but oh, how wrong we were! Another patrol car pulled in behind us, as well as the five or six motorcycle officers ready to go into action if we in any way resisted arrest and interrogation.

After all four of us emerged from our car, an officer "fleeced" each of us to determine if we were carrying any weapons. Since we were not armed, they did not put handcuffs on us. They took the car keys away from me and then one of the officers barked to the four of us.

"Come on with me; you've got a whole lot of explaining to do."

Flanked by police officers on all sides, we were taken up a flight of stairs, then entered a long hallway and were taken into an interrogation room. Instead of driving to Pensacola for a day of relaxation, sightseeing and fun, we found ourselves being treated as criminals!

Once in the interrogation room, sitting across the table from police detectives, we were told to just make it easy on ourselves and confess to the crime and tell them where we had hidden the four hundred dollars we had taken from the lady clerk at the small grocery store.

We tried to explain to the detective that we had never met the young lady (Joyce) before in our lives until about a half hour before we came out of that restaurant to get into our car to drive to Pensacola. We also tried to explain to them that her brother, Pub, was a native of Mississippi while Art and I were from the state of Washington (we had Washington license plates on our car) and that we were ministers who had just concluded a twenty-five night tent revival crusade in a rural area of Alabama to the north of there.

Assuming that we were criminals, they did not believe a word I was saying to them but tried repeatedly to convince us that we should make it a little easier on ourselves by coming clean and confessing to the robbery.

Coincidentally, the real robbers were three men and a woman driving a green, out-of-state Oldsmobile car, thus we fit their description. Now these detectives were not about to believe anything we were telling them, but were trying to break us down and get a confession of the crime. After thirty or forty minutes of group interrogation, we were taken, one at a time, into a nearby room to be cross-examined individually, which included being stripped down to our underwear and being thoroughly searched for evidence of the stolen money. That interrogation also included turning up our shirt collars to see if we had hidden currency there. A female officer conducted the "strip-down" search on Joyce.

To each of us, the interrogating detective would say again and again, "Just stop all the chattering and confess to this robbery. You know that you're guilty." When Art was being interrogated, the officer who had searched him found a piece of paper in his shirt pocket on which he had jotted down several scripture references while doing a topical study of the Bible, using abbreviations (such as Ps. 101:1, 2 or Dan. 12:2).

"Alright," the officer said to him, "you'd better come clean and tell me what all of this secret code means!"

"It's not a secret code at all, officer," Art explained. "I've been doing a topical Bible study and those are scripture references."

"Get out of my sight, you liar," the detective growled as he ordered Art to go back out into the room where the rest of us were. Apparently while all this interrogating was going on, other police officers were ransacking our car. They took the cushion out of the back seat and also took the battery out of the space where it was fastened in. But in the glove compartment they thought that they had found *concrete evidence* that we were indeed the robbers.

What they had found was an old (clean) sock of mine with $14.76 in coins in it, tied at the opening. The matching sock had a hole in it and I used it to wipe the dipstick off whenever I checked the engine oil. The loose change (pennies, nickels, dimes, quarters and fifty-cent pieces) were from the offerings of the Bright Water tent meetings, which we had decided to keep in the glove box for an "emergency" fund.

The four of us were all seated at the table in the larger interrogation room when the chief detective emerged from a side door, threw the sock on the table in front of me and growled.

"Now, Mr. Wise Guy, how are you going to explain this one and when are you going to confess to this robbery and tell us where the rest of that four hundred dollars is hidden?"

"Very simple," I responded. "I've already told you that Art and I just concluded a twenty-five-night tent revival in the rural community of Bright Water, Alabama. This change is from the nightly offerings, that's all."

"That takes the cake," he said mockingly. "You're the slickest-tongued thief I've ever met. You've got some wise answer for everything, don't you?" he said insultingly.

"No, sir, officer," I said. "I'm a Christian and a minister of the gospel. I don't tell lies. What I've told you is the absolute truth!" At that, he left the room muttering.

"You may be slick-tongued, mister, but you're not going to talk your way out of this! We've got the goods on you!" After nearly four hours of this kind of interrogation being repeated again and again, the detectives decided to have the lady who was robbed that morning at gunpoint come to the police station and make positive identification that we were indeed the robbers. We were ordered to stand up against a wall and look straight ahead as the victim of the robbery was ushered into the room.

"Now, take a good look at these four," the officer instructed her, "and then tell us that these are the ones that robbed your store at gunpoint."

Under my breath I was praying. "Oh, Lord, don't let it be a cross-eyed lady with poor eyesight, anxious to crack this case, who'll say, 'Oh, yes, officer, that is them!'" But upon taking one brief look at the four of us she blurted out, "Oh no, that's definitely not them. I'd recognize those robbers anytime—these are not them!"

We all breathed a sigh of relief and smiled at the lady as she turned and followed the officer who had brought her there back out of the room. Shortly thereafter the chief investigating officer came back into the room.

"I guess we're going to have to let you go."

"So, is that all?" I asked him.

"Whatta ya mean, 'Is that all?'" he muttered. "We don't apologize to nobody! We're just doing our job and since the four of you fit the description of the suspects, we hauled you in. Period!"

"But why did you wait until the last thing to bring in the lady who had been robbed?" I asked him.

"Look here, mister," he growled back with a mean look on his face. "I don't have to explain anything to you or anybody else, so get out of my sight or I'll lock you all up." Just then another officer of considerably better disposition entered the room.

"Here's your 'money sock' back and the keys to your car. Please follow me now and I'll take you to your car."

More than happy to get out of that interrogation room, we all followed this officer down a long hallway, then down a flight of stairs, and into the parking garage of the headquarters building. There was our little two-door '88 Olds with the trunk lid up, both doors open, the hood up, and the back seat cushion out and tipped up against the back of the front seat. The floor mats had been rolled up. Everything in of the glove compartment had been dumped out on the passenger seat, with the lid in the open position.

When I started to lower the hood of the car I noticed that the battery cover was off and lying on top of the carburetor breather

cover. By this time I was really beginning to feel righteous indigna-
tion toward the Mobile Alabama Police Department! We also discovered that their search team had attempted to remove the head
liner inside the car. What a revolting situation this had been for
Art and me and our two friends.

We did drive on to Pensacola that afternoon for a shortened
time of sightseeing before returning to Mobile to drop off Pub's
sister Joyce and then return to the Cedar Creek area of south-
eastern Mississippi.

Before leaving for Kansas the next morning we shared this bi-
zarre story of being falsely arrested and detained for over four hours
with Billy and Patsy Sparks.

"I think I would have threatened them with a lawsuit if that
had been me," Brother Sparks suggested. "After all, false arrest and
unlawful detainment are a pretty serious charge," he added.

It sure enough was a serious situation to the four of us at the
time, but after a while we just chalked it up to experience and
added it to our repertoire of unusual and unforgettable experiences as we continued to pursue the will of God for our lives and
to serve our generation by proclaiming God's message of redemp-
tion through the merits and mediations of our Lord Jesus Christ.

Worthy of mention concerning the Bright Water Tent Revival
Crusade is the fact that several generous offerings had been sent to
us through the Ministerial and Missionary Alliance "Tent Revival
Fund," which proved to be lifesavers for Art and me. No bills were
left unpaid and after reimbursing the Sparkses for food, laundry,
etc., we still had enough left over to make it back to Kansas.

What a "never-to-be-forgotten" experience it was for Art and
me during those five weeks in the "Deep South." I'm sure it was
the same for our dearly beloved friends, Billy and Patsy Sparks and
their infant daughter, Brenda. Art and I had been the only guest at
Brenda's first birthday party in November!

By the time we reached my parents' home in Kansas, Art and I
had decided to return to Seattle for the holiday season and to spend

a couple of months there before returning to Alabama for our next tent crusade in the spring of 1953.

A very pleasant surprise awaited Art and me when we arrived back in Kansas. My parents, along with Pastor and Mrs. (Ruby) Neilson, had decided to attend *The Voice of Healing* Convention that was to be held December ninth through eleventh. Since we had both developed a genuine interest in that institution and the men whose ministers were reported in its monthly publication, *The Voice of Healing*, we were eager to learn how much it would cost us to go with them to this convention.

"It won't cost you a cent," Dad informed us. "The Neilsons and your Mom and I have decided to invite you to go along with us and we will cover all of your expenses."

"*Really?*" I exclaimed joyfully.

"Yes," Dad assured us. "We'll be leaving early Tuesday morning, so get packed and ready to go!" We were more than happy to accept that most welcome invitation and at once made preparations for the convention.

Since Pastor Neilson's car was a four-door and somewhat roomier than ours. He drove us all to Dallas. We arrived there in mid-afternoon, located a hotel near the site of the convention, and checked in. We had a short while to eat dinner, rest a little, and then get dressed for the opening service of the convention at nearby Fair Park Auditorium.

For Art and me, a couple of young, itinerant evangelists, this convention was truly an inspiring and unforgettable highlight in our early ministerial careers.

Chapter 10

THE "GREAT COMMISSION" GETS PERSONAL

Most outstanding and unforgettable by far, for me at least, was the stirring and challenging sermon preached by missionary evangelist T.L. Osborn in that opening night service of the convention, Tuesday, December 9. In fact, that message delivered by Rev. Osborn has affected my life and ministry profoundly from that day to this.

Actually, when Rev. Osborn first began preaching that immortal sermon there was nothing flamboyant or dramatic about his delivery or preaching style that might lead one to believe that a masterpiece was about to unfold. However, by the time he had concluded his sermon and started making his appeal I was stirred to the very depth of my soul. The anointing of the Holy Spirit so was mightily manifested as he preached and was now making his appeal that I found myself responding.

In his sermon, Rev. Osborn presented the plight of untold millions of heathen people around the world who were living in dense spiritual darkness, waiting, as it were, for messengers of the Cross to come to them with the Good News that they could be saved by believing in and calling upon the Lord Jesus Christ for salvation.

"Some of them are old men and women now," Rev. Osborn declared. "All of their lives they've waited for the 'Good News' of the gospel, but no one has come to them. Soon they'll pass onward, into a Christless eternity, doomed and lost forever—all because no one had yet heard the Master's high call to "Go into *all the world* and preach His gospel to every creature."

"They could not be here tonight to tell you of their sad plight," he continued, "nor could they speak your language if they *could* be here—but I am here for them," he said. "I love these unreached people and have dedicated my life to reach them with the gospel message. Now, what about you?" he probed. "Those of you who may not, as yet, have found your place in His program, why don't you get up out of your seat and come down here to the front of this auditorium and dedicate yourself to this great unfinished task?"

It was precisely at that moment that I sensed a definite tug of the Holy Spirit at my heart to get up out of my seat and go forward—just as Rev. Osborn suggested. I had never considered becoming a missionary, nor had I ever felt a call to be one. On the contrary, I had somehow developed the opinion that missionaries, by and large, were probably ministers who couldn't make it on the home front so decided to go abroad and be missionaries. How I had ever come to such a foolish conclusion, I haven't a clue.

But on that night of December 9, 1952, there in the Fair Park Auditorium in Dallas, Texas, I felt love's constraint like I had never sensed it before in my life. Something deep within my innermost being seemed to say, "Get up and go, doubting nothing," so I, along with my colleague, Art, did just that.

Art and I had been sitting in a small balcony on the right side of that large auditorium. We quickly stood to our feet and made our way down the stairs onto the auditorium floor and down the aisle to the edge of the raised platform, where we joined scores of other men and women with whom Rev. Osborn prayed a powerful prayer of dedication. As I stood there near the platform that night it seemed that "the fountain of the deep" of my soul erupted. I wept so many tears of joy and consecration at that altar until I didn't know where they were coming from. A great cleansing took place in my heart and soul and I found myself saying, "Yes, Lord, I'll go anywhere you want me to go, even if it is to the ends of the earth!"

Although I did not understand the depth of meaning in all that transpired in my heart on that December night in 1952, I would be made to understand it a few months later. Actually, it was like another part of a giant puzzle was carefully and deliberately coming together in my life and walk with God, and I began "to apprehend that for which I had been apprehended" of God.

Every service of this three-day convention provided inspiration and blessing for all of us and we returned to Cheney on Friday "filled to overflowing." A young deliverance preacher in one of the daytime services ministered personally to my precious mother and she received a miraculous healing from the Lord as the result of it.

A few days after returning to Cheney from the convention in Dallas, Art and I departed for Seattle. We drove straight through, stopping only to refuel, eat. Driving night and day, we made the journey in about thirty-eight hours.

Returning to our home church in Seattle, we were warmly received both by the youth group and by the adults of the church. We were also afforded an opportunity to report on our four month evangelism tour and its many experiences by Pastor McAllister ("Brother Frank" as he was known by to the constituents of his church body). We were also invited to be co-speakers at the youth's annual Christmas banquet.

Shortly after New Year's of 1953, Pastor McAllister approached Art and me about the church board's decision (and his decision, as well) to ordain us and to grant full ministerial recognition to both of us.

"Well," I responded to that suggestion, "we have already been ordained back in Kansas, but thank you and the church board for your thoughtfulness, anyhow."

"Oh, that's perfectly alright," he continued. "We would like to ordain you as representatives of this church. It's OK to be ordained more than once," he explained. Then, (as Peter when he responded to Jesus offering to wash his feet said, "Not my feet only, but my whole body!"), Art and I said, "So be it!" Thus, on that first Sunday of 1953 Art and I were *doubly ordained* (that is to say, ordained for the second time).

Several friends within our home church conveyed their apologies to Art and me, conceding that they had been wrong in their assessment of our decision to step out into full-time ministry without first receiving formal training. It seemed evident this time that "the good hand of our God" was upon these two young "budding" evangelists, they said.

It was during these two-plus months in the Seattle area that Art and I started planning an old-fashioned Southland "brush arbor" crusade for the month of August of that year. A Christian realtor friend who attended our home church owned a vacant lot in an ideal meeting location, which we started checking into. Mr. Cantrell, the realtor, was very much in favor of our idea of using his large, vacant lot for this prospective Brush Arbor Crusade and thus gave us the "green light" to go ahead with plans for same. What a blessing!

Without a doubt, this planned Brush Arbor Crusade was a part of God's plan for Art's and my ministry, as well as for the salvation of a number of young people, among whom would be my two people very close to my heart.

"What Mean These Things, Lord?"

From time to time, I had shared with a few close, trusted friends and relatives the experience I had on that morning of August 19, 1952, in northern Missouri when the "stranger" appeared in our automobile. It seemed that everybody had a suggestion as to its meaning—perhaps it was an angel, or it was the Lord, etc., but never did anyone's suggestion satisfy my quest for the meaning of this very significant event in my life. I was totally persuaded that it did have a profound meaning and thus was very eager to have it revealed to me. Yet this was not to be until approximately nine months after I had experienced that strange visitation

Many times in prayer and anguish of soul I would cry out to God, pleading for a revelation concerning that experience—even to the extent that at times I fought against the foolish temptation to become upset with Him for not showing me its meaning. When at last the revelation did come, it was glorious and awesome!

It was the first week in March, 1953, when Art and I set out for the Midwest to begin our second tour of evangelism, during which time we would again experience God's miracles of protection, provision, intervention, and providence. Kansas would again be our first stop. Since my parents' home had become somewhat our headquarters in that region, after driving day and night from Seattle, we again settled in there for a few weeks.

During the month of March Art and I were afforded numerous opportunities for ministry, one of which was a week of special services at a rural church in the Webster Community, south of Augusta, Kansas.

Since we had made the decision to conduct a Brush Arbor Crusade in the Burien area of South Seattle during the month of August, we composed a "letter of invitation" to send to pastors and churches in that area. The letter was printed on our "Morlin-Ott Evangelism Crusade" letterheads and sent to dozens of pastors and churches—announcing the coming crusade and inviting both participation and attendance. Our letter was printed by *The Cheney Sentinel*, a weekly local newspaper. Once that letter was mailed out, the thought of our forthcoming Brush Arbor Crusade became increasingly exciting to us, thus we were earnestly praying each day for God's blessing for the crusade, especially for souls to be saved.

By late April of 1953 we'd decided it was time to return to Mississippi and Alabama in order to resume tent revival crusades there since the weather would now be conducive to such events. After retrieving our gospel tent from the farmer's barn where we had stored it for the winter, we erected it on the outskirts of the small town of Toxy, Alabama, preparing to conduct our next salvation/healing crusade.

Our friends, Reverend and Mrs. Billy Sparks, had moved back to Texas by this time, so Art and I were truly "on our own" for this crusade. We managed to obtain the approval and cooperation of an Assembly of God pastor in the area for the crusade. The lady from Toxy who had attended our Bright Water Crusade the previous month of November invited Art and me to stay in her small hotel during the tent crusade. It was a two-story building with a restaurant, lobby, and living quarters for the owners on the ground floor and the guest rooms on the second floor. The accommodations were complimentary, as were our meals during our stay there. That, of course, was a distinct financial blessing to us, especially considering that the total amount of offerings for the nine nights of the crusade, held April 30 through May 8, totaled $29.40.

One shocking discovery Art and I made during the Toxy Tent Crusade was the intense contempt (and even hatred) toward black people in that area. Even the Christians there were guilty to some extent of this kind of contempt. When I suggested to a local pastor that we might have a section of the seats designated just for "colored" folks, he vehemently objected, saying, "You let one 'nigger' under that tent and you'll find out that not one white person will come to your crusade!"

Needless to say, we were both shocked and saddened by this terse, harsh, and unchristian declaration. One morning, as we were eating breakfast in the restaurant at the hotel, the owner's husband, a non-Christian, came into the dining area and asked if we'd mind if he joined us, to which we responded, "Why not!" We were seated next to a window on the street side of the dining area, which looked out on the main street of the town.

This seemingly calloused man, during the course of conversation with us said, "You all see that there sign across the street?" (He pointed to a speed limit sign.)

"Yes," we both responded to his question, after which he spoke again.

"Well, I killed a 'nigger' right there a few weeks ago." (He was the town Constable.) Shocked by what he had just said, I responded, "You did! Why?"

"Well, he was running and when I hollered 'halt' and he didn't stop, I stopped him permanently!"

Although we held our peace outwardly, on the inside we wanted to pronounce a curse upon this hard-hearted, calloused man. But, of course, that was not ours to do. We felt assured that God would deal with him in due time.

Since we would not be conducting a service under the tent on Sunday morning, Art and I had accepted an invitation to minister at the Cedar Creek Community Church in Mississippi that morning. And, since there was not a gas station in the town of Toxy, we left a little early in order to stop for gasoline in the town of Melvin, Alabama, seven miles from Toxy.

Melvin was a sawmill (lumber) town and we felt sure we'd be able to gas up there. To our surprise, however, the streets of Melvin were "rolled up" on that Sunday morning—nothing was open anywhere in town. So now we were faced with a dilemma. There would be no point in us going back to Toxy, yet by this time the needle on the gas gauge was almost completely on empty. Except for a "miracle of provision/multiplication," like we had experienced in Fort Madison, Iowa, in August 1952, we found ourselves walking somewhere for fuel when the gauge registered "empty." This was a precisely accurate gas gauge!

From Melvin to Cedar Creek was about twenty-one miles, so what would we do now? Our only answer to this dilemma was to trust God for another "miracle of multiplication," so we just shut the engine off and paused for a time of earnest, believing prayer.

Confident that God had heard our prayers and that He would perform another "miracle of multiplication," we proceeded on down the country road leading to the Cedar Creek Community Church. Needless to say, Satan showed up to try to get us to waiver with reference to our faith, but we refused to succumb to his temptations, thus we remained steadfast and unwavering in our trust.

After traveling about eighteen miles from Melvin with the gas gauge resting completely on empty, we both sensed (or became aware of) a supernatural blessing that was about to unfold. As we approached the next intersection of a dirt township road I suddenly sensed a strong urge to slow down and to make a left turn onto that narrow, red dirt road, which I did. From a natural standpoint, this decision made no sense at all since the church we were going to was straight ahead. But since I had already learned from previous experiences that when the Holy Spirit speaks, it is always the wise thing to do that which He directs, I made the left turn and proceeded forward on that red dirt road.

Once again, common sense would have said that this was really a foolish decision, and my eyesight certainly would have confirmed that it indeed was since all we could see up ahead was a slight hill rising before us. However, confident that I was obeying the leading of the Holy Spirit, I continued to drive up this slight hill.

Upon reaching the crest of the hill we were made to realize why the Spirit had bade us to make that left turn onto this dirt township road! There, ahead of us a few hundred yards on the left side of the road, was an old-fashioned gas pump (the kind with a transparent glass tank on the top with the gallon marks calibrated on the glass and a lever on one side with which gasoline was pumped up over the top and down into the glass tank).

As I drove our car up to the pump and stopped there, an elderly Negro man emerged from a small building nearby.

"Can I help you fellows?" he asked.

"You sure can!" I replied. "We're completely out of gas and still have a ways to go to the church where we are to preach today. Could we buy some gas from you?"

"Why, of course you can," the old gentleman replied. "How much do you want?"

"How about ten gallons?" I responded.

"Sure enough," he said, moving the pump handle back and forth, pumping ten gallons of gas into the clear glass bowl and then releasing it into our gas tank through a hose and nozzle. Gravity caused the gasoline to flow down into our gas tank, with air bubbles rising upward occasionally in the reddish-colored fuel as it was emptying into the tank.

We paid the kind old gentleman for the gasoline, thanked him for the favor, spoke a blessing to him, and then drove on to the Cedar Creek Community Church, rejoicing and praising our Wonderful Lord for yet another miracle in time of need. And even though it was not a huge, earthshaking miracle, yet we knew that the Lord God had once again intervened on our behalf, thus we burst into a time of praise and thanksgiving to Him for His gracious kindness to us.

After a good morning service at the Cedar Creek Church, in which the Presence of the Lord was very real and present, Art and I were invited to a home for Sunday dinner, and then went back to Toxy to conduct the evening service under the gospel tent.

Our tent revival crusade in Toxy was not one of any specific significance, but was indeed another learning experience for Art and me. For certain, the Toxy Crusade seemed much harder than the Bright Water Crusade we had conducted the previous November.

After the final night service in the town of Toxy, we returned chairs, a piano, and other items to the country church that had loaned them for the crusade. We did not have a power pole for the Toxy Crusade as we had been granted permission to connect to electrical power at a nearby house.

By the time we attended to all of the necessary details of winding down and had dismantled the tent and placed all its parts into our trailer, it was nighttime. We could have stayed another night at the hotel in Toxy, but preferred not to, so once everything was loaded up we got into our car and had a good discussion, followed by a time of earnest prayer for guidance from the Lord with reference to where to go next. We knew that the gospel tent was ours for one more crusade, so the focus of our prayer time was, "Lord, *where should we go now* for the next tent revival crusade?"

Led by His Spirit

How long we prayed, I'm not sure, but it was for a considerable duration. Then, suddenly a sense of peace seemed to pervade our spirits somewhat simultaneously. I knew in my own heart that I had received a sense of divine guidance and Art related to me that he had also received the same from the Lord.

In honor, preferring my best friend and colleague in ministry, I spoke to Art.

"What has the Lord shown you?" I asked him, but he responded by saying, "You tell me first what you feel led to do and then I'll tell you if it is the same impression I've received."

Reluctantly I consented to go first, so I told Art that I felt impressed that we should go to South Florida. To that, Art let out a shout of praise and with a gleam on his countenance he responded, "That's the same impression I received!" Thus we were in perfect agreement as to where to go next. Of course, it would again be *uncharted territory* to us as neither Art nor I had ever been that way before.

After carefully looking at our road map we calculated that the shortest route there from Toxy was to drive south a few miles, then turn left (east) on Alabama State Highway 21. Having made that decision, a time of prayer for traveling mercies and blessing was the next order of business. By this time, darkness had settled over the entire area about us. Thick, black clouds had formed in the sky above us and lightening began flashing, followed by loud claps of thunder. By the time we concluded our prayer time, heavy rain was falling— much like the rainstorm we had been through on August 18, 1951, in northern Missouri. After all, it was springtime in the Deep South, the time of year when rainstorms were common.

Despite the downpour of rain, visibility was reasonably good so we proceeded on our journey, not realizing the severe dilemma in which we would soon find ourselves. As planned, I turned the car and trailer eastward onto Alabama State Highway No. 21, but without any warning or notice the pavement ended and within a matter of seconds our car and trailer were axle-deep in sticky red mud. Every effort to back the car up or move it forward was totally futile. We even got out of the car to push, with hopes that the tires might gain traction with a bit of extra force. They didn't.

By now our clothes were soaked and our shoes completely covered with thick, red mud. Realizing that our efforts were futile and that we were *once again* in a genuine dilemma, we agreed that what we needed now was another miracle; thus we entered into a time of earnest, fervent prayer.

How long we were engaged in prayer I am not sure, perhaps two-and-a-half to three hours, yet after a considerable space of time our prayers of entreaty slowly changed into prayers of praise and thanksgiving. The Presence of the Lord began to pervade our entire beings until all we could do was weep and worship Him. Apparently the rain stopped sometime while we were deeply engrossed in prayer and worship, but we were oblivious to that fact. When we finally came down out of the *Glory cloud*, to our utter amazement and delight our car and trailer were sitting on the pavement headed back in the direction we had come from (west). No one had come along on the highway where we were bogged down in the mud for those several hours, so we knew that our rescued position had to have been a miracle of Divine intervention!

In writing about this miracle now, one that has never ceased to amaze me across all the years since it occurred, I go on record declaring that I would have *nothing* to gain and everything to lose by faking or falsifying this account. Truly, it was another of God's supernatural interventions on behalf of a couple of young, sincere preacher boys longing to be in His perfect will and to be used of Him. Thus, I've often referred to this incident as a "Miracle of Rescue!"

After reworking our proposed route to Southern Florida we were on the road again—sometime after midnight. As was our policy, we drove night and day until we reached the outskirts of Miami. However, en route to Miami we had another unexpected situation develop that could have been very tragic.

We had stopped in Tallahassee, Florida, to refuel and to eat lunch at a café before continuing on our journey. I was again at the wheel, driving east out of Tallahassee on U.S. Highway 90. Approximately five miles out of the city limits I suddenly felt the car lighten and surge forward momentarily. Instantly, I looked in the rearview mirror and noticed that the tent trailer was no longer behind the car!

For a moment I nearly panicked, slamming on the brakes. Seconds later the trailer, with the tent, aluminum poles, steel stakes, etc. on it, rolled up alongside the right side of the car as if it were passing us on the shoulder of the road. Then the trailer hitch thrust into the ground, literally standing the trailer up in a vertical position as it came to a complete stop. The weight of the steel tent stakes (old car axles) completely broke out the front end-gate of the trailer.

A "miracle of mercy" had occurred in that, when the trailer broke loose from the car's bumper, it veered off onto the shoulder on the *right* side of the road. Had it veered off onto the *left* side of the car, it would have slammed into an oncoming Greyhound bus loaded with passengers that was passing beside us at that precise moment.

Some people would say, "That was merely a coincidence, not a miracle!" But to us, it was a "miracle of mercy," for had the trailer plunged headlong into that oncoming bus, it most probably would have caused severe injury or even loss of human life. Too, Art and I would undoubtedly have been facing a liability so great that it could have curtailed or even ended our ministries, thus I still give praise to the Master for what I refer to as His "Miracle of Mercy." Truly the good hand of our God was with us on that occasion as He delivered us out of a great tragedy and all the subsequent consequences that might have been!

After getting the bumper hitch repaired at a machine shop nearby and getting the front end-gate of the trailer back in place, we continued our journey toward Miami, arriving on the outskirts of the city around noon the following day.

We stopped on Miami's north side at a motel that gave us a very reasonable rate—two dollars a day. The motel room also had an attached garage that fit our need with reference to the tent trailer. There was also a nice swimming pool at the motel, which we both enjoyed as a means to "cool down" in the area's hot weather. Trusting God to reveal a location on which to erect the gospel tent for another revival crusade, we paid up for a week's stay at the motel.

Finding a location for a tent crusade, however, proved to be a real challenge, so much so that we were denied a permit for same anywhere in Dade County. In the meantime, we had attended services at a couple of churches—one in Miami and one in Hialeah. While attending an evening service at an Assemblies of God church in Hialeah, the pastor announced the showing of the Oral Robert's film, *Venture into Faith* at a sister church in Miami the following Tuesday night. As we were exiting the sanctuary after the service I spoke to Art.

"We've got to go see that film!" He readily agreed and we made plans to attend.

It so happened that a young man overheard our conversation about going to see the Oral Roberts film. He interrupted to introduce himself to us and then to ask what he referred to as "a big favor."

"I'd love to see that film, too," he exclaimed. "Would there be a chance that you fellows could come by my house and pick me up on your way to that church?" he asked.

"Why not," I responded. "We'd be glad to do it."

He jotted down his name and address and after giving us directions for locating his house, we agreed that we'd see him on Tuesday evening at around 6:15 P.M.

By the time Tuesday evening rolled around Art and I realized that our funds were dwindling much faster than we had anticipated. We had only one more night paid up at the motel where we were staying. Too, it seemed that we were "up against a brick wall" with reference to securing a permit to erect our tent for a gospel crusade. But we were determined not to allow this new dilemma to dampen our spirits or hinder our faith in God. After all, He had shown Himself mighty in our times of need before, so we knew that He could do it again. And, "do it again" He did, indeed! It happened on this wise:

Before heading out to the church where the film was showing, we fell to our knees in our motel room and cried out to the Lord for His help and provision. Then, we drove away to pick up Richard at his house on our way to see *Venture Into Faith*. Upon arriving at Richard's house no one came to the door, apparently not realizing that we were there.

"Rather than honking the horn, I'll get out of the car and go knock on their front door," I said to Art. When the door opened, Richard's wife greeted me.

"Come on in. Richard is just about ready," she said. I stepped inside and closed the door behind me as the wife disappeared momentarily into a hallway. I assumed that she had gone to let her husband know that we were there to pick him up, which she might have done. But when she returned to the living room, where I was standing near the door, she handed me a sealed envelope and lowered her head.

"The Lord spoke to Richard and me to give you this," she said. Feeling surprised and a little awkward, as we had never known these people before meeting them at the church in Hialeah on Sunday night, I replied, "Well, thank you." I accepted the envelope and then slipped it into the inside pocket of my jacket. About that time Richard emerged from his bedroom.

"OK, I'm ready now," he said. After kissing his wife goodbye he got into the car and we drove to the church.

The film was a tremendous "faith booster" for Art and me. We were both deeply stirred by this remarkable, feature-length film which documented many of the exploits of faith in the ministry of Rev. Oral Roberts, at that time one of the foremost evangelists in the world.

How much money we put into the offering that night I don't recall, but this much I distinctly remember. After driving our newfound friend, Richard, home and then returning to the motel where we were staying, we sat down and talked about what we had seen and of what a blessing the documentary of Oral Roberts' ministry was to us at that time. We then began to discuss our financial need and to face up to the plight we found ourselves in. For some reason, and probably in the excitement of the film's afterglow, I had forgotten about the envelope I'd received earlier in the evening from Richard's wife.

After pooling what money we had left, including loose change (it amounted to the grand sum of two dollars), it was just enough to pay for one more night's lodging. We also had over half a tank of gas in our car. This was the sum total of our assets at that time. But, rather than to bemoan our plight, we decided we would lay our two dollars out on the table, lay hands on it, and then pray for another "miracle of provision."

After a time of earnest, believing prayer concerning our needs, we agreed that we should now begin to thank God in advance for the miracle we had asked Him for, not yet realizing that He had already performed it. Right in the middle of our time of praising God for what He was going to do to provide for our needs, I suddenly remembered the envelope Richard's wife had handed me some hours earlier.

"Oh," I said, "You know something, Art? Richard's wife handed me an envelope when I went up to the door to pick him up for the film. She said that the Lord had told them to give it to us."

I reached into my inside jacket pocket, took out the envelope, opened it, and sure enough there was the very miracle that we needed—five crisp twenty-dollar bills! The discovery of this totally unexpected cash was cause for further rejoicing in the Lord and praise for His great faithfulness. Once again, our Wonderful Lord had shown Himself to be a "very present help in our time of need."

A friendship soon developed between us with Richard and his wife. We were later invited to stay with them, which we did for the duration of our stay in South Florida.

During the days ahead, as we continued our pursuit of obtaining a permit and finding a location to set up our gospel tent, we met a man named Mr. Andrews, a Christian businessman who owned a roofing company in Miami. Mr. Andrews needed a few helpers in his business at that busy time of year and thus offered Art and me a job, which we accepted with the understanding that our employment would be only short-term.

We thus worked for about ten days in the hot sun of Southern Florida. The work was hard and we both got sun-burned real good (or should I say *bad!*), but the extra income was a blessing as the expenses incurred preparing for our tent revival crusade were more than we had anticipated.

During those days of getting everything in order for the crusade our newfound friend, Rev. Gaynor Blowin (senior pastor of Hialeah Assembly of God Church), invited Art and me to attend a fellowship meeting of Assembly of God ministers of that area at a church in Fort Lauderdale, with him, on the night of May 11, 1953.

Little did I realize what would transpire in my life that night, but it indeed became a *"night of destiny"* for me. Upon arriving at the church where the fellowship meeting was to be conducted, we were met by the host pastor, who invited us to sit on the platform with a number of fellow ministers participating in the event. It was, of course, a gesture of ministerial courtesy on the part of the host pastor to extend this invitation to Art and me as visiting fellow ministers, which we appreciated.

After the service had been called to order and a Prayer of Invocation offered, the host pastor asked each of the twenty or so ministers seated on the platform to stand and introduce themselves. Among this group of ministers were newly appointed Assemblies of God missionaries to Japan, Rev. Fredolf Sondeno and his wife, Ardel. I had never met the Sondenos before, nor have I ever seen them again since that night, but in the providence of God they impacted my life deeply. Or, putting it more accurately, the Holy Spirit used them to stir my soul to the depths that night as they were called to the podium to sing a song. As long as I live, I shall never forget the song the Sondenos sang in that fellowship meeting that night: *Harvest Is Passing.*

I do not recall having ever heard that song before, but on that night of May 11, 1953, in Fort Lauderdale, Florida, God used it to break my heart and to bring me to a place of submission concerning His will for my life in an area I did not yet even understand. As Rev. and Mrs. Sondeno sang the song with anointing and inspiration, I suddenly began weeping: "Harvest is passing. Night draweth nigh. Millions are dying. Oh, hear their cry! Bowed down and burdened, with no one to care. Soon they'll pass onward to eternity."

As those words poured forth in lyric, suddenly it was as if the weight of the whole world were upon my shoulders. I began to feel a tremendous sense of urgency and responsibility gripping my soul—*the call of human need!*

The sermon I had heard Rev. T.L. Osborn preach at the Voice of Healing Convention on December 9, 1952, began to resound in my mind and soul as I listened to the words of that song.

"A thousand million souls living in heathen darkness around the world," the speaker said, "are waiting for messengers of the Cross to come to their countries, colonies, and islands of the Sea; to their towns, villages, and boroughs with the message of the risen Christ. Some have waited an entire lifetime, but no messenger arrived. Soon they will pass onward into eternity . . ."

"Is it fair," he asked, "for so many of us to hear the gospel over and over again when these underprivileged are still waiting for their *first* opportunity to hear about Jesus?" he pleaded in that stirring sermon.

The words of the missionaries' song, combined with the words of Brother Osborn's sermon, seemed to speak to me so forcefully that I felt deeply indicted by the Holy Spirit, thus found myself weeping uncontrollably.

Oh, it won't last, my first thought was. *I'll soon regain my composure and be OK.* But as the conviction intensified, I continued to weep all the more vehemently. Tears were streaming down my cheeks until I was beginning to feel embarrassed about my composure. It finally reached the point where I felt I was becoming a distraction so I slowly got up and left the platform, exiting the church through a side door near the back of the building. Art followed me out, attempting to console me.

"What's wrong, Gail?" he asked.

"I'm not sure, Art," I sobbed. "The words of that song seem to have arrested me. I feel indicted of the Holy Spirit I guess—I just can't help myself right now. Please bear with me, Art," I said. "I will be alright after while, OK?"

We'd gone to the church parking lot, gotten in our car, and were just sitting there for some fifteen or twenty minutes as I sought to regain my composure. Finally I spoke to Art.

"Why don't you go back into the service? I'll just stay here in the car and wait for you. Maybe I'll get back to normal by the time the service is over." But Art refused.

"No, Gail, I think we should go back to our room now." We drove away from the church in Fort Lauderdale and returned to Hialeah.

I later felt that I owed Art more of an explanation concerning my unusual behavior at the fellowship meeting in Fort Lauderdale, but I was at a loss. I couldn't seem to find the right words to say. It was like I was in a daze. We finally agreed to dismiss the matter and go to sleep for the night.

By morning I was much more settled in my spirit but still could not forget the night before at the fellowship meeting, especially the song, Harvest Is Passing. In fact, I have never forgotten that service or that song and am certain that I never shall!

Indeed the night of May 11, 1953, was a "night of destiny" for me, although I did not understand its meaning until later. In retrospect now, the events of that night were another piece of a giant puzzle that was slowly coming together in my life. In a few more days the full picture would be made clear to me.

Art and I had accepted an invitation to dine with our friend Richard and his wife at their home the following Friday evening, May 15, 1953. After enjoying a delicious home-cooked meal, we all lingered around the dining room table, visiting and sharing life experiences. Their three small boys had been quite rowdy and disruptive and so were sent into the living room to play, their mother having to go into the room several times to settle them down.

During the course of our visit around the table Richard and his wife asked Art and me to tell them about our background—where we were born, raised, etc. They inquired about our ministry—the places we had preached, the churches we had ministered in, etc. Between the four of us, we kept a dialogue going for twenty minutes or so.

Eventually, I started telling them about the unusual experience that Art and I had had in Northern Missouri on August 19th of the previous year, much like I had told it to a few close friends and family members over the course of the preceding nine months. I related to them that it seemed like everyone I told this story to had a suggested interpretation, yet none, to that point, had ever satisfied my quest for the meaning of the experience.

I told our new friends of how, over and over again, I had besought the Lord to give me the interpretation of that experience, but that the Heavens only seemed as brass each time I prayed that prayer. I further confessed that I had to fight against the temptation of becoming upset with the Lord because He was seemingly ignoring my heart's cry concerning this matter. Then suddenly I stopped talking, as if I had been struck speechless.

At that point, Art, thinking I had lost my place in giving the account of that experience, took up where I had left off and continued telling the story. But, he too, got only a few words out of his mouth when suddenly a supernatural Presence descended upon all of us like a Glory cloud. Once again, I began to weep, almost uncontrollably. But this time a sweet peace accompanied my weeping, so much so that I felt as though I were about to be raptured. In a matter of seconds all four of us in that dining room were laughing, crying, shouting, and worshipping the Lord all at the same time in concert. It was very similar to our experience in Northern Missouri on August 19th of the previous year.

As it had been on that occasion, a supernatural and holy awe seemed to come in waves. Just when it seemed that one wave of

Glory was beginning to subside, another wave would sweep over us. This continued for about the space of three hours or more before the Glory cloud slowly lifted and the four of us began to return to normal again. Yet all during that time when the Divine Presence overshadowed us, none of us were able to converse. All we could do was weep, laugh, and worship the Lord in a glorious concert of praise.

It wasn't until the Glory cloud finally lifted that I was able to tell the other three about the revelation I had received at that moment when I seemed to freeze while relating the Northern Missouri experience. At the time when I suddenly stopped relating my story to Richard and his wife, it was because these words had come pouring into my mind and spirit—words that were burned into my soul forever! And here is the message I received in those words:

"The man that appeared unto you in your car that morning was one of your heathen brethren appealing unto you to bring the gospel to him!"

Again, I want to make it clear—I did not hear an audible voice on this occasion. In fact, I have *never* heard the Lord speak to me audibly. However, the times I have heard from the Lord have always been perhaps even clearer than if they had been spoken in audible tones so that I could hear them with my physical ears! Hence these somewhat strange words were literally *burned* into my spirit, as it were. As long as I live, I will never forget the moment they were given to me by a supernatural manifestation of the Holy Spirit there in the dining room of our friend Richard's home. Nor shall I ever forget the words that were dropped into my spirit on that unforgettable evening of May 15, 1953!

When the cloud of Glory that had fallen upon the four of us lifted somewhat, I was finally able to relate to the other three there at the table the words that I had received by Divine revelation, which in turn precipitated another round of weeping, praying, laughing, and rejoicing that lasted for at least another thirty minutes.

Something interesting happened during that time frame of some three-and-a-half hours or more, which I think is worthy of mention. The three rowdy little boys who had been playing in the living room seemed to have been "zapped" during that time. When it dawned upon the mother that she had not checked on them or heard even a "peep" out of any of them for several hours, she quickly went to check on them.

"Come in here, you guys," she said as she beckoned to us with her hand. "I want you to see something unusual!" When the three of us got up from the table and went into the living room, there lying on the floor, like cordwood, were three little boys!

"The Lord must have put them to sleep for us," Richard suggested with a sort of snicker. Perhaps so!

When the four of us returned to the dining room and seated ourselves around the table again, I felt compelled to share what was going on in my spirit and in my heart. I started by alluding to the experience Art and I had had in Northern Missouri the previous August. One unforgettable feature of that experience was the face of the man that appeared unto me in our car on that early morning. His complexion and his hair were dark and the look on his face had haunted me for nine months. It was a look of entreaty or of appeal. He never said a word, and then he literally vanished when I doubled up my fist to hit him, leaving me somewhat stunned and stupefied, yet fully understanding that his appearance had a significant spiritual meaning and purpose. During the months that followed, although I yearned in prayer to have the vision's meaning revealed to me, no such revelation had come.

Looking back, I would finally realize how the Lord of the Harvest was working in my life to bring me to a place of surrender and willingness to think differently about the direction of the ministry He had called me to.

A Four-Piece Puzzle

The experience in Northern Missouri on that morning of August 19, 1952, was the first piece of a "four-piece puzzle" that would finally be completed on the night of May 15, 1953,—approximately nine months from the time of that initial experience. It has often occurred to me that nine months is also the gestation period for childbirth (from conception to birth).

The second piece of this "four-piece puzzle" was that unforgettable service at Fair Park Auditorium in Dallas, Texas, on the night of December 9, 1952, in which Rev. T.L. Osborn preached that immortal sermon calling "reapers" to the whitened fields of the harvest of human souls around the world. For even though I had not yet at that point in time seriously considered going abroad to preach the Gospel of Christ to the unreached peoples of the world, I was stirred very deeply by that sermon, as well as by the demeanor of the speaker, for Brother Osborn preached with undeniable authority and Holy Spirit anointing. From that night forward I could not forget his sermon or that service.

I replayed that service over and over again during the next five months. Even when I got back to Seattle about ten days after hearing Brother Osborn preach, I visited my beloved pastor, Rev. Frank McAllister, and told him about that stirring sermon and unforgettable service. Being in attendance was truly one of the high points of Art's and my first "tour of duty."

So, with the vision of that stranger's face that appeared to me in our car and the compelling appeal made by Rev. T.L. Osborn that night always fresh on my mind, a culmination of events and circumstances was bringing me closer to a time when all would come into focus and become clear to my mind.

The third piece of this giant "four-piece puzzle" would then fall into place on the night of May 11, 1953, at the Minister's Fellowship Meeting in Fort Lauderdale, Florida, when Rev. and Mrs. Fredolf Sondeno sang the song, *Harvest Is Passing*. Without any prior notice or warning, God would use that song to break my heart over the plight of the heathen in far away places and make me willing to say, "Yes Lord, I'll go where You want me to go. Not my will, but Thine be done!"

Now—four days later—the final piece of this giant puzzle would finally come together, making clear to me the meaning of the other three. God was calling me to the "regions beyond" to declare the unsearchable riches of Jesus Christ to the underprivileged and unevangelized of my generation; to leave my comfort zone and "security blanket;" to take a giant step into the unknown. It all seemed to overwhelm me at first, while at the same time giving me a tremendous sense of direction accompanied by an unspeakable peace of mind and joy of spirit. Even though it would be a while before I finally "launched out into the deep," my mission was now clear, for I had heard the call of human need and had responded by saying, "Yes, Lord, I'll go!"

"That Face . . ."

It was not until January, 1957, that I finally found my way to a mission field to preach Christ to those of other lands, languages, cultures, and situations, but the beginning of a worldwide quest for souls truly happened there in the dining room of Richard and his wife's home on that Friday night of May 15, 1953.

Hence the reason I have chosen to think of this experience as "The Bomb Shell" is because it has probably impacted my life and ministry as much or more than any single experience I've ever had. Of course, void of the August 19, 1952, experience in Northern Missouri it would have been without meaning. On the other hand, *that* experience was without any clear meaning until this experience was realized. Truly, these two experiences have been "mountain peaks" in my walk with my Blessed Redeemer.

Since that time, the coming together of what I chose to call my "giant four-piece puzzle," this Divine Visitation in my life has been the constraining force that has literally taken me to "the four corners of the earth," proclaiming the unsearchable riches of Christ to untold peoples throughout the world. And an almost sacred (at least to me) observation wherever I have gone throughout the world to preach the gospel is that I've seen that "*face*" over and over again in foreign lands. It usually happened when I was least expecting it— almost always while preaching through interpreters and when the anointing and Presence of the Holy Spirit was strongest.

There in the crowd or audience of hearers I would see the face of the stranger who appeared to me in my car that early Tuesday morning of August 19, 1952, in Northern Missouri. To me, this has always been a confirmation of God's special call to missionary evangelism and thus a precious matter never to be taken or spoken of lightly. I have seen that face in Brazil, Argentina, Bolivia, Mexico, Guatemala, British Honduras (now Belize), Puerto Rico, Japan, Formosa (now Taiwan), Hong Kong, the Philippines, Java (or the Republic of Indonesia), Singapore, India, Pakistan, Jordan, Israel, Russia, and China.

· ·

Chapter 11

"WITH SIGNS FOLLOWING:"
GUIDANCE AND MINISTRY

All the while that Art and I were in the Miami area of Florida, in addition to obtaining a permit plus finding a location to erect our gospel tent, we were also planning for the Brush Arbor Crusade in the south end of Seattle for the month of July. One day in May while driving down a street in Hialeah, Florida, Art and I were discussing our plans for the upcoming Brush Arbor Crusade. I had just been praying for my two unsaved brothers, Lester and Dwane, as I had been doing every day (sometimes several times a day) since the time God gave me the "night vision" at the National Fellowship Camp Meeting in Joplin, Missouri, in August, 1952.

"Wouldn't it be wonderful if both of my brothers would accept Jesus as their Savior at this upcoming Brush Arbor Crusade?" I said to Art.

"That would be awesome!" Art responded. At that point in time, Dwane was in Seattle (living with our older brother Louie and his family), but Lester was still in Germany, winding down his tour of duty. I knew that his tenure with the U.S. Army should be about over and that he would soon be coming home, but did not know just when.

While discussing the upcoming Brush Arbor Crusade and the fact that my two brothers were yet unsaved, suddenly the Holy Spirit seemed to overshadow me and these words came pouring into my mind and my spirit:

"Because you have been obedient to the leading of My Spirit and have faithfully and earnestly prayed for Lester and Dwane's salvation, I, the Lord your God, shall grant unto you the desire of your heart. If you will continue to walk before me in obedience and will return to Seattle to build the Brush Arbor which you have envisioned and will be faithful to preach My Word there, I will save those two brothers in that crusade. Only obey and do as I have impressed upon your heart to do and you will see My strong arm made bare!"

Needless to say, a feeling of exhilaration and great joy came over me while driving down the street at that time. In the excitement and exhilaration of the moment, I related to Art the revelation I had just received; thus we rejoiced together as Art had become my "partner in prayer and believing" for Lester and Dwane's salvation. We worshipped and magnified the Most High God for His great goodness and mercy!

From that moment on, each time I started praying for Lester and Dwane, as I had done night and day for the previous nine months, I found that I could no longer pray as I had prayed before. Now, rather than pleading for the Holy Spirit to draw them unto Jesus that they might be saved, I found myself thanking God, by faith, for their salvation—as if they had already called upon Him. After all, I had received that "Blessed Assurance" from the Father that He would save them in the upcoming Brush Arbor Crusade in Seattle, so now it was time to begin thanking Him by faith for their salvation.

Now, to praise Him in advance for Dwane's salvation was rather easy. After all, I had been instrumental in getting him out of Kansas and up to Seattle the previous month of September.

The real challenge to my faith was thanking God, in advance, for saving Lester since he was yet a soldier in the U.S. Army, stationed in Germany. Although I did not know it at that time, he would be returning to America within about three weeks and would be discharged from the Army. And, since he had lived all of his life in Kansas prior to being inducted into the Army, I was also unaware that he would be returning to Kansas after being discharged; not to Seattle, Washington. Too, I had said to God (in unbelief), "If You can save Lester, then I know You can save anyone!" I was convinced that Lester was a hard-hearted young man. I had seen him whip men much bigger than himself. I also knew that with his bare fist he had knocked several men completely unconscious. His first "knock out" was at age fifteen—and a semi-pro boxer was the victim!

I had heard Lester scream at our dad: "I hate you and I hate that church you go to and I hate all those other hypocrites that go to that church!" I was not saved at the time, but I hurt on the inside for our dad on that occasion. True, Dad had been a hard, mean man himself before he came to the Lord and was saved. I knew that he now loved the Lord and that he loved that little church in Cheney where he had been gloriously saved a few years earlier. I also knew that he loved his fellow Christians who attended that little church.

Probably nothing could have hurt Dad more than those harsh words that Lester barked out at him on that occasion. Our dear Mother was standing in the background weeping over the argument and the hatred that Lester was breathing out in a fit of temper. Remembering some of these things, I had concluded that Lester would certainly be a "hard nut to crack!" Not many weeks hence, however, I would learn how very wrong I was in my assessment of my brother Lester. Yes, I would get a fresh glimpse of the grace of God in action!

After several weeks of perseverance in our efforts to secure a permit to erect the gospel tent somewhere in Dade County (the Miami-Hialeah area) for an evangelistic crusade without success, we went into the next county north of Dade—Broward County. At last, a tent revival crusade would become a reality! Along U.S. Highway 441 in West Hollywood, Florida, we found a vacant lot suitable to erect a tent on. We also were able to secure permission to use that lot as well as a permit to set up the tent for the purpose of an evangelistic crusade in Broward County.

Our newfound friend and ministerial colleague, Pastor Gaynor Blowin of the Hialeah Assembly of God Church, was "a friend indeed" to us. He allowed us to use a piano from his church for the crusade (a great blessing for me as I had been the accompanist for congregational singing, on the guitar, for our first Alabama tent crusade). Pastor Blowin also allowed us to use the folding chairs from his church for seating inside the tent. Too, a number of his members came and helped us canvas the area several miles around the site of the gospel tent. His church had also paid to have ten thousand hand bills advertising the tent crusade printed. *What a blessing!*

The crusade commenced on Wednesday, May 27, 1953, and continued through Monday, June 8. We were pleased to have a number of souls saved, as well as several notable healings during this ten-day revival crusade. Many members of the Hialeah Assembly of God Church attended the crusade nightly, assisting Art and me in many ways, especially the lady who played the piano for us.

After the crusade was concluded, it was "take down and return time" again. We received notice that a fellow minister in West Texas, also a member of the Ministerial and Missionary Alliance, had requested use of the tent that we had now used for four crusades and was to begin his use of it on June 21st. We thus needed to depart South Florida quickly in order to deliver the tent to this brother. After returning all the chairs, the piano, and other items we had borrowed for the crusade, we dismantled the tent and packed all the parts onto our trailer.

Before leaving for Texas, Art and I took a few days off for rest and relaxation. For sure, our experiences in South Florida were "never-to-be-forgotten" learning times for both of us. We shall always be grateful to our loving Heavenly Father for allowing us the privilege and blessings that were afforded us during our stay in that area, especially for the spiritual blessings and divine revelations that we had received during that time.

On Saturday, June 13th (Art's 21st birthday) we bade farewell to our friends in the Greater Miami area and left for Texas and Kansas. We arrived in Spearman, Texas, on Monday, June 15th, and met Brother Orville Fullbright, the minister who would be next to use the gospel tent.

Since it was late afternoon when we arrived in Spearman, we were invited to be overnight guests at the Fullbright's home—a welcome invitation to both of us. During our visit that evening, Brother Fullbright asked if we would consider allowing him to use our trailer since it was "tailor made" for transporting the tent. Of course, we were glad to oblige, especially since we had been pulling it for some 1,500 miles!

Our friends Billy and Patsy Sparks were now pastoring a church in the town of Booker, Texas (about forty miles east of Spearman), so we stopped by to visit them before driving on to Cheney, Kansas. It was an enjoyable time of reminiscing with the Sparkses about our experiences in Mississippi and Alabama the previous fall, as well as sharing with them our experiences in Toxy, Alabama, and South Florida that spring.

Upon arriving at my parents' home in Cheney, I was pleasantly surprised to see my brother Lester there. While Art and I were in Florida, Lester had been discharged from the Army and had returned to Kansas where he was staying at our parents' home. Oddly, it was his *second* time returning to our parents' home after being discharged. Just after his release from the military, he'd purchased a car somewhere in Kentucky, driven to Kansas and stayed with our parents for only a few days before deciding to drive to Seattle, Washington. But after only a few days in the Seattle area he'd decided he didn't like it there and so had driven back to Kansas; thus he was there when Art and I arrived at my parents' home the evening of June 16th.

Now, the fact that Lester had already gone to Seattle but had not stayed there was a severe challenge to my faith, for I had just received a "word from the Lord" while in South Florida that if I would obey Him He would save both Lester and Dwane there in the upcoming Brush Arbor Crusade. Of course, Dwane was already in Seattle, but now *what about Lester*? To say the least, this gave cause for a lot of earnest and fervent prayer on my part concerning Lester!

While residing with my parents for a few weeks before leaving for the Northwest, Art and I were invited to preach from Sunday, June 28th, through Sunday, July 5th, at a pioneer work on Wichita's South Side. Rev. Albert Durham and his wife Ava had leased an abandoned hardware store building, renovated and remodeled it, and then opened it up for services. Art and I were the first evangelists invited to minister at this new church that became, and still is, a strong church in that section of Wichita.

As we were accustomed to doing, Art and I rotated nights while preaching there in Kansas that week. Admittedly, my faith had waned a little concerning my brother Lester, thus Art and I invited him to attend this revival crusade in Wichita in which we would be preaching. To my surprise, he accepted the invitation and attended two of the night services. I was earnestly praying that Lester might surrender his life to the Lord while attending those two services, but it was not to be—even though Art and I both had given "gripping" appeals during the altar calls the two nights he attended. He did relate to us at a later date that he had been under strong conviction each of those two night, but had not responded to the promptings of God's Spirit.

The Wichita Revival Crusade concluded on Sunday evening, July 5th. On Tuesday, July 7th, Art and I would be leaving for Seattle to begin final preparations for the Brush Arbor Crusade. Before leaving that morning I did my very best to convince Lester to go along with us, but to no avail.

"I wouldn't live in Seattle if they gave me the whole State of Washington!" he declared.

Although I didn't tell him so at the time, that declaration by my brother pierced my very soul and caused my faith to waiver, at least temporarily. I even offered to pay all of his expenses for the trip if he'd go along with us (driving his own car, of course).

"No thanks," he said. "There's no use trying to get me to go. I hate Seattle and have no desire to go back there again."

My seventeen-year-old sister, Janice, did go along with Art and me to Seattle. She had been there with our parents in the summer of 1951 and was excited to have the opportunity to go again, especially in light of the upcoming Brush Arbor Revival Crusade.

As we drove away from my parents' home that morning, bound for Seattle, I was both excited and heavy-hearted. Within my spirit I silently questioned the Lord. "Did I not hear You say to me while I was in South Florida that if I would be obedient to do the thing I have set out to do that You would save both of my brothers in the Brush Arbor Crusade?"

I even entertained the idea, momentarily, that maybe it was just "wishful thinking" on my part rather than a "word from the Lord." Regardless, we were now on our way to Seattle and were determined that we would indeed build this Brush Arbor and would conduct a fourteen-day evangelism crusade in it.

Thank God, my doubtful thoughts were of a short-lived duration, for after we had gone only a few miles from my parents' home, God spoke to my heart again, very vividly. It was both a rebuke and an encouragement to bolster my faith.

"Did I not reveal to you that I will save both Lester and Dwane in this Brush Arbor Crusade if you would obey Me and do as I have shown you to do? Only believe and do not doubt and surely you shall see My power manifested and you shall have your heart's desire!"

What an awesome faith-booster! What a magnificent encouragement! Like Abraham of old had said, my own heart spoke, "Against hope, I will believe in hope, for with God, all things are possible!"

Shortly after arriving in Seattle, Art and I, along with several volunteers, started making preparations for the Brush Arbor Crusade—somewhat of a novelty in the Pacific Northwest though a relatively common thing in the Deep South.

A Christian gentleman and friend, Mr. Joe Cantrell, had previously agreed to allow us to build the Brush Arbor structure and to conduct the crusade on a large vacant lot owned by him. So, after checking with Mr. Cantrell again, we began clearing the lot (mowing the grass and removing debris). Once the lot had been cleared, the construction of the Brush Arbor got underway. Mr. Cantrell had given us permission to harvest any and all timber needed to build the structure since there were plenty of fir trees on the back side of the property.

The structure, some fifty by ninety feet, consisted of upright poles around the outer perimeter, plus two rows equally spaced on the inside. The poles were planted in the ground like posts. Then a network of poles of smaller diameter was placed horizontally to form the roof area, held up by the vertical poles, after which brush was placed over the top of the horizontal structure. When the structure was finally completed the area beneath the arbor was large enough to accommodate five hundred chairs.

It took a week of hard work to complete the project, but we felt a sense of gratification when the work was all done for many people had commented to us that it was a very impressive structure with a distinct symmetry about it; quite attractive, too! The location was very good as it was situated at the intersection of South 136th Street and Des Moines Way (an arterial road in the Burien area of South Seattle). The site was easily accessible and the structure easy to identify.

Without question, this concept of a "brush arbor" structure was a somewhat different, even novelty approach to evangelism in the area. There had been a few tent crusades in the Seattle area (Oral Roberts for one), but never a "brush arbor" as far as we were able to ascertain.

On Friday evening, July 17th, after putting the finishing touches on the brush arbor, we all returned to Louie's house. While hanging up saws in Louie's garage and putting away the tools we had used, we heard Louie's six-year-old son, Jimmy, let out with a big "war whoop" documenting Lester's arrival. "It's Lester! It's Lester!" he shouted. Louie, Art, Janice, and I all came out of the garage rather hurriedly to see what all the commotion was about. And, sure enough, it was Lester in his green, four-door, 1941 Plymouth sedan. He had barely been able to make it up the slight hill to Louie's house because the clutch of his car was almost completely out.

When he opened the door and stepped out of his car, the first words out of his mouth were, "I must be losing my mind. I said I wouldn't come back here if they gave me the whole State of Washington, but here I am!"

Of course, the rest of us knew why he was there; it was unquestionably by Divine appointment. After Janice accompanied Lester into Louie's house, Louie, Art, and I went back into Louie's garage and had ourselves a "Brush Arbor Spell!" We had closed the garage door and spent a few minutes worshipping and praising God as we thanked Him for bringing Lester there just three days before the start of the Brush Arbor Crusade.

Worthy of mention is how it came about that Lester had returned to Seattle. He had been working for our dad on the farm in Kansas. The wheat harvest would normally have been over by this time, but rains had caused several delays; hence it was still in progress. On the day that he decided to go back to Seattle, another rain caused yet another delay in harvesting the wheat. Dad had gone to Kingman to buy some parts for his combine, so Mother decided to go with him. Lester was invited to join them, but he declined, so Dad said, "We'll see you when we get back home. OK?"

"Sure, that's fine," Lester replied.

Shortly after Dad and Mother had left, Lester decided, on "the spur of a moment," to take off for Seattle. He told us later that a sudden, unexplainable notion had hit him to go back to Seattle. So, he just packed up his few belongings in a couple of cardboard boxes, loaded up his guitar and amplifier, and wrote a brief note to let Dad and Mother know where he had gone. He then got behind the wheel of his car and started his journey toward the Pacific Northwest.

When our parents got home that afternoon and found Lester's note, they were shocked and a little saddened. They didn't understand why he did not wait until they got home before leaving. But they were also hopeful that his decision was in accordance with the "word" I had received from the Lord while I was in Florida concerning his salvation; that he would surrender to the Lord at the Brush Arbor Crusade and be saved.

When Lester arrived in Seattle that Friday evening, I knew in my heart that his totally unexpected arrival there was nothing short of a miraculous answer to nine months of earnest, intense, intercessory prayer for his salvation and that indeed his sudden decision to come back to Seattle was of the Lord. I am totally convinced that God put it into his heart to do what he did for soon he would bow his knees to the Lord Jesus Christ and accept Him as his Savior and Lord.

Monday, July 20th, was a busy day. The first service of the crusade would begin at 7:00 P.M. Five hundred rental chairs had been delivered and placed under the arbor that day. A center aisle had been created in the placement of the chairs. The raised platform was readied with sound system, a piano, lights, and an altar bench consisting of a log at the front of the wooden platform.

Art insisted I preach the opening service. The crowd was quite small that night—perhaps twenty or twenty-five people, all Christians. So, my appeal at the conclusion of the sermon was for every believer present for that first service to gather around the altar area and pray for a harvest of souls in the succeeding days of the crusade. We also prayed earnestly that the Presence of the Holy Spirit would be the outstanding characteristic in each service.

As the second night's service was just getting underway, my heart was hopeful as I observed my brother Lester coming in among the crowd and seating himself about ten rows back from the front. The crowd was somewhat larger that night and Art was the preacher. At the conclusion of the sermon, he invited any and all persons desiring a blessing from the Lord—healing, encouragement, prayer for unsaved loved ones, etc.—to come forward for prayer. Everybody present that evening responded to this invitation except my brother Lester and Art's brother Marvin.

Louie and I had knelt side by side on the platform and were engaged in some "heavy duty" prayer when suddenly we heard the sound of a familiar voice there at the altar behind us. He was crying out, "Please God, be merciful to me. Forgive me of my sins and save me!"

We both raised our heads at the same time and to our delight, it was indeed Lester calling upon the Lord for His salvation! Alongside Lester, praying *for* him and *with* him was Art's brother Marvin, a dedicated Christian and minister of the gospel. Then, of course, Louie and I soon joined with him in praying for our brother. It was impossible for us to keep back the tears of joy. Our sister, Janice, Louie's wife, Irene, Art and many others soon joined in on both the prayers for Lester, as well as a time of rejoicing over his salvation!

After some time in earnest prayer, Lester stood up to his feet, wiping away tears as he boldly declared, "Praise God! I'm saved now! I am a child of God!" What an awesome blessing that was to me! That for which I had earnestly prayed for nine months and then praised God for, by faith, for several weeks, had finally become a reality!

We were all amazed when we learned afterwards that Lester had been sitting there in his seat just waiting for someone to come to him and personally invite him to accept Jesus as his Savior and Lord. It was equally amazing to all of us to learn that Art's brother Marvin had been sitting nearby, silently praying for the prompting of the Holy Spirit to go to Lester and talk to him about the Lord. Marvin began the conversation by asking Lester if he was a Christian.

"No," he answered, "but I sure want to become one." Then Marvin suggested, "Why don't we go up to the altar and pray?"

"OK, I'm ready!" Lester responded, and that's all it took as they both came forward and knelt there at the altar to pray.

What a night of rejoicing that was! When we got back to Louie's house we called our parents back in Kansas to tell them the wonderful news of Lester's conversion. It was, indeed, a blessed surprise to Dad and Mother because they too believed that it was the Lord's doing— the fulfillment of that blessed assurance and prophetic promise made to me in South Florida only a few weeks earlier.

The crowds increased each night until by Friday, July 24th, almost every seat was filled. It was my night to preach again and my topic would be, "*The Second Coming of Christ.*" I had spent most of that day fasting and praying for the anointing of the Holy Spirit to rest upon me as I would be preaching on a subject that had become very dear to my heart. I was also earnestly and fervently praying that my brother Dwane would be drawn by the Holy Spirit to attend the service that night as he had not yet made an appearance at any of the previous four services. Of course, I was also interceding in prayer for him to come to the point of surrendering his life to Christ. In my spirit, I had a strong witness that this would indeed be a "moment of truth" for my younger brother, the only member of the Ott family who was not yet saved. However, my faith would indeed be challenged before Dwane's salvation would become a reality.

After a stirring song service, prayer time, offering, and special music, I stood up to preach. I was at once aware of a special, powerful anointing of the Holy Spirit that had come upon me as I boldly proclaimed, "This same Jesus shall come again in the same manner that He ascended to Heaven from the Mount of Olives in Jerusalem nearly two thousand years ago. And if your heart is not right with Him when He does," I warned my hearers, "you'll be *left behind*, because He is coming to take His Bride away at His appearing."

Obviously the devil didn't like what I was preaching that night because he must have put it into the hearts of three young boys, ten to thirteen-years-old, to hide out in a thicket off to one side of the main arbor and let out periodically with shouts, boos, and even profanities.

I asked a couple of ushers to try and stop their nonsense, which they attempted to do with only a fair degree of success. When at last I had concluded my sermon and began giving an altar call, these boys started throwing rocks and sticks onto the top of the brush roof of the arbor. Fortunately, no one was hit by any of the rocks, but the disturbance was such a distraction until I paused to warn these boys that they were inviting the judgment of God upon their defenseless heads. That seemed to be the "clincher" as they at once stopped their disturbance.

As musicians played and sang *Just As I Am*, I continued my appeal for any and all unsaved persons present to get up and come forward to accept Jesus Christ as Savior and Lord. I was so hopeful that Dwane would respond, but up to this point he remained unmoved. He and a girlfriend were seated near the back of the crowd that night, possibly positioned for an "easy exit" if things got "too hot." Finally, about the time my heart was beginning to sink, up jumped Dwane, along with his girlfriend, and down the aisle they came! Then, to my surprise, about the time they were halfway to the altar, out of the thickets to my left came the three boys who had been creating the disturbance earlier.

My first reaction was that they must be coming to try to disrupt the altar call, so again I addressed my remarks from the pulpit to them.

"Boys, if you are coming in here to mock or to create more disturbance, you will be stopped." But no sooner had I given that warning than I noticed all three of them weeping. Indeed, God had gotten hold on their hearts and Holy Ghost conviction had gripped them; hence, they too were coming forward to be saved.

So once again it was a time of personal happiness and joy for me. I had dedicated my life to reaching lost souls for Christ. And, even though I was thrilled to see five come to the altar on that Friday night, I was especially joyful to see the final fulfillment of "the word of promise" that the Lord had given me concerning Lester and Dwane's salvation. After nine months of fervent, intercessory prayer for them to be saved, followed by several weeks of thanking God in advance that they would both be saved in the Seattle Brush Arbor Crusade, at last both were in God's fold!

As for the three young boys who came in out of the woods that Friday night and gave their hearts to Jesus, they divulged that they had indeed come there earlier in the evening to hide out in the thickets of the wooded area around the Brush Arbor structure from which they intended to do anything they could to disrupt the service. And *disrupt it they had* by shouting, by making obscene gestures, by screaming and throwing rocks and sticks. They also related to us how that after I had started preaching about the Second Coming of Christ they had crouched down in the thickets and listened with keen interest to a topic that not one of them had ever before heard. By the time I made the appeal for sinners to come forward and accept Christ as Savior, (and following my second warning to them personally), they were under the brush arbor responding to the appeal.

Rev. Ray Isaacson, a local pastor, also attended the service that night, so he took these three young boys "under his wing" and got them into church and Sunday School, where they became grounded in the faith. Several years later I saw this pastor and he related to me with great delight that all three of those young men were still going on with the Lord.

Had no one else been saved in the Brush Arbor Crusade besides my two brothers, it still would have been worth every prayer prayed, every effort put forth, and every dollar spent to make the crusade a reality. I do not say this selfishly because I am aware that every human soul is important to God. He is not willing that anyone perish; no, not one! (2 Peter 3:9) Jesus Himself once declared that just one human soul is worth more to God than the entire material world with all its vast wealth and resources (Mark 8:36–37).

Now the dream that I had had at a camp meeting in Joplin, Missouri, nearly a year earlier, the nine months of earnest praying, the weeks of thanking God, by faith, for my two brothers' salvation, coupled with the "word of promise" that God had dropped into my heart in South Florida, had all culminated there under the brush arbor in South Seattle!

The phone call to our parents in Kansas was "the icing on the cake" for them. What a week—the last two members of their big family were now saved and "in the fold."

The crowds continued to grow as the crusade advanced, until its concluding and perhaps "crowning" service on Sunday afternoon, August 2nd. Although I had preached in the opening service of the crusade, yet because that was the smallest crowd of any of the services, it was agreed that I would preach the concluding one. And, because of the substance of the message I would deliver on that Sunday afternoon, I asked Art if he would preach both on Friday and Saturday nights. This was so I could devote those days to fasting, prayer and studying for the "grand finale" service on Sunday afternoon.

My topic for that service was "*The Harvest Call.*" Because I had been on a total fast since the previous Thursday evening, I was uncertain whether I would have the strength to stand up on that hot August afternoon, thus I besought the Lord to infuse me with His strength for that very special service. And He did just that! I was determined that, by the grace of God, I would deliver the message that God had laid on my heart.

As the *moment of truth* arrived for me to stand up and deliver the burden of my heart, I felt quite weak physically, but strong spiritually.

After Art introduced me as the speaker for this final service of the Brush Arbor Crusade, I rose from my chair, feeling a little weak in my body but strong in my resolve to deliver the burden of my heart for that service. I sensed an unusual anointing of the Holy Spirit resting upon me for that occasion as I moved to my position behind the podium. The place was packed out, with many standing on the outside of the structure, as I read my text and then announced the title of my message.

The strong conviction of my heart for that message was born out of the four awesome experiences God had given me over the past year concerning the spiritual plight of the heathen throughout the world. Although I preached for a full hour that Sunday afternoon there did not appear to be any restlessness or boredom among the people present. Admittedly, my presentation was patterned somewhat after that unforgettable sermon I had heard Rev. T.L. Osborn preach in Dallas, Texas, on December 9, 1952.

At the conclusion of my sermon I gave a somewhat emotional appeal calling for any and all who would be willing to come forward and dedicate their life to reaching the unreached of our generation for the Lord Jesus Christ. I expressed a deep-seated desire to pray a prayer of dedication and consecration with them at the altar.

Out of the crowd of some five hundred, seven young people responded and came forward. Some were weeping noticeably, among whom were Art's younger brother, Stan, and my sister, Janice.

Regrettably, only one of those who responded to the appeal that afternoon ever made it to "the regions beyond."

After completing Bible school training, Stan Morlin (and his wife, Sharon, and their children) went to Central America as missionaries to preach Christ to the peoples of Honduras and Costa Rica. Heaven alone knows how many precious Central American souls will be in God's eternal celestial city (the New Jerusalem) because a thirteen-year-old boy heard the call of human need in that afternoon service and responded obediently to that call. At the time of this writing, Stan Morlin and his wife Sharon are seasoned "missionary statesmen" with many years of dedicated service to the Spanish-speaking peoples of Central America behind them.

At the conclusion of the Brush Arbor Crusade, the next order of business was the dismantling of the structure. Just as the building of the Brush Arbor amounted to considerably more work than erecting the gospel tent, so the tearing down of the arbor took much longer, but we didn't mind. We felt more than rewarded. The salvation of my brothers, Lester and Dwane, and the call of God that came to Art's younger brother, Stan, made every effort and expenditure seem *as nothing*. Then, of course, the other conversions, healings, and blessings that were experienced by many who had attended made it all the more rewarding to us.

After returning the rental chairs, the borrowed piano, and the other items used in the crusade, we then tore down the structure. Once dismantled, we secured a burning permit from the local fire district and the old brush arbor went up in smoke. But even though the arbor was gone, beautiful memories of what happened within it lived on.

There was *one* area in which we experienced a considerable "short-fall"—expenses of the crusade compared to income. Although we did receive freewill offerings in each of the crusade services, we had determined in advance not use any high-pressure tactics or "gimmicks" in order to meet the expenses of the crusade. The total amount of all offerings received was *three hundred and eleven dollars and sixty-eight cents*—barely enough to pay for the rental of the five hundred chairs. And since expenses exceeded seven hundred dollars, Art and I found it necessary to find work in order to pay off the remaining unpaid bills.

The job we found was with a contractor who built custom homes. We were able to work together most of the time and our title was "building laborers." The work was hard, but the pay was sufficient, so we were able to pay off all of the outstanding crusade bills!

Courtship Comes A' Calling

Although Art and I had a policy of not dating any young ladies while out in evangelistic endeavors (even though the opportunity to do so was always "clear and present") we were now at home in Seattle and once again attending services at our home church. So, during a period of considerable inactivity with reference to ministry, we both started dating eligible young ladies.

On the Sunday following the conclusion of our Brush Arbor Crusade (August 9th, 1953), I asked a beautiful young brunette if I might have the pleasure of taking her home after the Sunday evening service.

"Yes, but you'll have to ask my Dad if it's OK," she replied, and I did.

"OK," he said, "but I want you to have her home by ten o'clock." To that I agreed, and then Barbara ("Bobbie") and I went to a little drive-in hamburger place for some food and refreshments.

It was a pleasant experience. After walking her to the door of her home I asked her, "What about tomorrow night?"

The young people of our church had conducted a worship service at a Masonic home for the aged at Zenith, Washington, for many years.

"Can I pick you up for the service at Zenith?" I asked.

"Sure," she responded, "I'd like that." So I bade her goodnight and went home to my brother Louie's house. As I drove home I seemed to sense that this was the young lady for me! Of course I would do a lot of praying and heart-searching before deciding conclusively about the matter, but that Sunday evening of August 9, 1953, would be the beginning of a lifelong relationship between Miss Barbara Bagley and myself.

August 22, 1953, was Bobbie's nineteenth birthday. By this time we were seeing each other more often—sometimes two or three times a week. For her birthday I gave her a bottle of perfume. For sure, I knew very little about perfumes and practically nothing about the likes and dislikes of young women. It was some time later that I learned that "Apple Blossom" was not exactly her favorite fragrance. However, she accepted it with gracefulness and gratitude, avoiding any hurt feelings.

By December, we were going together quite steady and had even talked about matrimony—but I had not yet proposed to her. Before "popping that question" I wanted to feel that marriage would be God's will for me and for her, and that she was *the person* whom God had prepared to be my life's companion.

In early December my brother Louie and I took on a contract to go to the East Coast (South Carolina and Florida) to pick up two new Plymouth cars that were being repossessed. We would drive them back to Seattle for the dealership that had sold them. And since it was the time of year for the annual *Voice of Healing* Convention, we decided to go by way of Chicago, the site of the 1953 convention, so as to attend same. We had invited a close friend, Arthur Erie, to go along with us. The three of us traded off driving times, thus we drove straight through to Chicago. It had been my hope that my colleague, Art Morlin, might be able to go to the convention with us, but he had to decline due to another commitment.

We arrived in Chicago the day the convention started and put up in a hotel nearby the convention center. It was an excellent convention, but somehow it didn't seem quite the same to me without my buddy, Art, being there too, as he had been the previous year in Dallas.

After the convention concluded, our friend, Arthur Erie, took us to the Chicago airport and then drove Louie's car back to Seattle. Louie and I boarded a flight to Jacksonville, Florida, where we picked up the first car we were to drive back to Seattle. Of course, we had with us the necessary documents for the release of the two vehicles.

Once we secured the release of the first vehicle, we then drove north to Jacksonville, South Carolina, where we picked up the second vehicle. From there we became a two-car caravan, driving all the way across the United States to Seattle, by way of Cheney, Kansas, where we enjoyed a brief visit with our parents and younger siblings before continuing the journey.

That old adage, "Absence makes the heart grow fonder" was certainly the case for Bobbie and me during this nine-day journey. We were both missing each other a lot, so my return to Seattle was a happy time for us. By this time, mid-December, I knew that Bobbie was the girl that I wanted to marry. So, after seeking God in prayer concerning His will in the matter, I felt that I had His "approval," and finally popped the question.

"Will you marry me?" Her answer was a definite, "Yes! but you will have to ask my parents for their consent."

It was a joyful moment for both of us that evening when we mutually consented to be married, although a wedding date was not yet set. At that time, Bobbie was nineteen-years-old and I was twenty-one. We had been out for a little drive.

Upon arriving back at Bobbie's home, I mustered up the nerve to ask her father, Clarence Bagley, for his daughter's hand in marriage. Expecting a lecture from him, I was somewhat taken back when he answered, "you'll have to ask her mother." Now, that was a little unnerving for me, as I had not anticipated an answer like that. So, leaving Bobbie's father in their living room, I went out into the kitchen where her mother, Thelma, was and rather sheepishly reported to her.

"Your husband said I'd have to ask you for permission to marry your daughter, Bobbie. So, how about it?" I asked.

"Well," she said, "I guess it'll be OK, but I want you to promise me that you will support her so that she doesn't have to work."

"Oh, yes, ma'am," I said back to her. "You have my promise. I will support and take good care of her; you can be sure of that." And so Bobbie and I had the "green light" to proceed with plans for our wedding.

During the holiday season, Bobbie and I spent a lot of time together discussing and planning our future together. I made sure to point out to her that I had the call of God on my life for full-time ministry. To that, her response was that she had always secretly dreamed of marrying a minister or a missionary when she grew up. Her older sister, Allison, had married a minister (Rev. Donald Duncan), in 1949, and she had hoped to do likewise.

In the meantime, Art, Lester, and Dwane had also fallen in love with three other young ladies in our church and had each proposed matrimony to their respective ladies.

Among the many facets of Bobbie's and my planning for our wedding day, an engagement ring was the next matter for me to attend to. So, after getting off from my job on Wednesday, January 13, 1954, I decided to go downtown Seattle to look at engagement rings at the Benn-Tipp Jewelry Store. After finding what I thought was the perfect ring, I inquired about a financial plan. Much to my surprise and utter delight, the manager of the store approved me to buy the ring that I was most interested in. After paying a down payment and signing a purchase agreement, he allowed me to take the ring with me that evening.

I was so excited that I couldn't wait, so I went straight to Bobbie's house and asked her if I could take her for a little ride. She seemed to detect the gleam in my eyes and thus perceived that I had something exciting to share with her.

"I'll be back in a little while," she told her family. "We're just going for a little drive."

After driving a few blocks from her home, I parked the car on a hill overlooking the houses on her street. I told her to close her eyes until I said "OK, you can look now!" When she opened her eyes, there before her eyes, glittering in the light from a nearby streetlight, was a beautiful, half-carat diamond engagement ring!

What a thrill and delight that was for the darling of my life who, in a few more months, would become my wedded wife! From that evening on we began making plans for a December wedding. The date would be December 10th of that year (1954), and the place would be our home church, of course. We talked at length about my being a minister, trying to be very realistic about the fact that it would not always be a glamorous life, but if lived together within the will of God, would be a happy one.

I also wanted to make sure that Bobbie understood that Art and I would be leaving for the Midwest once again around the middle of February to resume our evangelistic outreach in that area, thus we would be apart for several months.

"You have to realize that the call of God on my life for the ministry must come first. Convenience and being together would have to be a secondary consideration," I told her. Thus it was that we established an understanding and agreed to make the best of being apart for several months.

Special events for Bobbie and me before Art and I would leave for the Midwest again were my twenty-second birthday (February 8) and Valentine's Day, celebrated a few days early. For my birthday, Bobbie gave me a beautiful Bulova wristwatch, which would become one of my cherished treasures. For Valentine's Day, I gave her a gold, heart-shaped locket and chain. We made the most of our time together before I would tell her, "So long for a while. I will hold you in my heart until I can once again hold you in my arms!"

On Friday morning, February 12, 1954, after picking Bobbie up at her home and driving her downtown Seattle to her job with the Kemper Insurance Company, I kissed her goodbye and then drove back to Tukwilla to pick Art up at his parents' home. We then drove to Louie's house to pick up his wife, Irene, and two children, Delores and Jimmy, as they were to ride with us to Kansas to join Louie (who was at that time preaching in a revival crusade at a church in Wichita).

Everything went fine except for a minor accident on Monarch Pass in Colorado when another vehicle collided with our car, causing minor damage. We arrived at my parents' home at Cheney, Kansas, on Monday, February 15th. As had been the case during our two previous outings in 1952 and 1953, my parents' home would again be our headquarters in the region during our tenure there. All mail and phone calls were directed to us there.

This, our third evangelistic tour, would be different than the first two outings. We no longer had a gospel tent for revival crusades, thus had to rely on invitations from pastors to minister in their churches.

Of course, Pastor Earl Neilson was very gracious in affording us opportunities to minister in his church on several occasions, as were other pastor friends in the area. However, these engagements were always on weekends or a mid-week night, thus we had a lot of "off days" in between when we were not actively engaged in ministry. This became a matter of serious concern to both of us, as our hearts' desires were to be "full-time" in the ministry. It became a matter of frustration and we found ourselves fighting discouragement.

Then on the morning of March 29th, while hauling cattle feed from a field to the barn for my Dad, Art began to open up his heart to me. And although I was aware that something was troubling him besides our periods of inactivity with reference to the ministry, he had not as yet divulged the matter to me—until that morning. It concerned his engagement to his Barbara in Seattle.

Even though he had given her an engagement ring and they were planning to be married some time in the future, he was beginning to have serious doubts about it being the will of God for him. Thus he bared his heart to me that Monday morning about the matter. Actually, this came as no surprise to me although I had not said a word to Art about it until that time.

"Art," I said, "I probably wouldn't have told you this if you hadn't opened your heart to me about it, but I've also had an uneasy, doubtful feeling about this matter." After a lengthy, heart-to-heart discussion about his feelings, Art spoke.

"Gail, I've got to go back to Seattle and break off this engagement."

"Can't you do that by writing her a 'Dear Barbara' letter?" I asked him.

"No," he responded. "I don't feel right about handling it that way. I've got to go back home and take care of this situation personally." So, as soon as we had completed the job for my Dad, Art and I drove to the Greyhound Bus Station on U.S. Highway 54, two miles north of Cheney. The bus that would take him on the first leg of his journey to Seattle would be stopping there to pick up passengers at 8:30 P.M. that evening, so Art purchased his ticket for the trip back to Seattle.

Having packed up all of his belongings that afternoon, he bade my family farewell before we left to go to the bus station for his trip home. It was a sad moment for me when my best friend and colleague boarded the bus, as we bade each other farewell that Monday evening of March 29, 1954. I knew, however, that this was something he would have to attend to before he advanced further in the ministry.

The plan was that once Art had attended to the "breakup" with his Barbara, he would return to Kansas to join me once again. Yet I somehow had a "gut feeling" that he might not return. That feeling turned out to be accurate, as Art had made the decision to enroll in Northwest Bible College of the Assembly of God in Seattle (now called Northwest College and located in Kirkland, Washington).

As the bus pulled away with Art on board, a sinking feeling, even a sense of loss and loneliness, seemed to almost overwhelm me for a few moments. A lump seemed to form in my throat as I realized that my beloved friend and colleague was departing.

Driving back to my parents' home on the farm all alone, a myriad of thoughts seemed to parade across the stage of my mind. All of the great times Art and I had enjoyed together and the many awesome experiences we had been privileged to share came to remembrance. It would be different for me now, however, as I would be "going it alone" with reference to the ministry God had called me into.

I could not but thank God that He had by Divine Appointment brought Art and me together two years earlier in Seattle. I felt compelled to say, "Thank You, Lord, for all those good times and wonderful experiences You allowed us to enjoy together during those two years." It had been one grand experience for us to learn together to walk by faith and to trust God implicitly in all things.

Seeking His Voice

But what would I do now that that chapter in my life as a young minister had been closed? One thing for certain was the fact that God had called me into *full-time* ministry; thus I knew that this was not the end, but rather the beginning of a new chapter in my walk with the Lord. An inevitable "turning point" had now been thrust upon me. With God's help I would somehow rise to the occasion and meet this new challenge, trusting wholly in Him.

Entering the town of Cheney, I stopped at a grocery store to purchase a can of orange juice. This I did because I felt challenged to seek God again with fasting and prayer for His help and guidance for the weeks and months ahead. For sure, I knew that I needed to believe God for new doors to open before me. I was not content with just occasional opportunities to preach on weekends and in mid-week services. Thus I felt deeply challenged to seek God in prayer and fasting, beseeching Him to open doors of ministry to me so that I could be a full-time evangelist. A can of orange juice would be used to break the fast once I had heard from Heaven.

My brother Louie had purchased a small camping trailer house while in Kansas and had left it at our parents' farm when he and his family returned to Seattle. It would become my altar and place of seclusion during the days of my protracted fast. After letting my parents know of my intention to enter into a time of fasting and prayer, I told them that unless there was a death in the family or some terrible tragedy, I did not want to see or talk to anyone until I had received an assurance from the Lord concerning my heart's desire.

Mother was a little concerned lest I do myself physical damage by going too many days without food. I assured her that I wanted God's favor and blessing even more than life itself.

"Please don't worry;" I told her. "God will take care of me. I know He will!"

So, with a supply of water, the can of orange juice, and a can opener, I went into Louie's little travel trailer, shut and locked the door that same evening that Art left to go back to Seattle. There I would remain in complete seclusion for the next eleven days, searching the Scriptures and seeking God in fervent, earnest prayer that He might do a great work in my life.

As I poured out my heart to the Lord in prayer and supplication, I found myself saying over and over, "I know there's more, Lord, and I'm going to stay right here, shut in with You, until I have a further assurance that my prayers have been answered."

After three days, I began to feel very weak physically, but I was determined that I would not be denied. After six or seven days I would black out temporarily whenever I stood up. Many times the devil tried to make me believe that I was going to die if I didn't end this fast. But I repeatedly rebuked him.

"Get behind me, Satan. You are a liar and the father of lies. I will continue to fast and pray until I have a clear assurance from God that my petition has been granted! So, I command you in the Name of Jesus Christ to depart from me!" And God honored the authority that I was exercising over the devil according to His Written Word!

Although I prayed about many things and for many people during those eleven days (especially for Bobbie and Art), my main focus was for God to open doors of opportunity for ministry on my behalf and that He might endow me with a new, fresh anointing of the Holy Spirit.

Of course, Bobbie was apprised of my fast, and although she too had concerns for my health, hoping that I would not be foolish in that which I was doing, was resigned to my absolute insistence that this was the next major step in my walk with God.

I had arranged a little mailbox just outside the door of the small camping trailer so as to keep in touch with Bobbie. We had been writing to each other frequently, so this would allow that contact to continue even during my days of fasting. Mother agreed to act as my "mail carrier," both picking up and mailing my outgoing letters, as well as delivering incoming mail to me.

It was at about 8:00 P.M. on Friday, April 9th (the eleventh full day of this fast) that I suddenly felt a deep, settled peace come over my whole being. A blessed assurance began to flood my soul so that I was made to know that I had finally prayed through and that my petition had been granted. At that precise moment, I sincerely believe that God dropped the spiritual gift of faith into my heart, supernaturally emptying me of any and all doubt concerning the matter that I had been seeking Him about.

Although I was very weak physically from eleven full days of fasting, my heart was full of joy and gratitude. A new sense of certainty and expectation seemed to sweep over my soul as I worshipped the Lord with praise and thanksgiving at that time. I now knew that I knew that I had heard from Heaven and thus a sense of complete satisfaction filled my heart and mind. Even though details as to how God's answer would be revealed were yet to unfold, I knew that something good was about to happen. Something good was on its way!

Having full assurance in my heart that I had heard from Heaven, I opened the can of orange juice, thus breaking my fast. As I sipped the orange juice slowly to avoid developing a stomachache, I thought to myself, *how glad I am that I didn't 'throw in the sponge' and give up before the answer came!* The orange juice provided me with enough nourishment and strength that I rested quite well that night.

On Saturday morning, April 10th, I was awakened around 5:00 A.M. when Dad turned on a bright yard light that was mounted high up on the windmill tower. I knew that he was at the barn to milk cows. After washing my hands and face and getting dressed, I went over to the house, greeted my mother with a hug, and announced to her that I had heard from heaven!

"Would you be so kind as to cook a small breakfast for me?" I asked Mother.

"Of course I will," she replied. "What would you like?"

"How about an egg and a piece of toast," I responded.

"I'll have it for you in a few minutes," she said. "You just be seated at the table and make yourself comfortable," she instructed me. After Mother set the food she had cooked for me on the table, I thanked her for her kindness, offered a prayer of thanks to the Lord for the food, and then proceeded to eat. As I was eating my food, I heard Mother exclaim, "Wonder who that is this time of morning?" She had noticed a car coming from the east with its headlights on, turning into the driveway.

As the car came to a stop just a few feet away from the kitchen door, I heard Mother say, "Why it's Brother and Sister Durham from Wichita!" She opened the kitchen door and greeted the Durhams while they were getting out of their car.

"What brings you dear people way out here to the farm at this time of morning?" Mother asked.

Pastor Albert Durham's immediate reply was in the form of a question.

"Sister Vera, would you have any idea how we could get in touch with your son, Gail? God woke both Ava and me up in the night and spoke to us to contact Gail Ott about coming to our church to preach a revival meeting."

Somewhat amazed about what she had just heard Brother Durham say, she answered, "Why, yes, Brother Durham, he's sitting in here at the table eating a bite of breakfast right now. Won't you folks please come on into the house?"

"Oh, praise God!" Brother said as he entered the room where I was seated.

"We had no idea where you might be at this time. In fact, we wondered if you might have gone back to Washington State again."

By this time I had finished eating the food that Mother had prepared for me, so I said to the Durhams, "Why don't you sit down here at the table with me so we can visit."

As the Durhams sat down at the table with me, Mother asked them if she could fix some food for them, but they gracefully declined her offer.

After Brother and Sister Durham each related to me how the Lord had awakened them during the night about contacting me for a revival crusade at their church, I then informed them of how I had been fasting and praying for the past eleven days, beseeching the Lord to open up doors of opportunity for ministry to me. I told them that at around eight o'clock the previous evening, my prayers had been answered and how God had dropped the spiritual gift of faith into my heart, causing me to know that my petition had been granted.

"Little did I realize, however, just how quickly I would see the unfolding of God's answer, which came to me just about nine hours ago!" I exclaimed. We all rejoiced together at the timing of this miracle. Even Dad, who had come in from the barn, got in on the celebration of praise!

How amazing all of this seemed to me! Here I have been fasting and seeking God in earnest, fervent prayer for the past eleven days. Then, just a few hours after receiving the assurance that He has heard my prayers and that the answer is on the way, Brother and Sister Durham are awakened in the night and directed by the Holy Spirit to seek me out for just that purpose—ministry!

I felt the way I think those saints in Jerusalem must have felt when they were praying without ceasing for Peter who had been imprisoned by Herod the King (Acts 12:1–17). *While they were yet in prayer*, Peter was there knocking on the gate at the house where they were praying! An angel of the Lord had come and set Peter free from the prison and from his impending doom.

Although I had felt absolute assurance that my prayers had been answered, it was still amazing to me to see how quickly and beautifully the Holy Spirit had orchestrated this whole thing. Was it a mere coincidence? *Never!* I am totally convinced that I was privileged to witness a beautiful manifestation of God's faithfulness and that I was privileged to be the recipient of a Divine provision.

After we mutually agreed on beginning the revival crusade the following Wednesday evening, April 14th, to continue through Sunday, April 25th, we prayed together before the Durhams left to drive back to their home in Wichita (about 25 miles). On that same day (Saturday, April 10th) my uncle, Rev. Paul Bailey, called and invited me to preach in his church, The New York Tabernacle on New York Street in Wichita, across the city from Full Gospel Evangelistic Chapel, the next day. This was to me, like "putting the icing on the cake!" Oh, how quickly the Lord responds to the cries of our heart when we really get in earnest with Him. How faithful He is indeed when we truly turn to Him, trusting to Him with all our heart. I can say without hesitation that I have found it so!

Equally amazing was the fact that this preaching engagement with the Durhams in Wichita would be only the beginning of a succession of "opened doors" for me with reference to my ministry. Does that mean that other pastors contacted me that same Saturday (April 10th) about coming to their churches to minister in revival crusades? No. But the way future events unfolded was to me nothing short of amazing.

Here is how it all came about: While preaching for the Durhams in Wichita, the wife, daughter, and son-in-law of a pastor in Bentonville, Arkansas, attended one of the revival services in which I was preaching. They were on a tour, visiting a number of churches in several states for the purpose of advertising their upcoming "Wildwood Dale Youth Camp" near Bentonville. The pastor's wife, Mrs. Charles Dale, came to me after the service that evening and asked if I would consider coming to Bentonville to preach a revival crusade in their church there. From that conversation, a crusade was scheduled for me to preach at this church, Wildwood Dale Chapel, beginning on Monday, May 10th. This crusade would continue through Saturday, May 22nd.

Between the close of the Wichita Crusade with the Durhams and the Bentonville Crusade with the Dales, I accepted preaching engagements in Cheney, Kansas; Webb City, Missouri; Seneca, Missouri; Anderson, Missouri; and Fayetteville, Arkansas. I also took off the night of Wednesday, May 19th, to return to Cheney so I could attend my sister Janice's high school graduation.

When I returned to Bentonville the following day, May 20, to resume the revival crusade there, Janice came with me. She loved to pray with people around the altars, especially people coming to accept Christ as Savior and Lord. She was a welcomed addition to my ministry for that summer.

While ministering in the Bentonville Revival Crusade, I received a phone call from a Rev. Claude Pruitt in Bokchita, Oklahoma, inviting me to come to his church for a revival crusade. I had never met or even heard of Rev. Pruitt prior to that phone call, nor had I ever heard of the town of Bokchita, Oklahoma.

Rev. Pruitt explained to me that he had written a letter to my uncle, Paul Bailey (Mother's youngest brother), asking him to recommend an evangelist, as he and his church were desirous to have a revival meeting. In response to Rev. Pruitt's letter, Uncle Paul gave him my name and told him how to get in touch with me in Bentonville.

From a conversation by phone with Rev. Pruitt, I accepted the invitation to come to Bokchita to begin a revival crusade on Sunday night, May 23rd, which would continue through Saturday, June 5th. Looking back, the Bokchita Crusade was one of the most blessed of all the churches that I was privileged to minister in that summer of 1954. Truly, it was a time of Divine Appointment and spiritual refreshing. It seemed like heaven came down and touched the entire crusade from the very first service through the grand finale on Saturday night, June 5th. Brother Pruitt and his good wife were wonderful people to work with in ministry.

My sister, Janice, stayed with the Pruitts in their home; they had two daughters. One was close to Janice's age. I stayed in the home of an older couple for the fourteen days of the crusade.

One of the things that made the Bokchita Crusade very special was that I was asked to officiate in a water baptismal service for the new converts. Thus on the Saturday afternoon, before the concluding service in Bokchita, I was afforded the honor of baptizing six of the eleven new converts in a creek nearby the church. That, of course, was a "first" for me.

Besides the eleven converts that came to Christ during the Bokchita Crusade, twenty-seven were baptized in the Holy Spirit. Several people testified of receiving notable healings from the Lord as well. It was indeed a gratifying crusade for such a relatively young, itinerant evangelist.

The reason I concluded the Bokchita Crusade on Saturday night was that my cousin, Joan Settle (Aunt Stella's oldest daughter), was getting married in Kingman, Kansas on Sunday afternoon, June 6th. Since I had lived with the Settles during my junior year of high school, I had become close with the family, thus wanted to attend the wedding, which also happened to be on my Dad's fiftieth birthday. Too, I would be leaving for Seattle with my brother Lloyd and our mother on Thursday, June 10th, to attend my brother Dwane's wedding. Dwane had asked me to be his best man for the ceremony. Needless to say, I was also excited about seeing my sweetheart, Bobbie, again as we had been apart for four months.

We arrived in Seattle on Saturday, June 12th, at about 11:00 P.M. We all stayed at Louie and Irene's house during our time in Seattle. The first thing I did that Saturday was to go to Bobbie's house. It was a glad reunion, even though it would end about a month later when I would return to the Midwest to resume preaching in revival crusades. The Lord would open doors for four more church revival crusades that would take me through Saturday,

October 3rd. Dwane and June (Lubking) were married on Saturday night, June nineteenth. It was a nice wedding and I enjoyed serving as Dwane's best man, especially since I had led him to accept Christ as his Savior less than a year earlier.

Mother, Lloyd, and I were Sunday dinner guests at Bobbie's home on June 20th, the day before Lloyd and Mother would leave to go back home to Kansas. I had decided to stay in Seattle for a few weeks, then ride back to Kansas with Louie and his family.

The days seemed to pass by very quickly. Bobbie's vacation began on Saturday, July 19th, so we would have more time together to plan our wedding, have a good time and enjoy a few days together before I would depart for Kansas again on Friday, July 23rd, with my brother Louie and his family.

We arrived in Cheney on Sunday, July 25th. Upon my arrival, a letter awaited me from a Rev. Baker in St. Louis, Missouri, in which he requested that I call him about the possibility of coming there to conduct a revival crusade in his church. In his letter, he related that a mutual friend, Rev. William Kelly, had suggested that he invite me to come there to preach for him.

I did call Rev. Baker and we agreed on the date of August 15th to begin a revival crusade in his church. In the meantime, I would attend a fellowship camp meeting to be held in the city park at Meade, Kansas, which began on Thursday, July 29th, and continued through Sunday, August 8th. I was there for the entire camp meeting, with the exception of the final Sunday night service.

It had been my honor to speak in a large youth service at the camp meeting on Sunday afternoon, August 1st, and then, to my amazement, the camp meeting committee decided to ask me to be the night speaker for the next day's evening service (Monday, August 2nd). The reason I was amazed was because all of the other night speakers were older, more experienced, and better known than me. I would be the youngest and only single minister to be invited to be a night speaker. Although I felt honored and humbled to be chosen as a night speaker for the camp meeting, I did not take the assignment lightly.

In the hot, sticky August weather, I drove my car out into the country, parked under a large cottonwood tree, and there called upon God to trust me with a powerful anointing of the Holy Spirit to preach His Word in that evening service.

"Without that anointing, I will fail," I told the Lord. "I need You. Oh, I need You," I cried out. And, the Lord heard my plea.

That evening as I walked to the podium after being introduced as the speaker for the evening I sensed that anointing that I had prayed for resting upon me. The audience under the big gospel tent must have exceeded five hundred. But, I did not feel any stage fright—to the contrary; I felt "holy boldness" as I stood before the crowd to proclaim the unsearchable riches of Christ. For a twenty-two-year-old budding evangelist with no formal training, I felt highly favored by my ministerial colleagues and especially blessed by my Wonderful Lord and Master!

A pastor from the town of Ulysses, Kansas, who was in attendance that Monday night sought me out later, inviting me to come to his church to preach the following Sunday night, August 8th, which I did. Three other pastors in attendance that Monday night that I was guest speaker also sought me out to invite me to come to their churches to conduct revival crusades. In fact, two of these three pastors were also night speakers at the camp meeting. There was a different speaker for each of the eleven nights of the camp meeting. From those three invitations I would conduct revival crusades in churches in Perryton, Texas; Spearman, Texas; and Magnolia, Arkansas.

On Saturday, August 14th, my sister Janice and I drove to St. Louis, Missouri, as I would begin preaching in a revival crusade there on Sunday night, the fifteenth. Janice accompanied me there to be an altar worker during the crusade.

The church in St. Louis consisted of a "new start" congregation that was meeting in an abandoned store building that had been renovated, refurbished and transformed into a sanctuary. It was located in a somewhat "hard" area of St. Louis so was considerably different than the other churches I had preached in. To say the least, it was definitely a challenge.

The crusade in St. Louis concluded with a service on Sunday night, August twenty-ninth. Janice and I drove back to Cheney on Monday, where we would be for a few days.

On Wednesday, September 1st, we drove to Meade, Kansas, where I would preach that night and the next night before driving on to Perryton, Texas, to begin a revival crusade at People's Church, where Rev. Calvin Cook was the pastor. The Perryton Crusade began on Friday night, September 3rd, and continued through Sunday night, September 12th, with services every night.

While ministering in the revival crusade at People's Church in Perryton, I was afforded the privilege of ministering on a daily radio program several times. This was a first for me and I counted it an honor. The crusade in Perryton closed on Sunday night, September 12th. The next crusade would begin the following night at Union Church in Spearman, Texas, just twenty-six miles to the west of Perryton. Rev. Calvin Springer was pastor of the Union Church at that time. The Spearman Revival Crusade would be of a shorter duration, beginning on Monday night and concluding the following Sunday night, September, 19th.

My sister Janice accompanied me for both the Perryton and the Spearman Crusades. Her presence during altar calls was especially appreciated. God had blessed her with a special ability and anointing to be a distinct blessing to those seeking the Lord at the altar. The Spearman Crusade would, however, be the last revival meeting she would accompany me in. The final crusade for that year of 1954 would be at Bethel Church in Magnolia, Arkansas. Janice was unable to accompany me there.

Because my car was in need of repairs, I left it with a mechanic in Wichita while I took the train to Magnolia, Arkansas, on Saturday, September 25th. I was to begin a revival crusade there on Sunday night, the twenty-sixth. Rev. Grady Adcock was pastor of the Bethel Church in Magnolia at the time. He, too, had been a night speaker at the camp meeting in Meade, Kansas, in early August and had at that time invited me to come to his church in Magnolia to preach a revival crusade. The date of September 26th had been agreed upon for the crusade to begin. It would continue through Sunday, October 3rd.

While preaching in the crusade at Bethel Church in Magnolia, little did I realize that my brother Louie would succeed Pastor Adcock as pastor of that church a few months later. The Magnolia Revival Crusade was the seventh such crusade for me from the time I had gone before God in prayer and fasting on the 29th of March (six months previous), beseeching Him to open doors of ministry to me. Now, in addition to the seven revival crusades I was privileged to preach in during that six-month span, I had also been privileged to preach in several different churches on fourteen separate occasions in three states.

In retrospect, I've often wondered what course my ministry might have taken had I not set aside those days to fast and pray for God's blessing and direction for the ministry He had called me to! This I do know, that "God is faithful and is a rewarder of those who diligently seek Him" (Hebrews 11:6). I have found it to be abundantly so. Even in the realm of financial support, He supplied my every need during those wonderful days, the spring, summer, and fall of 1954.

Since no further invitations to conduct revival crusades had been received, my focus then became Bobbie's and my wedding date just two months away. The date had already been set for Friday, December 10, 1954. After returning to Wichita by train from Magnolia, I picked up my car from the mechanic and began making plans to return to Seattle. Since Bobbie had asked my sister Janice to be one of the bridesmaids in our wedding, she would also be traveling with me to Seattle.

On the morning of October 11, 1954, we bade our parents and siblings farewell and then started on the journey. Just as Art and I had done on several occasions, Janice and I would also drive straight through (about 1800 miles). We found that two-hour shifts for each driver seemed to work quite well. We arrived in Seattle early in the morning on Wednesday, October 13th, early enough for me to pick Bobbie up at her home and drive her to her job in downtown Seattle.

Since Louie no longer lived in Seattle, I would be staying with my brother Dwane and his wife June until Bobbie and I were married. Janice had been invited to stay with a family from our church, the Caseys, so I took her there. Carol Casey, about Janice's age, would also be one of the bridesmaids in our wedding.

Bobbie's brother-in-law, Rev. Don Duncan, had arranged a preaching engagement for me that evening of October 13th, so getting some rest was imperative after some forty hours of driving with limited sleep. Both Dwane and his wife June worked at daytime jobs, so I was alone in their house that day, catching up on some much-needed sleep.

I did pick Bobbie up at her job that afternoon and then dined with her family before leaving for Yelm (near Olympia) to preach at the Assembly of God church there that evening. Within a few days I had found a job with the Boeing Company and was working "swing shift." This meant that I would see very little of Dwane and June except on weekends.

One afternoon, while waiting to cross the street at East Marginal Way in front of the main Boeing plant, I narrowly escaped being struck by a speeding car. At that time, I was the only pedestrian waiting to cross the street. As soon as the traffic light turned green, I stepped off of the curb onto the street. I had failed to notice an automobile coming toward me at a very high speed. I assumed that because I had the green light that traffic coming from my left would stop. Just as I stepped off of the curb onto the street a hand grabbed me by my left shoulder and quickly yanked me back—just in time to avoid being struck by the speeding vehicle that was being driven right through the red traffic light!

I literally *felt* the wind vortex created by the speeding car blow across my face and at once realized that I had come within a "whisker" of probably being killed. I quickly turned to thank the person who had grabbed me by the shoulder, preventing a tragedy, only to find no one there. Just then a strong awareness came over me that an angel of the Lord had rescued me from a certain tragedy!

One might expect to literally *fall apart* emotionally at a moment like that, but instead a wonderful peace came over me as I went on, praising and thanking God for His care and protection over my life.

At long last, Bobbie's and my wedding day arrived. The Church by the Side of the Road in South Seattle would be the place for the ceremony. There we would exchange our wedding vows, each receiving a ring from the other, and finally hear Pastor Frank McAllister say, "I now pronounce you man and wife, in the Name of the Father, and of the Son, and of the Holy Spirit."

Since I had served as best man for both Lester and Dwane in *their* weddings, my best friend and colleague in the ministry, Art Morlin, would be my best man, with Lester and Dwane serving as groomsmen for me. This was by mutual agreement so that no feelings would be hurt.

Ours was a beautiful and very meaningful wedding ceremony. I knew that it was for life!

After a brief honeymoon in Vancouver, British Columbia, Canada, Bobbie and I settled down in our little furnished apartment near our church. For the most part, my ministry during the next year would be primarily in the Seattle area, mainly preaching in a number of churches in the area. A revival crusade at a church in Kansas, originally scheduled for January, 1955, had been cancelled, thus no traveling for ministry would take place until the next year (1956).

It was mid-January, 1955, when the Holy Spirit awakened me in the wee hours of the morning. A tremendous burden gripped my heart concerning my brother Dwane and his wife June. They had decided to leave Seattle and move to Wichita, Kansas. I had tried to talk them out of making the move, but to no avail.

At the time I was awakened by the Holy Spirit I did not have a clue where Dwane and June were at that moment. Somehow I was made to know that they were in danger and that I should at once begin to intercede for them in earnest, fervent prayer. I at once rolled out of bed and fell upon my knees beside the bed, praying for them. Although I had no idea what kind of danger they were in at that time, I just knew that I was to intercede for them in prayer.

After a while, the burden became so intense that I began weeping and agonizing in prayer. This awakened Bobbie.

"Gail, what's wrong?" she asked me. "Why are you down on your knees crying?"

"I'm not sure," I sobbed. "I just got this heavy burden to pray for Dwane and June. They are in some kind of danger wherever they are. I don't know what it is, but I know that I am to intercede for them in prayer."

How long I travailed in prayer on behalf of Dwane and June in those wee hours of the morning I'm not sure—perhaps two and a half to three hours. All I know is that I felt like my heart would burst if I failed to pray, as I felt so burdened to do.

Finally, after two or three hours, the burden began to lift and a peace began to sweep slowly over my spirit. I was made to know, in the spirit realm, that whatever danger my brother and his wife were in, the danger was now passed. So, before getting back in bed to go to sleep again, I thanked the Lord for awakening me to pray for them and also for his deliverance of them from danger.

It was not until some time later that I learned what had happened that cold January night in 1955. What I learned indeed amazed me and truly made me to realize that God had trusted me to be a part of a great "miracle of mercy." I was deeply humbled by it all.

Here's what had happened. Dwane and June were driving their car somewhere in the State of Utah at the time I was awakened to pray for them. The temperature was somewhere around thirty degrees below zero in the area where they were. Their car had stalled and would not restart.

"We'll just have to wait here in the car and hope that someone traveling this way will stop to help us," Dwane had said to June.

"We wouldn't dare get out of the car and start walking. If we did, we'd freeze to death in a hurry."

But no one was out on that highway in those early morning hours, so all they could do was wait and hope that help might come their way. After about two hours or so Dwane had a notion come to mind.

"Put your foot on the clutch pedal and hold it down." He did that, but nothing happened. However, he continued to hold it down. Finally, after several minutes had gone by, Dwane said to June, "I believe that we're moving." And they were—ever so slowly. Although they were not able to perceive it in the darkness, the road ahead had a very slight downward incline to it and thus, with the clutch pedal down to break off the resistance, the car began to move.

As the car started moving forward, ever so slowly to begin with, Dwane began to realize that it was slowly but surely picking up momentum. Another fact that they were unaware of was that the highway was also gradually curving around to the right. As the momentum increased and the car was now coasting around the curve of the highway, in the distance they could see a yard light at a farmhouse.

Finally, their car coasted up alongside the farmhouse with the bright yard light on, so Dwane and June got out of their car and walked up to the farmer's house. After they had knocked on the door, the farmer opened it to see who was there. When Dwane explained their plight to the farmer, he invited them to, "Come in where it is nice and warm." Although Dwane and June were not aware of it, the farmer told them that they were probably less than half an hour away from being frozen to death. One of the common symptoms of death by freezing is an abnormal sleepiness that precedes death. Thanks to the graciousness of this good farmer, they got "thawed out" physically, got the car's engine started, and were on their way once again. Of course, the greatest thanks go to a gracious, merciful God who is ever-faithful—a God who never slumbers nor sleeps!

It has occurred to me at times how that I was blessed of the Lord so distinctly when the Holy Spirit awakened me that very early morning hour to pray for my brother and his wife. To be perfectly honest, I've also wondered at times what may have happened if I had ignored the burden to pray for my brother and his wife in that early morning hour? Would they perhaps have frozen to death? Or would the Lord have found another person to intercede on their behalf? These things we are not given to know. But one thing we are given to know is that with the Lord, "To obey is better than sacrifice" (1 Samuel 15:22). Thank God for His great love and mercy toward us!

Chapter 12

Rewards and Regions Beyond

P salm 127:3, NIV, states that, "Children are a reward from Him." The first of two such *rewards* that Bobbie and I received was a beautiful baby girl, born January 16, 1956, at Swedish Hospital in Seattle. We named her Sally Gail Ott. Four years and nine months later we would receive our *second* reward at the same hospital when Andrew Lewis Ott joined us on September 16, 1960.

Sally was nine months old when we drove from Seattle to my home town of Cheney, Kansas, where Bobbie would get her first taste of farm life. I had been invited to come to Cheney to preach a revival crusade in my little home church there—the same church where I had been ordained four years earlier.

Sister Pauline Parham was now the new pastor at the Cheney Mission Church. I had, of course, met Sister Parham four years earlier when Art and I had preached for her while she was the pastor of the Knox Street Full Gospel Church in Houston, Texas. God had used Sister Parham in giving guidance to Art and me, which culminated in our two tent crusades in Alabama.

Nine-month-old Sally made an immediate hit with all of my family and friends in and around Cheney. She was an absolute darling! It was the first time, but certainly not the last, for Bobbie and Sally to visit in Kansas while I preached the gospel.

Sent by the Savior

I had been blessed of the Lord in so many ways—with open doors for ministry, a beautiful wife, a beautiful daughter, many wonderful Christian friends and ministerial colleagues—yet there was still a *tug* at my heart. The cry of the heathen, the lost souls of humanity in the regions beyond America, again filled the eardrums of my "inner man."

Thus after returning to Seattle following our month or so in Kansas, in the fall of 1956, I began to make plans to launch out on my first missionary journey, which would be to the country of Brazil in South America.

I had taken some classes in Portuguese, the primary language spoken in Brazil. Rev. Harland Graham (brother-in-law of Pastor Frank McAllister) and his wife, Hazel, were seasoned missionaries who had already invested many years of their lives in the country of Brazil. Knowing of my heartfelt calling to evangelism, they graciously invited me to come to Brazil to minister. For starters, they arranged a schedule of engagements for me in Northern Brazil. It would be my first experience in missionary evangelism (preaching through interpreters).

I departed from Seattle on the first leg of my journey to Brazil on January 16, 1957—our daughter Sally's first birthday. After a very special party for Sally at Bobbie's parents' home, the family drove me to the Seattle airport, where I would board a plane for San Francisco. There was no Brazilian consulate in Seattle at that time. I'd have to go to San Francisco to secure my visa and other necessary documents to enter the country of Brazil.

After securing these in San Francisco, I took a Greyhound bus from California to Cheney, Kansas. At home in Cheney, I would again seclude myself locally in a vacant house that belonged to my parents and spend the next eight days in fasting and prayer, seeking God, as Elisha did, for a *double portion* of His power and anointing on my ministry in Brazil.

Once I gained peace in my heart about the upcoming mission to Brazil, I broke the fast and accepted my parents' offer to drive me to Houston, Texas. I would minister in two churches in that area before continuing on to Miami by bus, there to depart for South America. Although I was missing Bobbie and Sally terribly by this time, it was an enjoyable few days with my parents. They were able to be with me for the special services I preached in greater Houston, and their support meant the world to me.

Soon enough, Dad and Mom left Houston for Kansas, and I boarded a Greyhound bus for Miami. Many hours later, my friend Richard and his wife met me at the bus station and took me to their home. I spent a few days in Miami securing passage for the sound equipment I was taking to Brazil, as well as making other arrangements for the journey. I would celebrate my twenty-fifth birthday in Miami.

Since I would be in town for a few days before flying out to Puerto Rico en route to Brazil, Richard and his wife invited me to go to a "healing crusade" being conducted in a vacant store building in Hialeah. When we arrived at the meeting, the place was packed—with some 400 people in attendance!

Having just spent eight days in fasting and prayer, my level of spiritual alertness was definitely elevated. I say *that* to say this: While most everyone present in the service seemed to be mesmerized with the would-be "deliverance" preacher, I soon became troubled in my spirit. I sincerely believe that the spiritual gift of the discerning of spirits (as described in 1 Corinthians, Chapter 12) was at that moment being manifested in and through me.

Shortly after the start of the pulpit ministry, under my breath (certainly not out loud) I began to rebuke the spirit of deception that I discerned was in operation through the minister in charge. I found myself saying in the spirit realm, "You spirit of deception, I rebuke and bind you in the Name of Jesus Christ!" It was at this juncture that the would-be *deliverance preacher* began to seem quite nervous. Soon beads of perspiration broke out across his forehead. Next, he began to tremble; before long he went down on his knees. Finally, he was lying out flat on the platform as if in a state of semi-unconsciousness.

Somebody ran to the phone and called for an ambulance. Soon a siren blared outside as the ambulance arrived at the building. In just a few minutes, medics had this preacher on a stretcher and were headed toward the ambulance, which whisked him off to a nearby hospital.

Most everyone at this meeting assumed that this evangelist had suddenly fallen ill. I, however, believe that I witnessed the power of the Lord in operation, binding a spirit of deception in a man who was feigning that he was telling people things about themselves supernaturally, when he was actually a "false prophet." At first, I felt somewhat guilty for what I had done (rebuked a deceiving spirit) unbeknownst to anyone else present at that meeting. Yet I knew that this was the work of the Holy Spirit praying through me, so I quietly pondered this in my heart.

After this preacher was taken away by ambulance, my friend Richard stood up and spoke.

"Hello, everyone. Say, here's a preacher! Why don't we have *him* preach to us?" At first I thought, Never. I wouldn't *think* of doing that, but then, a few seconds later, I seemed to sense the prompting of the Holy Spirit that I should consent to preach the Word of God to these waiting worshippers. I made my way to the pulpit and the Lord blessed the ministry of His Word.

Love in Many Languages

My first stop enroute to Brazil would be San Juan, Puerto Rico, where I would preach through an interpreter for the first time. My flight from Miami was late; thus by the time I arrived at the Church of God Bible School in San Juan the students were waiting in eager anticipation to hear the message God had for them through this young preacher from the United States.

The anointing of the Holy Spirit was strong upon both my Spanish interpreter and me that night. It was a *blessed* service. I spent the night (a short one) at the Bible School and slept in a bunk bed dormitory room with the male students. My flight out of San Juan the next morning was an early one, thus it was still dark when I arrived at the airport. En route to Belem, Brazil, that day, the plane would stop at the tiny island of Antigua, at Trinidad, and at all three Guineas (French, Dutch, and British) before finally arriving in Belem, a sprawling city at the mouth of the Amazon River.

After an overnight hotel stay in Belem my journey continued, with a couple of stops before finally arriving in Fortaleza, my first destination in Brazil. I sent a telegram from Belem to missionaries Harold and Ethel Matson in Fortaleza, giving them my flight information, thus I expected that they would meet me at the airport upon arrival there. To my surprise the telegram's speed was not quicker than my own. It arrived the day *after* I did! This was the first of many "different" experiences I would have abroad as I learned that things don't always get done elsewhere in the world as they do in the United States!

At the airport, I wrote down the Matson's name on a slip of paper and a taxi driver assured me that he knew where they lived, so I hired him to drive me there. After about three hours of driving all around the city of Fortaleza, I happened to see Dennis Matson (the missionaries' son) walking on a sidewalk. With my limited Portuguese and the cab driver's limited English, I got him to stop so we could pick Dennis up and thus be directed to the Matson's home.

Ethel Matson had to do a lot of negotiating with the "cabbie" to get my bill reduced to a reasonable amount, but it was finally done and our brief visit begun. I would return to Fortaleza a month or so later for open-air evangelism crusades. This would be only an overnight stay before flying on to Natal the next day. There I would begin two months of missionary evangelism in the country of Brazil.

It gave me a deep sense of satisfaction and fulfillment to *at last* be in the area of the world where I would begin a worldwide ministry of missionary evangelism. Missionaries Harland and Hazel Graham had everything in place for the first of several evangelistic crusades that I would minister in there in Northern Brazil. Admittedly, I was very excited and "fired up" for that first service in Natal! It would be held in a large gospel tent and had been well-publicized, thus a full crowd was on hand for the first service.

My scripture text was taken from I John, 3:8: "For this purpose the Son of God was manifested, that He might destroy the works of the devil." With this text as a "springboard" for my message, I posed the question: "What are the works of the devil that the Lord Jesus Christ came to destroy?" The answer: sickness, disease, and sin. Jesus said in John 10:10: "The thief [Satan] cometh not but for to steal, and to kill, and to destroy . . ." I pointed out that Satan steals our health through sickness, tries to kill our bodies through disease, and desires to destroy our souls through sin.

"And Jesus Christ is the same yesterday, today, and forever," I proclaimed (Hebrews 13:8). "He is still destroying the works of the devil today!"

It was a wonderful service. Many responded to the invitation to accept Christ as Savior. We also prayed for the sick and, each night, God honored our faith by healing all manner of sickness and disease.

That was the beginning of two months of intense evangelism in three cities in Northern Brazil (Natal, Recife, and Fortaleza). More than a thousand souls responded to the invitation to accept Jesus Christ as Savior in those services and scores of dramatic healings gave witness to the power of the Risen Christ.

One point of interest that marked these first international crusade services in Brazil, which I would later also observe in other countries, was my sighting in the crowds that attended of "that face"—the very one that I had seen on the morning of August 19, 1952, in Northern Missouri. Remarkably, it almost always happened when I was preaching under the anointing of the Holy Spirit

At times when I was not thinking about it at all, that's when I would see "*that face*"—one I shall never forget!

Since Northeastern Brazil was so near to the equator, the intense heat took a toll on me during my time there. When I left Seattle on the sixteenth of January to begin this first missionary journey I weighed 185 pounds. When I arrived back in America two months later, I weighed only 145 pounds. However, I felt good for the most part. Eating the food abroad was my biggest challenge. Raised on simple fare in Kansas, it was easier for me physically to *fast* than to eat foods unfamiliar to my digestive system.

"With Signs Following . . ."

Perhaps the most notable miracle of healing during the first crusade services in Brazil was the restoration of sight to a seventy-year-old man in Fortaleza. This man had gone blind at age six and had groped in blindness most of his life. When his sight was restored he became ecstatic—running here and there, observing colors, people, etc. All who saw him shared in his joy and praise of God.

Since I had traveled to Brazil on a permanent visa in order to take sound and taping equipment with me, I had also traveled on a one-way ticket. Thus, in order to get back to America I had to trust God for a *financial miracle*. An airline ticket back to the U.S. would cost three hundred dollars, which I did not have. After seeking God in earnest prayer concerning the money needed to purchase my plane ticket home, a wealthy Brazilian businessman asked to buy my tape recorder (a reel-to-reel machine). I had bought it used for one hundred dollars in 1952 and had used it often. The Brazilian man offered me a sum equal to *three hundred U.S. dollars* for the recorder; hence a deal was struck and I had the funds to pay for my airfare back to America.

Bidding farewell to the Graham and Fusch families (Del and Jo Fusch and their three children were first-term missionaries working with the Grahams in Natal at that time), I boarded a Brazilian Airlines plane for the first leg of the journey home. We changed planes, boarding a larger aircraft, at Belem, then stopped in Caracas, Venezuela, before a flight to New York City. Arriving in New York, I put up for the night in a hotel near the airport before continuing on to Wichita.

Bobbie, her younger sister Corolyn Bagby, and our daughter, Sally, had traveled to Wichita by train, hence were at the airport to meet my flight. It was a happy reunion—except that it took a few days for Sally to warm up to her daddy. She wasn't quite sure who this "dude" was after nearly nine weeks' absence.

Purchasing a used car in Cheney, Bobbie, Sally, and I traveled extensively throughout the Midwest ministering at churches both in revival crusades and guest-speaking engagements. After awhile we were able to purchase a small camping trailer house, which would become our home for a few months.

At the conclusion of a revival crusade that I ministered in at the Knox Street Full Gospel Church in Houston, Texas in August, 1957, Bobbie and I, along with our one-year-old Sally and Bobbie's sister Corolyn (who had flown from Seattle to join us), drove to Cuernavaca, Mexico, where I was to minister in an evangelistic crusade outside of Mexico City. The crusade was conducted in a large church in a rural area called Progresso.

The evening of our first night enroute to Cuanavaga we were guests of my uncle, Orville Bailey (Mother's brother), and his wife in McAllen, Texas. I had never met this uncle prior to that evening. He was the owner of the Poinsettia Courts Motel in McAllen. It was a very nice occasion for us and for my uncle and aunt.

Arriving in Cuernavaca, Bobbie, Sally, and Corolyn would stay with Martha Meyers, wife of Missionary Statesman Wayne Meyers. Brother Meyers had invited me to come to Mexico for this crusade, had made all the arrangements for the meetings, and would also serve as my Spanish interpreter in them. In my opinion, Wayne Meyers was one of the most dedicated and dynamic missionaries I have ever met. He was used mightily of God in the country of Mexico in a ministry that spanned a lifetime.

During that ten-day crusade, hundreds of Mexicans responded to the invitation to receive Christ as Lord and Savior. We prayed for the sick and afflicted each night. Faith was strong and many notable and undeniable healings were wrought amongst those coming forward in believing prayer. We also encountered many demon spirits, over which we exercised our God-given authority by casting them out. On the concluding night of the crusade, Bobbie, Sally, and Corolyn were present in the service. Brother Meyers's wife, Martha, drove them a long distance to the crusade location.

On that final night, more than a thousand people crowded into the church building. The aisles were packed, while people stood lining the exterior walls and the platform behind the podium filled to capacity. The power of the Lord was present to heal the sick to an unusual degree. More than a hundred responded to the invitation to receive Christ that night!

Separation and Other Sacrifices

When we finally returned to the Houston area, we again lodged in McAllen at the Poinsettia Courts, compliments of Uncle Orville. We had parked our small trailer house on a farm outside Houston. The rice farmer was a dear friend of ours and was also the pastor of the Satsuma Full Gospel Church in the area (Rev. W.C. Stockdick and his wife, Floy).

Incidentally, in the interim since our parting, my dear friend and ministerial colleague, Art Morlin, had married Bobbie's older sister, Joan Bagby, on June 30, 1956. They were expecting their first child now, while we were in Mexico. When we arrived at the Stockdick farm on August 18, 1957, Bobbie and her sister called home to Seattle to inquire about the expected baby and learned that she (Kim Morlin) had been born that day. We took Corolyn to the Houston airport the next day to fly home.

For the next two months Bobbie and I, along with our eighteen-month-old daughter, were involved with ministry in churches in several states, primarily as itineration for my next missionary journey. This time it would be the tiny country of British Honduras along the Yucatan Peninsula of Mexico. I had been invited to conduct evangelism crusades in all five cities of that country by a Church of God missionary, Rev. O.O. Wolfe.

Bobbie and Sally would not be accompanying me for the month of ministry in British Honduras, so they boarded a Greyhound bus in Webb City, Missouri, to return to Seattle while I drove on to New Orleans, Louisiana, and boarded a flight to Belize, British Honduras. We gathered our courage, knowing we would be apart for some two and a half months this time. I would join them in Seattle near Christmastime.

In the late 1950s, British Honduras (population 69,000) was a British colony (it was since granted independence and renamed "Belize"). English was spoken there. God gave me a great ministry in that small country and I was privileged to lead many souls to a saving knowledge of Christ.

The Lord also spared me from death while staying in the home of the Wolfes' in Belize. I had washed some of my socks and underwear and had gone into the couple's backyard to hang them on a clothesline to dry. Later that day, a young man knocked at the door of the Wolfes' inquiring about a job of any kind. He was carrying a machete, so Brother Wolfe said, "Yes, I'd like to have the grass cut down in our backyard." While the young man was cutting the six to eight-inch-high grass down he killed five deadly poisonous snakes—near the clothesline where I had hung my clothes!

"You've been granted a miracle of deliverance from death," Brother Wolfe informed me.

"What do you mean?" I asked.

"Well," he said, "the young man with the machete knife just killed five deadly, poisonous snakes in our backyard right under the clothesline. If you had been bitten by any *one* of them you'd probably have been dead before you got to the hospital." All I could say was, "Thank You, Lord, for Your care and protection!"

Just as in Brazil and Mexico, I saw "that face" again while preaching in British Honduras—the face I had seen in our car in

Northwestern Missouri the morning of August 19, 1952. It seems that he almost always appeared *somewhere* in the crowd as I was preaching under the anointing of the Holy Spirit. To me, this has served as a repeated confirmation of the special call that was given to me by the Lord of the Harvest to take His gospel to the four corners of the earth. I count it a high calling and have never taken it lightly. Of course, all of the glory and praise and honor belong to Him. He has always been "The Message." I have only been "the messenger."

That same face I saw in Brazil, then in British Honduras, has appeared in crowds while I've been preaching the unsearchable riches of Christ in Argentina, Bolivia, China, Costa Rica, El Salvador, Formosa (now Taiwan), Guatemala, Hong Kong, India, Israel, Japan, Java (Indonesia), Jordan, Nicaragua, Pakistan, Panama, the Philippines, Russia, and Singapore.

The crusade in British Honduras concluded with a glorious meeting in a large church in the capital city of Belize on Sunday night, November 24, 1957. The following morning, I boarded a flight back to New Orleans, where I picked up my car, which I'd left with a pastor there while traveling.

From New Orleans I returned to my parents' home in Kansas. I would ride with my parents and youngest sister, Janie, to Seattle, and to be reunited with Bobbie and Sally in time for the Christmas holidays.

The trip from Cheney to Seattle was delayed a few days due to the tragic death of Pastor Pauline Parham's nineteen-year-old son, Charles. The death of Charles Parham was a tremendous shock, not only to his family, church, and many friends, but also to the entire community. When tragedies like this happen and we cannot understand why, we simply must trust God for "grace and help in the time of need," which is present in abundance to those who need it. I personally regarded Sister Parham and her family to be among my very closest friends and colleagues; her loss was keenly felt and the delay to pay our respects to her was no bother.

The drive to Seattle with my parents was pleasant and trouble-free. Naturally, I was very happy to be reunited with Bobbie and Sally. Right after Christmas, we all returned to Kansas. The car was a little crowded this time with six people in it, but no matter.

Our small trailer house was parked at my parents' farm, where I had also left our car. For the next eight months, we would be engaged in church ministry and itineration for my next missionary journey—primarily in Kansas, Oklahoma, Texas, Missouri, and Arkansas. In early October, we returned to Seattle, where invitations had come and arrangements were being made for my next missionary evangelism journey.

On this tour, I would be ministering in ten countries, beginning in Japan and concluding in Israel. From Israel, it was cheaper to continue on, traveling completely around the world, than to return to Seattle from Israel by backtracking, so this was what I would do.

Since I would be away for five and a half months on this evangelism tour, it was not advisable for Bobbie and Sally to accompany me; thus they would again stay behind.

Amazingly, the Lord had supplied the funds I would need to pay my plane fare for the entire trip around the world and back to Seattle! It came to $1,361.47. I purchased the flight ticket but, because of several unexpected expenses, I was almost flat broke. My flight from Seattle to Honolulu, Hawaii (the first leg of my journey), was scheduled to depart the Seattle-Tacoma airport at 10:30 P.M. on Monday, October 13, 1958. Bobbie's parents would drive us to the airport for my departure.

Bobbie, Sally, and I were riding in the back seat of her parents' car on the way to the airport. Realizing that I was almost flat broke and had no money to give to her and Sally, Bobbie questioned me.

"How are you going to be able to leave with no money in your wallet?" Looking at this situation in "the natural," it was kind of a scary! But I knew that the same God who had supplied *all* of our needs up until that time wasn't out of miracles, so I lovingly replied to my sweet wife.

"I don't know where it will come from, honey, but I know that the Lord will provide. Why, He could send an old lop-eared donkey up to me with the funds I need in his mouth, or maybe a bird out of the air, with just the right amount. I don't know how He will do it, but I know He will. He's never failed us yet and He's not going to this time! Only believe!"

Arriving at the airport terminal, I removed my suitcase and briefcase from the car and proceeded to the check-in counter. After checking in, we all went out to the waiting area at the departure concourse gate. When the time to board drew near, a gentleman picked up a microphone and announced that Pan American Flight #194 to Honolulu would be delayed due to a cloud of fog that had suddenly settled over the airport.

It will always be my firm belief that God caused that fog to appear and delay the flight. *Why?* Two different friends of mine were on their way to the airport to see me off. However, they had not taken note of the correct departure time; thus were about forty-five minutes late. Now, had the plane departed on time, I would have left financially broke, as well as had to leave Bobbie and Sally with no money for *their* needs. But, because a fog had delayed the departure of my flight, my two friends got there in time to do what God had laid upon their hearts to do—give me one hundred dollars each! Now I would be able to give Bobbie one hundred dollars and also have that amount to begin my missionary adventure.

No sooner had my friends gotten to the departure gate and given me their love offerings then the fog lifted. In a few minutes they announced over the P. A. system: "We will now begin boarding Flight #194 for Honolulu." That was the first of many financial miracles that the Lord would perform on my behalf during the five-and-a-half months I would be away on this round-the-world missionary evangelism tour.

Not only was I able to give Bobbie one hundred dollars before departing, but the following day she got a call from the Boeing Company, where she'd recently applied for work, that she had a job if she wanted it. Again the Lord proved Himself faithful, though He did allow our faith to be tested!

"Warm Christmas" in Tainan

After an overnight stay in Honolulu and a brief stop on tiny Wake Island, I finally arrived in Tokyo, Japan. My missionary friend, Al Winroth, met me at the airport there. The two of us immediately boarded a high-speed train at a nearby station to make the trip to Nagoya, Japan, where I would begin six weeks of ministry in that country.

Missionary Winroth had made previous arrangements for lodging with Rev. Manuel Zamora and his family. The Zamoras were independent missionaries from Canada. My first evangelism crusade in Japan would be conducted under a large gospel tent in Nagoya, a city that had been 89 percent bombed out and burned during World War II. A Japanese brother had been arranged to interpret for me during this crusade.

Unlike the South and Central American countries I had preached in, Japan was, for the most part, a "spiritually cold" nation. The spiritual darkness here was intense, and while in Latin American countries people readily responded to the invitation to accept Christ as Savior, the Japanese people were somewhat skeptical, reserved, and reluctant. Yet, when they witnessed the undeniable miracles of healing that the Lord wrought amongst the sick and afflicted, they *did* respond, although not in the large numbers I had witnessed in other countries.

In two weeks the tent meetings were concluded and I began an open-air meeting in a park in the city of Narumi. There were no chairs or benches, thus the listeners had to stand while I preached the Gospel of Christ (through an interpreter, of course). The crowds usually were in the hundreds. The Lord confirmed His proclaimed Word with signs following. Five blind eyes were healed and their sight restored. There were also six deaf ears opened, with hearing restored. Many testified of healings from tuberculosis, high blood pressure, heart disease, etc. Time and space do not permit a detailed report of each healing. However, there was one outstanding miracle of healing wrought upon an elderly Japanese man in the Narumi Crusade that I'd like to relate to readers.

This man, like most of the listeners at the Narumi Crusade, had never heard the gospel message before in his life. Except for one small Catholic Church, there was not one church in this city of 100,000 people, although there *were* a number of heathen temples and shrines and perhaps a thousand or more gods and goddesses for the people to worship.

This man was passing by the park one afternoon while I was preaching. He stopped and listened to the message of supernatural deliverance through the Lord Jesus Christ. He was very ill with a severe case of shaking palsy. He couldn't move one arm, which was quite stiff. He shook all of the time, but he listened very intently to the message. Then, when prayer was offered for the sick, he came forward. We laid hands upon him, rebuked the spirit of infirmity in his body, and prayed for God to heal him. The shaking stopped immediately. After a moment, he began to move the arm that was stiff and finally was waving it above his head. He was completely healed and saved!

The man returned the next day to testify of his healing over the loudspeaker.

"I am convinced now that this Jesus is alive and real," He exclaimed.

My last week in Japan was spent in Totsuka and Yokohama. In three special services in these cities some twenty or so people accepted Christ as Lord and Savior and a number of healing miracles were wrought amongst the sick. I was also privileged to preach the Gospel of Deliverance on five radio broadcasts in Japan, which had a potential of ten million listeners.

On December 2, I left Japan to fly to Formosa (or present-day Taiwan). Missionary Ruth Helgeson met me at the airport in the capital city of Taipai. We immediately boarded a train for the city of Tainan in Southern Formosa, where I would spend most of the month of December in crusades.

The Tainan Crusade began in an auditorium and was later moved outdoors to an open-air setting. Seventeen persons responded to the invitation to receive Christ in the opening service. Except for one week of meetings in the city of Hsin-Yeng, all of the meetings were conducted in the city of Tainan. Services in Taiwan were trilingual—a new experience for me. This is how it worked:

I first spoke in English. Sister Ruth Helgeson then interpreted into Taiwanese. Then, Brother Andrew Tsai translated the message from Taiwanese to Mandarin Chinese. The interesting fact about this was that Brother Tsai could not understand English at all. He had no idea what I had preached in English until Sister Helgeson put it into Taiwanese. It was an interesting experience!

While in Formosa I was awakened from sleep one night a little after midnight. A young Chinese man who was going into the Formosan Air Force the next day wanted to be baptized in water, and he wanted *me* to do the baptizing right then! Thus, I got out of bed and went out into the night to a place where there was water and baptized this new Chinese Christian. I later baptized fifteen others in a special baptismal service in the city of Hsin-Yeng.

Christmas in Tainan was indeed *different* for me. I preached in crusade meetings both on Christmas Eve and Christmas Night, with souls being saved both evenings. On Christmas Day it was a balmy ninety-degrees in Tainan—hardly a "White Christmas!"

Proclaiming Christ in China

On Sunday morning, December 28, I departed from Taipai for Hong Kong. A missionary, Rev. David Schmidt and his wife, Gwen, met me at the airport and took me to their home, where I would lodge for the next five days. That Sunday night I preached in an Assembly of God church in Kowloon, Hong Kong Colony. Gwen Schmidt served as my Mandarin interpreter for the service.

While in Hong Kong, Brother Schmidt took me on a most interesting trip to the small Portuguese colony of Macao. We went by boat at night. Our cabin had small beds, on which we slept adequately. The next morning the boat docked at the harbor in Macao. We disembarked for an interesting, four-hour sightseeing excursion before boarding the boat to return to Hong Kong that evening.

On New Year's Night, January 1, 1959, I had the privilege of ministering in a church in Tsum Wan, New Territories. Missionary Vera McGillauery had arranged the meeting, including a Cantonese interpreter. Three precious Chinese people accepted Jesus as Savior in that meeting. We also prayed for the sick there and "the power of the Lord was present to heal" (Luke 5:17).

The Philippine Campaign

On January 2, 1959, I left Hong Kong for the Philippines, where I would be busy in ministry for over a month. Church of God Missionary James Reesor met me at the Manila airport and took me to his home in Manila. Brother Reesor and I left the next morning by car to drive to the city of Cauayan, Isabela, about 250 miles north of Manila, where I would minister.

On Sunday night, January 4, we opened a campaign in the Cauayan City Center building. About two hundred people were present for the first service, which was delayed due to a defect in the lighting system. Brother Memerto Cortez, a young ministerial student at the Church of God Bible School on the outskirts of Cauyan would serve as my Ilacono interpreter. During the Cauayan Campaign, several hundred souls accepted Christ as Savior. There were also a number of notable healings during this campaign.

The farewell that the Bible school students and staff gave me at the conclusion of the campaign was memorable. Brother Memerto announced to me that they were going to roast a dog for this gala event.

"Really," I said. "Which one of these young dogs is it going to be?" I asked. There were four or five nearly full-grown pups there at the Bible school.

"Oh, no sir. You don't understand, sir," he replied. "It's going to be this old dog, the mama of this litter," he explained. "You see, she is old and is going to die anyhow," he went on to say.

"Oh, Lord, I need Your help right now!" I thought. Just then an inspiration hit me.

"Oh no," I responded. "You see, this old dog is my friend. I've been petting her and talking to her. You wouldn't honor me if we ate my friend for the farewell dinner. If you're going to eat her, please do so after I'm gone," I pleaded. It worked! The old flea-bitten mama dog was spared. We had water buffalo instead!

Again, I want to mention that in each of the ten countries I ministered in on this excursion, as it had been in South and Central America, I saw "that face" again and again in the crowds attending. In this way, the Lord encouraged, and indeed *ignited* me in my calling.

After the conclusion of the campaign in Cauayan, I returned to Manila, where I would spend a few days before flying to Djakarta, Java, to begin evangelism crusades on the most densely populated island in the world. While in the Philippines, I eagerly awaited word from Missionary Mark Buntain in Calcutta, India, the next country on my tour slated for a major evangelism campaign. The original invitation had come from a missionary who never returned to India, thus he transferred the invitation to Brother Buntain.

Doors Open in India

Several times while with Brother Reesor in the Philippines he suggested putting me in touch with an Indian medical doctor in the interior city of Kharagpur, India.

Each time I said, "No, I've got to wait until I get a response from Brother Buntain." Finally I sensed that this invitation was of the Lord, so I spoke to Brother Reesor.

"OK, why don't you go ahead and contact Dr. Bastia in India. If this works out, then I'll accept it as the will of God for my ministry in India.

Brother Reesor immediately contacted Dr. Bastia, recommending that he invite me to come to Kharagpur for an evangelism campaign. The very next day after Brother Reesor had contacted Dr. Bastia a letter came from Missionary Mark Buntain in Calcutta saying that he would not be interested in trying to have a campaign in Calcutta at that time. He did, however, invite me to preach a couple of nights at his church in Calcutta, which I did upon arriving there.

Soon a letter of confirmation came from Dr. Bastia confirming arrangements being made for an evangelism campaign in Kharagpur.

What is amazing about this contact made by Brother Reesor is the fact that Dr. Bastia had been fasting and praying for *two weeks* prior to receiving Brother Reesor's letter. His prayer to God was, "Please, Lord, send an American evangelist to Kharagpur without me having to send out an invitation; then I will know of a certainty that this is Your doing and not mine!"

When Brother Reesor's letter arrived, he was confident that it was a direct answer from the Lord, thus he rejoiced, broke his two-week fast, and started preparing for the crusade. Hence it was the firm conviction of my heart that the India Crusade was ordained of the Lord.

On February 7, I bade farewell to Brother James Reesor and his family and took my flight to Djakarta, Java. Upon arriving at the hotel in Djakarta I decided to send a telegram to Missionaries Bob and Marian Broadland, giving them my flight number and arrival time in Surabaja. They knew I would be coming, but were awaiting the flight information. To my surprise, three classes of telegrams were offered in that country—regular, urgent, and extremely urgent. Based on my experience of sending a telegram in the country of Brazil, I decided that I would go with the most expensive one—the "extremely urgent."

I felt confident that by sending it via Indonesia's fastest mode the Broadlands would be at the airport to meet me in Surabaja, especially since I was sending it two days prior to my arrival. Sunday, February 8th, was my twenty-seventh birthday. I spent the day in my hotel room, praying and preparing for the crusade meetings in

Malang, East Java. On Monday, February 9, I boarded Garuda Indonesian Airways Flight #770 at the Djakarta airport for the four-hundred-mile flight to Surabaja. Arriving there at about 11:00 A.M., I immediately scanned the crowd inside the terminal building, looking for my friends and contacts, Bob and Marian Broadland. They were nowhere to be found.

I decided to stick close to the entrance of the terminal building so that I could see them when they arrived. I thought they might have had car problems or gotten caught in a traffic jam or some other kind of delay. An hour went by and still no Broadlands. A second hour went by and there was no trace of Bob and Marian.

About then I began to have serious doubts about the arrival of the "extremely urgent" telegram I had sent on February 7 from the hotel in Djakarta. Yet I refused to panic. The only thing for me to do was just stay put at the Surabaja airport terminal building, which I did. Realizing that something was wrong, I began to call upon the Lord in silent prayer.

You've never failed yet, and I know I can depend on You in this situation, Lord, thus I will thank You in advance for Your intervention today. Amen. At approximately 2:00 P.M., a tall, slender American walked through the door, into the terminal building, and up to the ticket counter.

After checking in, he turned around and looked in my direction. Obviously he and I stood out like sore thumbs among the darker-skinned, black-haired Indonesian people who were generally shorter of stature than Americans. Anyway, the man walked up and began talking to me.

"You must be flying out to Manila on the same flight I'm going on," he suggested.

"No, sir," I replied. "I just came from Manila two days ago. I'm waiting for some friends from Batu to come pick me up."

"When did you arrive here in Surabaja?" he asked me.

"About 11:00 A.M. today," I replied.

"Well, did your friends from Batu know you were coming here?" he probed.

"Oh, yes, I sent them a telegram from Djakarta two days ago. They knew I'd arrive here today," I said.

This American, who was probably thirty-five to forty years of age, laughed.

"They may never get *that* telegram," he informed me. "This is Indonesia, not America!"

"Yes," I said, "but I sent it 'extremely urgent!'" He laughed again and informed me that all "extremely urgent" meant was that I paid more money to send my friends a telegram. He then began to make suggestions like, "I could tell you what bus to take, but since you don't speak Indonesian you could get on the wrong bus and end up no-telling-where." He went on to say that there was a train of sorts that ran down to Malang, but it was very undependable, and a taxicab was out of the question.

"You wait right here," this gentleman said to me suddenly. "I'll be back in a few minutes."

I watched as he went to an area where there were a few telephones. He picked up the receiver, put in some coins, and then dialed a number. In a few minutes he came back over to where I was sitting and introduced himself. We had not become acquainted until then. He went on to inform me that he was the manager of the huge Procter & Gamble factory there in Surabaja.

"I just called the factory and ordered my private chauffer to come here to pick you up and take you to Batu. It is about fifty miles from here and the roads are not like our roads in the U.S., so it will take a while, but he will get you there."

"But you've never met me before," I said. "How can you do such a tremendous kindness to a total stranger?" I asked him.

"It doesn't matter that we've never met before," he continued. "You're in a pickle and I want to see that you get to your friends' house!"

"Well," I said, "in that case, I will be more than happy to pay you for this great kindness."

"Oh, no," he responded. "Maybe you'll be in the position to help someone yourself someday," he suggested. "Just pass the kindness on—OK?"

"By all means," I responded. In a short while a big, four-door Chrysler sedan pulled up to the door of the airport terminal and my newfound friend said, "Here's your ride, young man." After loading my suitcase and briefcase into the car, I shook hands with this kind gentleman again, thanking him for this wonderful gesture and bidding him a pleasant flight and "So long." He then added one more word of instruction.

"Do not pay this driver one cent for driving you to Batu. He is paid very well by the company and is the envy of most Indonesian people."

"Alright, if you insist," I responded and then got into the back seat of the big Chrysler sedan, waving goodbye as we drove away. The chauffeur drove me right up to the front door of the Broadlands' house; curb-service! I got out, unloaded my suitcase and briefcase, and saluted him as he turned around to drive back to Surabaja. I had been with the Broadlands only about an hour when there came a knock at the front door. Who was it? The delivery boy with my telegram! By this time, I was fully aware of a miracle of assistance that my Blessed Lord had bestowed upon me that day of February 9, 1959.

Bob and Marian Broadland, whom I had known in Seattle, were overseers and teachers of a Bible school (Secola Alcatab) that was situated just across the road from their house. The drive from Malang up to Batu, mostly upgrade, was fascinating. Of all the places I have been in the entire world, this was probably the most beautiful. I have come to refer to that area as "a magnificent tropical garden." The island of Java, at that time, was the most densely populated land area in the world. Most of its people were poor, hard-working, and somewhat reserved.

I was privileged to have the opportunity of ministering to the students in the Bible school in Batu during the daytime and then in an evangelism crusade in the city of Malang in the evenings.

Rev. Don Peterson and his wife, Carol, were also missionaries in Indonesia, stationed in Malang at the time I was there. Don served as my Indonesian interpreter for the crusade in Malang. Both families, the Broadlands and the Petersons, were sent out to Indonesia from the Bethel Temple Church in Seattle.

Because of civil unrest in the Republic of Indonesia at the time I was there, I had a difficult time securing a visa to enter the country. In fact, my visa was limited to fourteen days. I also had to register with the police in East Java so that my whereabouts could be known all the while I was in the country.

The Malang Crusade was a time of blessing and victory. Souls were saved. Sick bodies were healed, and many of the saints there were encouraged in the Lord. Because I was required to be out of the country of Indonesia on or before February 21, Missionary Bob Broadland drove me to Surabaja to catch a flight back to Djakarta. To our surprise, there were no spaces left on any commercial flights to Djakarta on that day (February 20). After Bob explained to the airport security people that I had only one more day before I had to be out of the country, they arranged for the two of us to fly aboard an Indonesian military plane. It was an old twin-engine plane with lawn chairs for seats. The cabin was not pressurized, thus the flight was somewhat low to the ground. Just below where I was sitting was a hole in the fuselage. I could see the ground below through that hole!

We made it to Djakarta, where Bob had arranged for me to minister in the "mother church" that evening. He served as my interpreter. It was a large church and had a full crowd for that service.

On our way to the airport on Saturday, February 21, I was able to witness the unbelievable—a "bechek" (rickshaw) traffic jam! Bob explained that there were more than 28,000 of these rigs in the city of Djakarta alone, all vying to make a living by meeting the travel needs of the people.

After bidding my friend Bob Broadland farewell I boarded a Malayan Airways flight to Singapore where I would minister just one night in an open-air meeting. After arriving in the city of

Singapore, I was pleasantly surprised to be met by a representative of Malayan Airways, who handed me a voucher for free taxi service to and from the Embassy Hotel, as well as a complimentary night's lodging and meals at the hotel.

Sister Ruth Helgeson, the missionary I had worked with in Formosa, had contacted a missionary from Finland who lived in Singapore about arranging for me to preach there, which he did. Brother Ed's English was quite broken, but we were able to communicate. He met me at the airport and, after learning that I had been given a complimentary stay at the hotel, including meals, agreed to pick me up there at about 6:00 P.M. for the special service that night. To my amazement, this dear brother and his helpers had prepared a large vacant lot for that one night service with a platform, lights, public address system, etc.

It was a blessed service with souls being saved and sick bodies healed. Although they had never met me before, the people bestowed a great deal of honor upon me. It was a "never-to-be-forgotten" night for me. After the special service, Brother Ed took me on a night tour of the city of Singapore in his Volkswagen Microbus. One of the city's attractions was the yacht of Prince Philip of England (Queen Elizabeth's husband). The prince was paying a state visit to the city of Singapore. I did not see him, but I did see his wife, his mother-in-law and his sister-in-law at Windsor Castle in England about a month later.

Calcutta! By Way of Bangkok

Because of the way my airline tickets had been written back in Seattle, I would continue on my round-the-world journey the next day. My next stop would be Bangkok, Thailand. I would again be flying on a Malayan Airways flight to Bangkok. It so happened that one of the passengers on the flight from Singapore to Bangkok was actress Ann Blythe, who would be going on a tiger hunt safari in Thailand. All eyes were upon her aboard that flight.

Once again, I was pleasantly surprised to be met by yet another Malayan Airways agent in Bangkok, who informed me that I would be given two nights' lodging at a hotel in Bangkok, compliments of the airlines, which also included taxi service to and from the hotel and meals for the two days. Since I had no contacts in Bangkok, it would be a time of sightseeing and rest for me before continuing on to my next destination.

Even though I did not minister in the country of Thailand, while mingling amongst the teaming thousands of Thai people I would see "that face" in the crowd, which haunted me because I knew that I was for the most part in a heathen land. Buddhism was then the major religion in Bangkok. Lavish Buddhist temples abounded in this capital city. Fortunes of gold, silver, precious stones, and the like had gone into these heathen temples while all around them the poor people struggled just to stay alive. It was heartrending to see such stupendous spiritual darkness enslaving multitudes of people with little or no hope of a better life.

On the following Tuesday, February 24, I boarded a Pan American Airways flight from Bangkok to Calcutta, with a stop in Rangoon, Burma. At Rangoon, I did not disembark. When new passengers boarded the airplane in Rangoon, an older, somewhat heavyset American gentleman, a Mr. McCulley from Milwaukee, Wisconsin, sat next to me. He soon struck up a conversation. Noticing that I was quite young to be traveling alone, he ventured to suggest that I must be in some branch of military service.

"Yes, I am," I responded.

"What branch?" he asked.

"The evangelistic branch," I replied. "I'm a preacher of the gospel and am on a worldwide evangelism tour."

To that, Mr. McCulley smiled and said, "I'm really glad to meet you, young man. I am a Christian, too. In fact, I am to speak in a meeting in Calcutta tonight," he added.

"So am I," I told him.

"How interesting," he chimed in as he warmed up to me even more. As we visited en route to Calcutta, I was amazed to learn

253

that Mr. McCulley was a wealthy businessman. He was the owner of a large bakery in Milwaukee. He reached into his inside coat pocket and pulled out a tract entitled "Tragedy or Triumph?" He had written the tract himself. It was the story, in brief, of his son, who was one of the five American missionaries who were martyred by savage Indians in Ecuador, South America. He explained to me how he had tried to talk his son out of going on this missionary journey to Ecuador.

"I offered to turn my entire bakery business over to him if he would stay in Milwaukee and not go on this venture to Ecuador," he told me, then went on to say how his son had responded.

"I'm sorry, Dad, but this is what I feel God wants me to do. I must obey His call." Now, as he looked back upon the ordeal of his son's death, he had come to the conclusion that what seemed like a terrible tragedy, God had turned into a great triumph. Thus he was now traveling throughout the world telling the story of his slain son in various settings—churches, service organizations, etc.

The long flight from Bangkok to Calcutta, by way of Rangoon, was late arriving at the Calcutta airport. Both Mr. McCulley and I had speaking engagements in the city that night and were concerned about our late arrival. Since I was to speak in an Assemblies of God church, Missionary Mark Buntain, the pastor, had sent one of his men to the Calcutta airport to pick me up.

To my surprise, this Indian brother came onboard the plane before any of the passengers had disembarked and asked, "Is there a Rev. Gail Ott on this flight?" I immediately raised my hand.

"Yes, sir; that's me," I said.

"OK, then, sir, you come with me," the man said. So, I was the first passenger on the flight to disembark. It so happened that this Indian brother was a security officer for one of the main airlines (BOAC), and he was using his position of authority to hasten my release from immigrations, etc., so as to get back to the church where I was to preach that night. He asked for my passport, which I handed to him, and thus he quickly took care of all the paperwork for my entry into the country.

Then, as all the other passengers were waiting for their luggage, this brother took me to where the luggage was being placed on carts.

"Do you see your luggage anywhere here?" he said.

"Yes, sir," I replied. "That's my suitcase right there." He fetched it off of the cart and said to me, "Come on, my car is out in front of the building."

As I walked by Mr. McCulley, who was waiting in a long line to go through customs, he asked me, "How do you rate this kind of service?"

I stopped momentarily, tapped him on his rather large stomach with the back of my hand, and said, "Hey, man, it's not *what* you know that counts—it's *Who* you know!" The truth of the matter was, I did not know this Indian brother—had never met him before. It simply was another of the Lord's special blessings bestowed upon me.

The drive from the Calcutta airport to the church was a distance of about twenty miles and the road was quite rough. All the way to the church I was praying a prayer of desperation.

"Oh, Lord, if ever I've needed You, I need You now!" I felt like my head was spinning after a somewhat turbulent and long flight from Bangkok that day.

"Please, Lord, touch me with a powerful anointing of the Holy Spirit for this service tonight," I prayed. "I can't make it without Your help. I'll simply fail if You don't quicken me with Your anointing."

When we arrived at the church (a converted theater building) the people were singing choruses, just awaiting the arrival of their guest speaker from America. It was an upstairs auditorium, quite large, with a near-capacity crowd present. The brother who had driven me from the airport spoke.

"Just follow me," he said as he led me to the platform and introduced me to Mark Buntain. After embracing me, Brother Buntain said, "You're on, my brother" as he introduced me to the audience. I was given a round of applause, after which I read from the Scriptures and then prayed a brief prayer. I was dressed in my white suit, which I had hired a tailor to make for me in Manila, Philippines. The people were looking me over, not knowing what to expect from a twenty-seven-year-old stranger from the United States. No sooner had I started preaching when I realized that the Lord had heard my earnest plea in that car enroute from the airport to the church.

A powerful anointing came upon me; so much so that I felt as if I were walking on air. People were weeping and praising God throughout the congregation as the gospel message issued forth from my lips. I knew that I was experiencing one of the greatest anointings of my preaching ministry that night.

After the altar call and a time of prayer for the sick, Missionary Mark Buntain took me back behind the heavy velvet curtains, dropped his head on my shoulder, and wept almost convulsively for a few moments, literally saturating my left shoulder with tears.

"Young man," he said to me, "you will never know what this service tonight has meant to me!" I was humbled by Brother Buntain's words and happy that he had been so blessed by the preaching of God's Word. Since we had only corresponded by mail and had never met before, Brother Buntain had arranged for me to stay in a hotel not far from the church. I would be ministering again on Wednesday night before departing by train to the interior city of Kharagpur for an evangelism crusade there.

On Wednesday morning, Brother Buntain came to the Hotel Clacton where I was staying to take me for a brief tour on the back of his motor scooter. Among other points of interest, he took me to a large, vacant area, where we stopped and got off of the motor scooter.

"By the Grace of God, here is where we are going to build a hospital some day," he told me. "Well," I said, "I trust that your vision will come to fruition in due time. With God, all things are possible!"

"That's right, young man," he responded.

After a good rest and time of study and prayer, I was ready and waiting for the second service at the Buntains' church that Wednesday evening, February 25. Brother Buntain came to the hotel to pick me up and then drove me to the church for the second of the two special services in which I was to be the guest speaker. The second night was not quite as dramatic and power-packed as the first night service was, but was a gracious time in the Lord just the same. The people were very receptive and thus easy to serve.

On Thursday morning, Brother Buntain came to the hotel to pick me up and then drove me across town to the train station where I would board the "Madras Mail" train for the trip to Kharagpur. Since he was going away on a trip to Bombay that same day, we would not see each other in India again, so we embraced and said farewell as I boarded the train for the long ride to Kharagpur.

Confirmation in Kharagpur

On the train ride to Kharagpur from Calcutta, I had made friends with three British businessmen who were also bound for Kharagpur. As the train rolled into the station in Kharagpur and came to a stop I, along with the three British businessmen, disembarked and started walking on the wooden dock toward the train station when suddenly an Indian gentleman came running up to me, throwing his arms around me as he exclaimed, "Oh, Brother Ott, I'm so glad to see you! Welcome to Kharagpur!"

Somewhat taken back, I asked him, "How did you know who I was?" I had not sent a photo of myself to him. His immediate reply was, "Oh, my brother, God showed you to me in a vision. I knew exactly what you would look like! The only thing different was I thought you would be taller than you are."

That was at approximately 3:00 A.M. on Friday morning. Yet another surprise was the fact that quite a number of "believers" were there at the train station with Dr. Bastia at that early morning hour to welcome me to Kharagpur. It was clearly evident that their anticipation was high concerning the campaign that would begin on the evening of that day.

From the train station, I was taken to Dr. Bastia's home, a two-story bungalow-type house, where I would be lodging for the duration of my stay in Kharagpur. I was given an upstairs room with a nice single bed to sleep on. There was also a small desk in the room.

Dr. Bastia and his family all had first-floor bedrooms, thus I was the only person residing upstairs during my stay in their home. Dr. Bastia was a medical doctor. He treated many sick people each day in their living room, which was his clinic. Watching from an upstairs balcony I concluded that the doctor treated every patient with the same injection. Most of his patients were suffering from dysentery with flu-like symptoms. On a few occasions, when a patient of his was afflicted with a more serious illness, he would call for me to come and lay hands on them, praying for a healing from the Great Physician.

The crusade location was only a short distance from Dr. Bastia's home. A structure called a "pondal" had been erected at the site. It was somewhat on the order of the brush arbor in the U.S., with the exception that the roof material consisted of canvas rather than brush. It was a large structure that would accommodate several hundred people. There were no chairs or benches for people to sit on. The audience either had to sit on the ground or stand during the services. Some did both. The crowds swelled to over six hundred before the conclusion of the crusade.

Since Kharagpur seemed to be a "melting pot" for language groups, my sermons had to be interpreted into three different languages: Hindustani, Bengali, and Telagu. Dr. Bastia's niece, who was a linguist, did all of the interpreting, one language at a time. I had plenty of time to think about my next sentence during the triple interpretation.

Due to the lengthy interpretations, my sermons had to be short and to the point. And, of course, the theme of all my preaching was *supernatural deliverance*: "Jesus Christ the same yesterday, today, and forever" (Hebrews 13:8).

The response to the altar call and invitation to accept Christ as Savior was very gratifying each night. Hundreds responded. We prayed for the sick each night of the crusade (eleven days: February 26 through March 8). Many notable healings were wrought among the sick and afflicted for whom we prayed. Faith was strong and, "the power of the Lord was present to heal" (Luke 5:17). Truly, God confirmed His Word preached, with "signs following."

Several persons possessed with demons were set free during this crusade, as well. As it was in the city of Samaria when Philip went there to preach Christ to them, "There was great joy in that city!" (Acts 8:8) So it was in Kharagpur . . .

During my stay in the home of Dr. Bastia, I was never invited to eat a meal with his family. This was intentional on their part as their customs were so much different from those of Americans. They would all sit down on the floor in a circle with the food in the middle. They did not use silverware at all, but rather picked their food up out of the different dishes with their hands. Therefore, a maid would bring a portion of food up to my room at mealtimes each day. Admittedly, I had a difficult time eating foods that I was not accustomed to; thus I did a lot of earnest praying for grace each day. I knew that their feelings would be hurt if I refused the food they offered me, so I "forced" it down even though it did not agree with my taste buds.

One day, however, a bowl of some kind of meat was brought to me at lunchtime. I almost gagged trying to force it down. Then, I stopped eating and dropped to my knees in earnest prayer. "Lord," I prayed, "please help me. You know I'll throw up if I keep trying to eat this food. But, You also know that they'll have their feelings hurt if it is still in the bowl when they come to pick up the dishes. So, Lord, I beseech You, please help me now. I need Your intervention."

Just then a strong impression came to me to get up and look out the window, so I did. What I saw just below the window, rather close to the backside of the house, was a cow nibbling at the very short grass. This cow was so thin that her back was like a razor. You could almost count her ribs. But, the most unusual thing about this cow was the fact that there were five buzzards sitting on her back! It was as if they were waiting for this poor old cow to die so they could have a feast.

"Thank You, Jesus," I said quietly so that the people downstairs wouldn't hear me, as I began taking the meat out of the bowl in pieces and tossing it out the window. As those five buzzards swooped down off of the cow's back and quickly grabbed up those pieces of meat, I knew that the Lord had sent them in answer to my prayer!

Later that day, as I was writing a letter to Bobbie, I told her of how the Lord had sent me five buzzards to help me clean up my bowl of food. When she read my letter she laughed and laughed, as she had never heard a story like that before! It's comical now, but I was aware of a Divine intervention on my behalf on that day in Kharagpur, India.

Precious People

The crusade in Kharagpur concluded with a final service on Sunday night, March 8. It was a wonderful service in which the people gave me a stirring ovation to express their gratitude for my coming to their city to proclaim the "unsearchable riches of Christ" to them.

Around midnight I boarded the train to return to Calcutta. My heart was stirred to see several dozen people show up at the train station to bid me farewell. Some even ran alongside the train, waving goodbye to me and shouting expressions of appreciation until the train's momentum picked up enough to be moving faster than they could run. I'll never forget those precious people of Kharagpur, India. They were poor as far as this world's goods are concerned, but were rich in faith. Their sweet, gentle spirits made a lasting impression on this young evangelist from the U.S.A.

The train arrived in Calcutta around noon on Monday, March 9 . . . Since my flight to Karachi, Pakistan, would not depart until later in the evening of that day, I decided to do some sightseeing around Calcutta. Since I had a suitcase and a briefcase, I decided to call on the Buntain family to ask if I could leave my luggage at their home until it was time to depart for the Calcutta airport. The timing was perfect. I stored the luggage and was off—unprepared for some shocking scenes on the streets of Calcutta that would break my heart. The most heartrending sights were of little children lying on the streets, dying of disease or starvation. One in particular lay in the middle of the street causing traffic to weave in order to avoid running over him. Not only were there dying children lying on the streets, most with flies all over them, but there were older people as well.

I went into a little gift shop and found an Indian merchant who could speak English. When I asked him about these dying people on the streets he said, "Oh, this is Calcutta. We see this every day. If you were here in the evening, you would see men in ox carts coming along the streets, picking up the dead bodies."

"What do they do with the bodies?" I asked.

"They take them out along the Hoophly River and burn them," he replied. "It is an every day occurrence." Many of them were afflicted with the dread disease of leprosy. Indeed, it was an unforgettable sight.

Late in the afternoon I returned to the Buntain home to pick up my luggage. Mrs. Buntain was very gracious, offering me food and allowing me to use their bathroom to clean up and change my clothes before the flight to Karachi. I took a taxi from the Buntain's home at 2C Camac Street to the Calcutta airport and boarded an Air India flight to Karachi, Pakistan.

Christ Moves in Karachi

The Air India plane set down at the Karachi airport just before dawn on the morning of March 10. By the time I retrieved my luggage, missionaries Ruth Lindgren and Lela Holmes were there to meet me. Enroute to the Palace Hotel in Karachi, where I would lodge for the next six days, I was intrigued to see camels pulling huge wagons loaded with various cargos on the main highway from the airport into the city. There were also donkey carts on the road, bearing their burdens to various destinations in the city.

The Karachi event was amazing from beginning to end. It started when I met Ruth Lindgren and Lela Holmes at a meeting in the Bethel Temple Church in Seattle shortly before setting out on this round-the-world journey. They were preparing to leave Seattle to pursue missionary endeavors in Karachi. At that meeting, they spoke to me.

"Why don't you come to Karachi for ministry while you are in that part of the world?"

"I'd be delighted to do that," I responded. From this simple conversation the Karachi Crusade was set in motion. Ruth and Lela, neither of whom had ever married, agreed to contact me during my tenure in the Philippines and did indeed write to me there. In their letter, they asked me to suggest possible dates on which I could minister there. I am ashamed to say it, but while contemplating a short crusade in Karachi, I reasoned, *What kind of arrangements could two old maids make? They'll probably have some small cubicle on a side street with just a handful of people.* So, I suggested in my reply that I could come to Karachi for meetings from March tenth through the fifteenth. From there, a series of miracles began to unfold that led to the greatest evangelism crusade of my entire ministry.

Ruth and Lela set out to secure as large an arena as possible for the crusade services (not a little cubicle on a side street such as I had imagined.) They first tried to secure a soccer stadium for the meetings, but were denied a permit. Martial law was in effect in Pakistan at that time, thus prohibiting large outdoor events. Next, the two women went to the owner of Catrac Hall, a large convention-center-style building in the heart of Karachi. The owner, a devout Muslim, told them that the hall was booked up for over a year in advance, but that he would check the schedule to see if there were any days it might be vacant. To their delight, those exact days (March 10 through 15) were the only days the hall would be available until May of 1960! Although they held their peace while negotiating with the owner of the building, on the inside they were overjoyed! A series of incredible miracles would soon unfold to allow for an awesome crusade in Karachi.

A second miracle immediately followed this first one. When the rental fee for the hall was discussed, this Muslim owner told the ladies, "I must be losing my mind, but I'm going to allow you use the hall for a reduced fee. I don't know why I'm doing this," he went on to say, "because this is only one-fifth of the regular rental fee."

This owner may not have realized why he was renting Catrac Hall out for six nights at one-fifth the regular rental fee, but these two believing Christian ladies knew very well the reason why: God was answering their fervent prayers! In a letter Ruth Lindgren wrote to me while I was in India, she describes what was happening:

"The people are very anxious for you to come and they have been very busy (and I mean busy), making arrangements. It is not easy to rent halls here—yet everything from the start until now has been one big miracle of God doing the impossible. It's really been absolutely astounding! The set-up has been well planned. We will tell you more about it when we see you.

The hall accommodates around five to six hundred people. Thousands will *try* to come. We have a real assurance in prayer that God will move and bless. We want His power manifested and are believing Him for a real outpouring!"

Our next great miracle involved the selection of an interpreter. There was a fine British businessman who was a devout Christian who could have served as the interpreter, but for some reason Ruth and Lela didn't feel that he was God's man for the assignment, therefore they went before the Lord in earnest, fervent prayer about the matter.

On Monday, March 9, the day before the crusade was to begin, an Indian Christian brother showed up at Ruth and Lela's home in Karachi. He told them he did not understand why he was there, but only knew that God had spoken to him to come. The amazing thing about this was the fact that he was over a thousand miles north of Karachi when the Lord spoke to him about this. To obey would not be easy!

This brother may not have understood why he had made a journey that took him six weeks to complete, but the ladies understood clearly. He was sent of God in answer to their prayers. You see, as far as they could ascertain, he was the only Holy Spirit-filled Christian in that country (at the time, the world's fifth largest in population) that could speak both English and Urdu, the language of Pakistan.

This brother's arrival in Karachi was perfectly timed; the Lord's doing, undoubtedly. And I must say that of all the interpreters I've worked with throughout the world, I would have to rate him as *number one*. I say that because it was clearly evident that the same anointing of the Holy Spirit that rested upon me as I ministered the Word of God and prayed for the sick each night rested upon this brother with equal intensity.

My interpreter and I, along with Ruth, Lela, and the British businessman, arrived at Catrac Hall about a half hour before the first service was to begin. Several hundred people had already gathered outside the hall, waiting for the doors to open.

The public address system was set up and microphones were in place, readied for the opening service of the crusade to begin. The atmosphere was electrified with anticipation. Once the doors were opened, the eager people waiting on the outside rushed into the hall to find a seat. In a matter of minutes the place was filled to capacity. Once the hall was filled, martial law required that the doors be closed, thus each night many people had to be turned away. The British businessman served as the doorkeeper each night of the crusade and seemed to relish his assignment.

Perhaps we could also refer to the *attendees* of the Karachi Crusade as another miracle. Why? Because although Pakistan was a predominantly Muslim country, ninety percent or more of those who attended the crusade services were of a sect called the "Parsees." Their religion was heathen. They were "fire worshippers." Moreover, these Parsees, although by far a minority group, were the socially elite people of Pakistan.

The second, most numerous people group to attend the crusade services were Jewish people. Only a few Muslims attended.

The response to the gospel message was, for me, overwhelming. The invitation to accept Christ as Savior netted over one hundred souls the first night. My interpreter got so blessed and excited that he had to fight back tears of joy as he witnessed the spiritual hunger in the seekers. And God met them with His Presence.

One of the first miracles of healing was a twelve-year-old Jewish girl who was totally blind. As she came forward for prayer, the anointing of the Holy Spirit was strong upon me, as well as my interpreter, and I had an inner assurance that the Lord was truly going to confirm His Word preached with signs, wonders, and miracles. I had already challenged the audience concerning the reality of Jesus Christ and the fact that He is alive today.

"If Jesus Christ is alive today like I have told you here tonight that He is, then His Name has supernatural power," I reasoned. "So, when I lay these hands upon the sick in Jesus' Name, healings are going to happen.

"But," I continued, "if He is still dead, if He did not truly rise from the dead, then nothing will happen when I lay these hands upon the sick and pray for their healing in Jesus' Name." Apparently that reasoning made sense to the people, thus many of them came forward and stood in the prayer line, trusting to be healed of various sicknesses, diseases, blindness, deafness, etc.

As this twelve-year-old Jewish girl stood before me with her guide person (presumably her mother) at her side, I placed my two hands on her forehead with my thumbs lightly touching her eyes. I spoke quite forcibly.

"You blind spirit, I rebuke you in the name of Jesus Christ, and I demand that you come out of these eyes! You cannot resist the command of God's servant, for I bind you in the name of Jesus Christ and cast you out! Depart in Jesus' Name!"

My interpreter kept right up with me even though I did not pause momentarily, as when preaching. This precious, young Jewish girl immediately let out with a loud shout of joy and took off running and shouting.

"I can see! I can see!" She ran all the way around the hall on the outer aisle next to the walls. She stopped momentarily a couple of times to look at portraits hanging on the walls. They were portraits of the present and past presidents of Pakistan.

No one could deny this awesome miracle wrought by the Lord Jesus Christ, who Himself said, "Go ye into all the world and preach the gospel to every creature . . . and *these signs shall follow them that believe*; in my Name shall they cast out devils; they shall lay hands on the sick *and they shall recover*" (Mark 16:17, 18).

This outstanding miracle of the restoration of sight to a blind Jewish girl set the tempo for the next five nights of the crusade. There were so many miracles of healing each night that *miracles* became the norm for the crusade services. Time and space do not allow for the mention of the scores and scores of healings that were wrought amongst the sick and afflicted in the Karachi Crusade. Indeed it surpassed all other crusades that I had ministered in—*before or since*. Unquestionably, this was God's time for a harvest of souls in Karachi, Pakistan.

On the closing night of the crusade, with a more than capacity crowd packed into Catrac Hall, following the preaching of the Word I felt led to pray for the sick *before* giving the invitation to accept Christ as Savior. Among those who had come forward for the prayer for healing was a fourteen-year-old Parsee (fire-worshipping) girl who was born stone deaf and was also dumb. Her mother, who had brought her there for healing, explained to me through the interpreter that not once in the girl's entire life had they ever noticed even the slightest indication that she could hear a sound.

"If a bomb exploded somewhere behind her," the mother explained, "she would feel the concussion, but not hear the sound."

She went on to say that, as a child, the only way they ever knew that she was crying would be when they saw tears in her eyes.

"She has never uttered a sound," the mother told us. The moment of truth had now come, both for this dear mother and her fourteen-year-old daughter. At my invitation, they came up several steps and onto the platform. I spoke to the audience.

"Every head bowed, please, and every eye closed." At that moment, I placed the ends of my index fingers into both of the girl's ears and demanded, "You deaf spirit, come out of these ears in the name of Jesus Christ!" The girl stepped back, threw up her hands and smiled a beautiful smile of joy as tears began to stream down her face. The crowd had, for that moment, remained very quiet and still, but now, astonished by what they were seeing and hearing, began to come forth with a volume of praise to the Most High God!

Once I got this girl to settle down, I snapped my fingers near both of her ears. She immediately responded that she could hear that sound. She was so overjoyed that I was having a difficult time getting her to stand still so I could perform a final test of her hearing. I had her face the audience while I took off my Bulova wristwatch and placed it up to her left ear, while at the same time placing the palm of my left hand over her right ear. From the thunderous applause of the audience, I knew she had heard that watch tick. I repeated the same procedure with her right ear. The result was the same. She could hear my watch ticking with both ears.

Next I sat down on a stool in front of her, placed my hands gently on her throat, and demanded, with authority, "You dumb spirit, loose these vocal cords and come out of this girl! I rebuke you in the name of Jesus Christ whom I serve. You cannot resist this command for I cast you out in Jesus' Name."

My interpreter sobbed his way through this prayer rebuking the dumb spirit, allowing the audience to know what I'd said. Then, looking the girl right in the eyes, I spoke.

"Hallelujah!" Then, to the utter amazement of everyone in Catrac Hall, she repeated quite clearly what I had said!

It did not dawn upon me until later that perhaps, in the natural anyhow, this was a foolish thing for me to do. Why? Simply because there stood before me a fourteen-year-old girl who, by her mother's own word, had never uttered the slightest sound in her entire life. So it would stand to reason that one who had never heard or uttered a sound would need to learn how to utter sounds that would be audible! But this was *God's night* at Catrac Hall and it was His Blessed Holy Spirit at work, not this preacher.

Once again an ocean of praise from the hearts and lips of a crowd for the most part, heathen people went up to the God of Heaven. How amazing! How blessed that moment was indeed!

It was immediately after the miraculous deliverance of this child from deafness and a dumb tongue that the Holy Spirit prompted me to give the invitation to accept Christ. God being my witness, the response was so overwhelming that it was impossible to have the responders come to the front of the auditorium and gather around the platform, as had been the procedure the five previous nights of the crusade. Thus I instructed all who desired to make Christ their Lord and accept Him as their Savior to stand to their feet. At least four hundred people, mostly Parsees, stood to their feet and repeated the Sinner's Prayer after me. Oh, how precious was the Presence of the Holy Spirit at that moment! Tears of joy welled up in my eyes as I realized that there were angelic beings in the Glory World rejoicing at that moment over those who had denounced their heathen gods and turned to the Lord Jesus Christ in repentance and faith.

All the while I was praying for the sick on that final night of the crusade, and especially while ministering to the deaf and dumb girl, I kept hearing a commotion going on outside the doorway of the main entrance. I was aware that there were perhaps hundreds of seekers outside who were unable to get into the hall that night, but there was one woman in particular who was not going to be denied.

The British businessman who had become the crusade's official doorkeeper at Catrac Hall told this woman repeatedly that he could not let her in, but she refused to take no as an answer. The woman had brought her six-year-old son, hoping to have him prayed for. He was a hopeless invalid, stricken with polio from birth. She, too, was of the sect of the Parsees and had heard about all the healings that people were receiving at the crusade; hence she had brought her son in hopes of his deliverance from polio.

Since this woman simply refused to take no for an answer, nor would she go away, the doorkeeper began to sense that maybe the Lord wanted her to come into the hall so that her son could be prayed for. Thus, after securely locking the door, he cautiously approached the platform and beckoned for me to hear what he had to say. Moving over to the edge of the platform and kneeling down on one knee, I heard him speak.

"Reverend, there is a woman outside here who refuses to go away. She keeps knocking on the door. I've told her again and again that we cannot let anyone else into the hall, but she refuses to go away. Her son is crippled and she wants you to pray for him."

At that instant, the Spirit bade me tell the doorkeeper to let her come in. Once the door was open and she was inside the hall she quickly worked her way through the press of people who were crowded down in front of the platform and stood there before me, holding out the shriveled and twisted body of her six-year-old son. The first thought that raced through my mind at that moment was a fearful one: *This is a trick of the devil to make a mockery of my ministry and to try to refute the other miracles that the Lord has wrought upon so many people in this six-night crusade.* This hopelessly crippled boy's body was so twisted and deformed that I actually wanted to pray for an angel of mercy to come and take him to the glory world. But I knew that that was not *God's will.*

My faith was now being challenged like it never had been since the night God spoke to me about going to raise the five-year-old from the dead back in Kansas. I cried out in the spirit realm to God for help. And at that moment words came into my mind and spirit with crystal clarity. I began speaking to this woman through my Urdu interpreter.

"I'm going to lay my hands on your son and pray for him to be healed. Jesus Christ, whom I serve, has promised that these signs shall follow them that believe: 'They shall lay their hands on the

269

sick and they shall recover' (Mark 16:15–18)." I went on to tell her, "I am a believer. My interpreter is a believer. There are many believers here tonight. So, when we pray for your son to be healed, you too need to believe."

At that point, almost as if the thought had come to me by revelation, I continued by saying, "Jesus did not say that in every case the sick would be *instantly* and totally healed. Sometimes the healing is a process. Of course, when the healing is instant and complete, that is a *miracle* of healing." I continued by telling her that there were also "delayed miracles."

"Perhaps that is what God will grant to your son, so after we pray for him I want you to expect him to be healed. If it doesn't happen instantly, keep believing and trusting God that he *will* be healed and will be made completely whole!" All the while I was instructing her thus, she kept nodding in agreement. Then the moment of truth came. We laid hands upon the invalid boy, rebuking the spirit of infirmity in the Name of Jesus, demanding it to depart from his body. We prayed for the healing virtue of the Lord Jesus Christ to enter his body so that he might be restored to perfect soundness.

After the prayer, the little fellow looked more deformed and miserable than before, but I repeated my words to his mother.

"Now, I want you to *expect* your son to be healed. If it is not tomorrow, then perhaps it will be the next day. But however long it takes, keep believing and fully expecting that your son will be healed and will become completely normal." We prayed with this mother to accept Jesus as her Savior, which she gladly did.

After this episode with the persistent mother and her crippled son, the service was dismissed and the crusade was concluded. Another group would occupy Catrac Hall the next night, March 16, but for those six days of March 10 through 15, 1959, it was the Lord's house. Concerning this mother and the crippled son, it was in mid-July that a letter reached me from the British businessman who had served as doorkeeper during the Karachi Crusade. It concerned the crippled boy. The mother had located the British brother with a thrilling report, which he relayed to me now in detail in his letter. She told him that she remembered the words that I had spoken to her to, "expect your son to be completely and totally healed—and don't give up!"

According to the letter, this mother went into the little boy's room one morning about six weeks after the night we prayed for him. He was sitting up. His arms and legs were no longer shriveled and drawn up. He was completely normal. "A delayed miracle!" was the thought that immediately came to my mind *as tears of joy filled my eyes* when I read the British brother's letter that day.

Back at the Palace Hotel, where I had been lodging the week of the crusade, I was trying to get my suitcase packed and everything in order for an early morning departure. The Karachi Crusade had been a most satisfying and rewarding experience for me, so while packing up for my departure on Monday morning, I was rejoicing and praising God for that awesome final service.

It had been only half an hour or so since I'd returned to my room when a knock came at my door. I opened the door to find several Pakistani young men standing there; they had somehow discovered where I was staying. They had come, they said, to ask me to pray for them—some for sicknesses, others for situations in their lives, and two fellows for salvation. It was quite a touching experience for me and I felt humbled by the fact that in their great desire to receive a touch from the Lord God they had searched me out.

Although the Karachi Crusade was a wonderful experience for a twenty-seven-year-old American preacher, I had been away from my darling wife and daughter for a little over five months. I was anxious to return home to America and to my little family in Seattle. Bidding a fond farewell to Ruth Lindgren and Lela Holmes, as well as my interpreter, the British doorkeeper, and other friends I had made during the crusade in Karachi, I boarded the Middle East Airlines transport for my next destination: Jerusalem!

· ·

Chapter 13

JEHOVAH JIREH: AT HOME AND ABROAD

The flight from Karachi to Jerusalem would be making a couple of stops, the first in Kuwait City, Kuwait. This was primarily a refueling stop before continuing on to Beirut, Lebanon. In Beirut I would change planes for the flight on to Jerusalem, Jordan. The layover in Beirut would be more than four hours long so I hailed a taxicab and took a whirlwind tour of the city to pass the time.

Upon arrival in Jerusalem I was immediately singled out for interrogation. The fact that I was a young American male traveling alone gave rise to suspicion that I might be a spy for the government of Israel. The interrogation was lengthy and very confusing. The agents threatened to seize my movie camera, suspecting I might use it for espionage purposes. It took some strong persuasion on my part to talk them out of taking the camera, but I finally succeeded.

"If you believe that I'm a spy," I reasoned with them, "then why don't you just take my film? Why would you need to take my camera, also?" (Of course, I was praying under my breath that they would not take my film even though I had suggested that as a compromise.) This reasoning seemed to satisfy the agents. I was finally released and headed to the Ambassador Hotel in Jerusalem.

To be in the Holy Land, to walk where Jesus walked, to see the place where He was crucified, the tomb where His body lay for three days and then rose on the third day, as well as other places of interest, was almost overwhelming to my soul. I had to pinch myself at times just for a *reality check* that this privilege had been granted to me. Indeed, it was "the icing on the cake" of a wonderful five-month, around-the-world evangelism tour.

On my first full day in Jerusalem I hired a guide to show me around the city. When I told him I wanted to see Christ's empty tomb, he took me to a traditional site, which I knew very well was not what I wanted to see.

"Oh," he said, "there is a place outside the wall of the city called 'the Garden Tomb'—that must be the one you want to see."

"That's right," I told him, so he took me there. I decided I did not need the guide's services any longer, so I paid him for his time and let him go. The keeper of the Garden Tomb was a very gracious Arab man who was a born-again Christian. He had, at one time, been a banker in the city of Tiberius along the Sea of Galilee.

"We got out of Tiberius with little more than the clothes on our backs," he told me (during the war of independence between the Jews and the Arabs in 1948).

A friendship developed between Brother Matter, his wife, and myself that afternoon, which resulted in my having the privilege of preaching in the City of Ramalah that night. This dear brother made the arrangements by phone, picked me up at my hotel in his 1947 Chevrolet sedan (a gift to him from Evangelist Oral Roberts), drove me to Ramalah, and then served as my Arabic interpreter! There were several with whom we prayed for salvation that night.

The following day, Rev. G.M. Kuttab, a Church of God sponsored Arab missionary to his own country, came to meet me and also to take me on a brief excursion down to Jericho and the Dead Sea. My missionary friend in the Philippines, Rev. James Reesor, had contacted Brother Kuttab about my coming to the Holy Land, thus the connection.

That evening, March 18, 1959, Brother Kuttab took me to Bethlehem for a service in a small church. It was actually a home converted into a sanctuary. He served as my interpreter for that service. It was a very rewarding experience for me to have preached His Gospel in the city of our Savior's birth.

"No Man's Land"

On Thursday, March 19, I went to the United States Embassy in Jerusalem, Jordan, to secure a certificate from the Consulate that would allow me entrance into the country of Israel. Brother Kuttab then drove me to a location where tourists desiring to cross over the boundary from Jordan to Israel were required to walk across a buffer zone called "no man's land."

I bade farewell to Brother Kuttab, picked up my suitcase and briefcase, and strolled across this strip of vacant land, making certain not to turn around and look back as I had been warned I would be shot if I dared look back. They told me at that crossover point that I would never be welcomed back into any Arab country if I actually crossed that buffer zone into the Jewish State of Israel. *That was a somewhat scary experience*, but I made it across!

A mutual friend had put me in contact with an American-born Jew, Rev. Herman Pencovic, who had come to live in the country of Israel for the purpose of establishing a Christian ministry there. Missionaries, as such, were not allowed to come to Israel from other nations.

Once across "no man's land," Rev. Pencovic, a very gracious brother in the Lord, met me at a pick-up point and took me to his home, where I would stay until departing for Europe on Monday, March 23. Brother Pencovic gave me a grand tour of the Israeli sector of Jerusalem. In the afternoon, he assigned one of his assistants, a survivor of the Holocaust, to take me on a walking tour of the "Old City." We went to the Wailing Wall, to the Tomb of King David, to the Upper Room, to a museum of the Holocaust, as well as hitting several other points of interest. An older Jewish lady who had taken me on the walking tour would also serve as my Hebrew and German interpreter for both services that Sunday, March 22, before my impending departure.

Reverend Pencovic, with his wife and family, was serving as pastor of a relatively new Messianic Jewish congregation in Jerusalem. Their home was a large brick building, and their living room was the sanctuary. The reason my message was interpreted in German as well as Hebrew was that several of the constituents were Jews who had recently immigrated to Israel from Germany and were, at that point, Hebrew language-learners. My ministry to this Messianic Jewish congregation was primarily to encourage them to stay right in there and "fight the good fight of faith!" It was again a gratifying experience for me to have the honor of preaching the "unsearchable riches of Christ" in the city where our Blessed Redeemer had walked, was tried, and then crucified for our (my) sins.

Early on Monday morning, March 23, Brother Pencovic drove me to a bus station where I would travel the fifty or so miles from Jerusalem to Tel Aviv by bus. From there I would fly on to Athens, Greece, then on to Rome, Italy. The travel from Jerusalem to Tel Aviv would be the only leg of this journey, completely around the world, by surface. With the exception of surface transportation from one airport to another in Paris, London, and New York City, the entire journey was made by airplane! Of course, I did travel by car and by train in some of the countries I visited on this tour.

Athens, Milan, Vienna, Zurich, Paris, and London

There were several hours of layover time in Athens, thus I took a bus into the city so that I could go on a walking tour of the famous sites there. From Athens, I flew to Rome, Italy, where I would stay overnight at the YMCA for the modest price of two U.S. dollars. From Rome, I flew to Milan, Italy, then on to Vienna, Austria. In Vienna, I again had a four-and-a-half hour layover; thus I took a bus into the city for a mini-sightseeing and souvenir shopping tour. From Vienna, the next stop was Zurich, Switzerland, where I again lodged at a YMCA for a reasonable cost of two dollars. Because I arrived in Zurich after dark on that Tuesday night,

March 24, and then left for the airport again before daylight the next morning, I did not see much of that city.

From Zurich I flew to Frankfurt, Germany, where I had a change of planes for the flight to Paris. The drive by bus from airport to airport in Paris allowed me to see many sights, the most prominent of which was the Eiffel Tower. From Paris, I flew to Brussels, Belgium—again for a change of planes. The flight from Brussels to London was originally scheduled to be by helicopter, but due to adverse weather conditions that flight was cancelled, thus the flight was by airplane. The flight from Brussels arrived at the airport in London at dusk, hence all passengers staying overnight in London were transported by bus to a terminal in downtown London. By the time we arrived, it was dark. Retrieving my suitcase, I went to Pan American Airways ticket and information counter to inquire about the departure time for New York City the next day (Thursday, March 26th).

I was excited about this transatlantic flight for two reasons: first, because I was anxious to get home to my wife and daughter; and, secondly, because the flight to New York would be by Boeing 707 jet. This would my first-ever flight on a jet-propelled airliner! I eagerly anticipated the flight. The agent told me that I would need to check in at BOAC's London office the next morning to learn the departure time.

At this point of my journey, I was almost broke. I had exactly $2.10 to my name. Unexpected transfer fees, airport taxes, bus and taxi services across Europe had depleted my already dwindling funds so that I was near "the bottom of the barrel" at that point. But for some reason I refused to panic. Rather, I prayed a brief prayer of faith, asking the Lord for another miracle of provision. Having prayed thus, I had no fear. A sweet peace of assurance came over my whole being, thus I was simply waiting and watching to see how the Lord would meet my needs.

True, I tried to help the Lord perform the miracle I needed, but it didn't work. I told the Pan American agent that in Singapore and

Bangkok, the carrier I had traveled on had provided me with complimentary accommodations, plus transfers to and from the hotels.

"You're in Europe now, mister," he informed me. "We don't do those things here."

"Well," I replied, "I didn't think it would hurt to ask." Just then, an accommodating British gentleman who had overheard my conversation with the Pan American agent asked me if he could be of any assistance.

"Yes, perhaps you can," I replied. "Could you tell me where the YMCA is and what bus I could take to get there?"

"Of course, I can," he replied. "But the YMCA is completely across London from here. You wouldn't want to take a bus there; it would cost you a small fortune. What you will need to do is to take the 'underground"—it is very cheap; you can ride all over London for ten cents!" He then continued.

"Here, follow me to the end of the block and I'll show you where to get on the underground [subway]." He told me which tram to take and then said, "Be sure to count the stops and get off at *stop number twelve*. The YMCA will be right there when you come back up onto the street. If you don't get off there, you'll end up far, far away from the 'Y.' OK?"

I thanked him for his kindness, went down the stairs to the underground terminal, and waited for the tram he had told me to take. Fortunately it was the very first one to stop at that terminal. I paid my ten cents, got on board, and then very alertly counted every stop. At stop #12, I got off the tram and climbed the steps up to the sidewalk.

Sure enough, there a few blocks from where I stood I could see the big neon sign: "YMCA." As I proceeded to walk toward the YMCA, to my left I noticed another neon sign: it read "BOAC." I reasoned that if I would go there first and then to the YMCA, I could perhaps check my suitcase for the flight to New York and thus spare myself from carrying it to the "Y" and back the next morning. Little did I realize that I was about to find out just how the Lord was going to do wondrous things for me! When I walked into the BOAC building, an agent at the counter asked me, "May I help you, sir?"

"Well, I hope so," I replied, and then asked if I could possibly check my suitcase in for the flight to New York the next day, Friday.

"May I see your ticket, please?" he asked before answering my question. I then handed him my ticket and he began to peruse it.

"Where will you be staying tonight?" he asked.

"Well," I replied, "I'm not sure, but I think it will be at the YMCA."

"What?" he exclaimed. "Do you mean to tell me that you are flying to New York on Pan American and they are not putting you up in a hotel here in London tonight?" he asked in apparent disgust.

"No, sir," I replied. "I already asked a Pan American agent at the downtown terminal and he told me, 'We don't do that in Europe.'"

At that the gentleman said to me, "Sir, please have a seat right over there while I make a phone call." After about ten minutes he returned to the counter and summoned me.

"Here are some vouchers," he said, handing them to me. "One is for a taxi to take you to the Mount Royal Hotel for your lodging tonight. Another is for the room, another for your dinner tonight, another for breakfast in the morning, and the last one is for a taxi to bring you back here tomorrow morning for transfer by bus to the airport for your flight to New York."

"Wow!" I exclaimed, "How do I rate all of this?"

"Well," he replied, "I called Pan American and gave them a piece of my mind. I told them if this gentleman were flying on a BOAC flight tomorrow he would have a complimentary hotel room, meals, and transportation to and from the hotel, as well! So, the Pan American agent told me, 'Go ahead and issue him the necessary vouchers; Pan Am will pick up the tab for it all.' I've already called for a taxi to take you to your hotel and I believe that it is out in front right now," he told me.

I thanked him for his kindness in making all of these arrangements for me and then loaded my suitcase and briefcase into the taxi and away we went on a twenty-minute drive to the hotel. As the taxi pulled up to the entrance door to the Mount Royal Hotel did it ever look good to a poor, tired young preacher! I had been told that no tipping was necessary for the taxi or hotel staff as this was all complimentary.

After checking into my room I went down to the dining room for a delicious steak dinner. What a blessing! I had a very comfortable, full-sized bed in a spacious room rather than a small cot in a dinky cubicle at the YMCA with only public restroom facilities. I knew that all of this was totally undeserved on my part—it was, indeed, another blessing from my Wonderful Lord!

After enjoying a good night's rest and a delicious breakfast in the dining room on Thursday morning, March 26th, I checked out at the front desk, asking the clerk to call for the taxi to take me back to the BOAC terminal for transfer to the airport. The blessing continued. The taxi driver asked if I had seen much of London while there. I told him that it was already dark when I arrived in London last night, thus I had seen very little of it.

"In that case, let me show you around London a bit on our way back to BOAC," he said. "OK?"

"That would be terrific," I said. "I would enjoy it immensely!" He drove me in front of Buckingham Palace, by the Parliament Building, the London Tower, the London Bridge, Piccadilly Square, Westminster Abbey, and several other points of interest. When we arrived at the BOAC terminal building I thanked this gracious cab driver for his kindness in giving me such a nice tour of London.

"Don't mention it, chap," he replied; "My pleasure!" After unloading my luggage, the cab driver drove away. In a short while a transfer bus arrived at the BOAC terminal to transport Pan American passengers to the airport for the flight to New York. Upon arrival at the London airport, we all proceeded to the Pan Am check-in counter.

The agent there asked all the passengers to come up as close as they could get for a special announcement concerning the flight to New York. "I regret to tell you this, but there is going to be a five-and-a-half hour delay in the flight," he informed us.

"Oh, no," I blurted out.

To that the agent addressed me by saying, "Listen here, friend. It is costing this airline over $500.00 an hour for that plane to be late. Believe me, when the mechanical problem has been corrected it will be in the air, I promise you." Having been gone from home nearly five and a half months already, I was naturally disappointed to hear the man announce a five-and-a-half-hour delay. But at the same time I wanted the plane to be safe! I asked the agent to please forgive me for my lack of patience.

The Pan Am passengers for this flight to New York were taken to a large waiting room where we could sit on comfortable chairs while waiting for our aircraft to arrive from New York. No one seemed overjoyed about having to wait that long, but since there was no choice, we were all resigned to try to make the best of it.

In a little while, however, the boredom would be banished as the agent came again into the room.

"How would you folks like to go on a tour of Windsor Castle while we're waiting for our aircraft to arrive from New York?" The response was unanimous, so soon a large bus arrived to take us there.

It so happened that on that very day, the Thursday before Easter, Queen Elizabeth, her sister, and the Queen Mother were at the castle. We were told that on a Thursday before Easter, many years previously, Queen Elizabeth the First had washed the feet of a randomly chosen peasant at the castle, thus it was now being repeated by Queen Elizabeth II on this particular day. The timing was perfect for no sooner had we joined the crowd outside the King George VI Cathedral (a part of the castle), when the doors opened and out came the Royal Family. I was within twenty feet of the Queen, her mother, and her sister when they emerged from the Cathedral. It was really a very interesting and exciting experience.

Three shiny Rolls Royce sedans were waiting just to the left of the sidewalk leading out of the church. Each of the royal ladies got into a separate vehicle to be whisked away from the adoring crowd.

The visit to the castle wasn't the end of the tour. Across the street from the castle was a big hotel. All of the Pan Am passengers who had come to Windsor for the castle tour were treated to a delicious steak dinner in the hotel dining room before returning to the London airport. All of this certainly helped us pass the five-and-a-half-hour delay without boredom! After the meal at the hotel in Windsor, we were escorted back to the airport terminal building just in time for the flight to New York.

In a short while an announcement was made.

"We are now ready to begin boarding Pan America Flight 101 bound for New York City." That was music to my ears! I was eager to get onboard. As I've always done when flying on airplanes, I bowed in silent prayer, asking the Lord to give us a safe and enjoyable flight.

Once all passengers were onboard, the 707 jetliner taxied to the end of the runway and then paused for clearance for take-off from the tower. Once clearance was given, the pilot gave it full throttle and soon that magnificent machine was airborne and I was homeward bound!

The flight to New York was of about eight hours duration, which included a brief refueling stop in Gander, Newfoundland. By the time the flight arrived in New York and the airplane was parked at the terminal gate, it was dark outside. This meant that I had missed my flight on to Seattle. But, it wasn't all bad. Pan American Airlines gave those passengers who had missed their continuing flights complimentary lodging for the night in a very nice motel near the Idlewild Airport (later renamed John F. Kennedy International Airport). Included with the accommodations were meals and transfers.

On Friday morning, March 27th, my ticket was rewritten and I was given first-class passage from New York to Seattle by way of Chicago. Thus, upon arriving home in Seattle I still had the two dollars that I'd had when I arrived in London from Brussels! How amazing! It had to be the Lord's doing.

My arrival at Seattle International Airport on that Friday evening of March 27 was indeed a happy time for me, as it also was for my darling wife, Bobbie. Sally, now three, was quite reluctant to warm up to me at first, but after a while everything was OK and I could hold her and hug her. Five and a half months was a long time to be away from home, and it was an especially a long time for a young husband and father to be away from his family. The same was true for Bobbie and Sally. It was a great sacrifice for them as well.

Although I knew that I was doing the will of God by going on this World Missions venture, it seemed like I had been gone for five and a half *years* rather than five and a half months. Bobbie's parents, her sisters, and their families, my dear friend Art Morlin (now Bobbie's brother-in-law), my two brothers Lester and Dwane, as well as several other close friends were at the airport to greet me and welcome me home. All of this made me feel that I had truly been blessed of the Lord. I was humbly thankful that He saw fit to use me as He had on this venture.

Now that I was back home with my family, as I looked back on the overall ordeal of the missionary journey, I could not help but be amazed and extremely thankful to God for the many ways in which He had blessed me and provided for my every need. I will pause at this juncture to recount some of those blessings.

The first great blessing was that God gave me a wonderful wife and helpmate who was willing to sacrifice nearly half of a year of our young married life in order for me to go forth to preach Christ in ten nations around the world. When the rewards are meted out at the Bema Seat of Christ one glorious day, I sincerely believe that Bobbie's reward will be every bit as great and perhaps even greater than mine because she was willing to stay behind so that I could go forth. It would not have been feasible or possible for her to have been at my side on that journey, but she was with me in prayer.

The next blessing was that He kept His hand upon my precious little daughter, Sally, whom I loved with all of my heart and missed so very much while I was away. By this time in her life, I had been away from her and Bobbie for the equivalent of a full year (counting the Brazil, British Honduras, and this World Missions venture). I've always felt that I owed her an honor because of this, even though she was too young to realize what it was all about.

The next blessing I am grateful to my Wonderful Lord for is the way He opened up many doors of ministry to me on this journey—especially since not *all* of those doors had opened before I left the U.S. to begin this venture, especially the Indian and Pakistani Crusades. Also, I'm grateful for the multiple miracles that went into bringing each crusade into being. I truly found that, "He is able to do exceeding abundantly above all that I could ask or think" (Ephesians 3:2).

Yet another awesome blessing was the way in which God supplied all of my needs. When I embarked upon this venture, I had no firm commitments of financial support, yet every time a need arose the funds would come in. The arrangement for my financial assistance was that whenever a love offering came in, which was mostly by mail, Bobbie would deposit it in my "Missions Account" at the bank and then inform me by letter of the same. I in turn would be able to write a check for the amount that had come in, after which my missionary friends would get it cashed and converted into the currency of whatever country I would be in. This was nothing short of *supernatural supply*, as far as I am concerned, because every need was met. From the support offerings that had come in, I was able to pay most all of the expenses involved in the crusades that I conducted.

But, the greatest of all the miracles, great or small, was the "harvest of souls" which the Lord permitted me to have a significant part in! I attribute much of that harvest to the fact that the Lord "confirmed His Word with signs and wonders" (most notably the many miracles of healing wrought among the sick and afflicted—especially the opening of the deaf mute child's ears and the loosening of her tongue on the final night of the Karachi Crusade). The four hundred or so souls that prayed the "Sinner's Prayer" for salvation following that supernatural deliverance was the single-greatest altar call response I've ever been able to witness or experience in a ministry spanning over five decades.

When I think of His blessings during that five-and-a-half-month missions venture, I feel like the Psalmist David must have felt when he wrote of God's mercies towards him with the pen of inspiration: "If I should count them, they are more in number than the sand" (Psalm 139:1). Health, strength, many new friends, honor, favor. The list goes on and on. What a wonderful, gracious, and loving Redeemer we serve!

Evangelism: At Home and Abroad

Since the title of this book is *I Have Been Young*, it has been this author's intent to especially chronicle events and miracles that were experienced in my younger days. I will skip much of the personal, day to day matters so as to focus on events related to the ministry God has called me to.

Returning home to Kansas, I continued to preach in churches and answer invitations to minister in special meetings at the request of many pastors. After conducting a revival crusade at the Full Gospel Chapel Church in Rockdale, Texas, from July 1 through 12, 1959, my dear friend and colleague Art Morlin and his wife Joan (Bobbie's sister), along with their two-year-old daughter Kim, came to the Midwest to partner with me one more time in a gospel tent revival crusade. Rev. Earl Pruitt, then pastor of the Full Gospel Church in Seneca, Missouri, had invited Art and me to set up a tent on the high school campus in Seneca and hold an evangelistic crusade. Pastor Pruitt obtained the proper permits to do this.

A farmer in Spearman, (West) Texas, had purchased a 40'x 60' tent for the sole purpose of lending it to ministers for evangelism crusades, thus we contacted him about using his tent. Brother Bernard Barnes was very gracious, affording us the privilege of using that tent free of charge. All we had to do was drive to Spearman to pick it up. And then, of course, return it to him once our purpose was fulfilled.

The Seneca Crusade was duly advertised and services were well attended each night. It was like old times for Art and me, although we each had a wife and young daughter this time. Souls were saved and the sick were ministered to during the ten-day crusade. When the crusade was concluded, we dismantled the tent and hauled it back to Spearman to return it to the farmer who owned it.

While Art and his family were still in the Midwest, he and I decided to accept an invitation to evangelize in Mexico. It had been a little over two years since my crusade in Progresso, thus I was eager to return to that area. Too, this would be a final, united evangelistic thrust together with my friend, colleague, and now relative, Art.

We began our month of ministry in Mexico by ministering in a week of services in the city of Cuernavaca, located south of Mexico City. I had had considerable experience speaking through interpreters, but this would be a new experience for Art. Because we were knit together in purpose and plan, this worked out beautifully. We saw many souls come to Christ in Cuernavaca and many sick people healed by the power of the Lord.

Our next crusade together would be in the city of Pachuca, northeast of Mexico City. This crusade of a week's duration was in a large church in Pachuca. During the week of the crusade there, we were guests in the home of a wealthy Mexican businessman. Once again, as we alternated nights of preaching in this crusade, we were blessed to see a "harvest of souls" as our emphasis was always on *salvation first* and healing second. A young Mexican minister served as our interpreter for the Pachuca Crusade.

One very touching event that occurred during the Pachuca Crusade was a wedding. One evening as Art and I arrived at the church early, a wedding ceremony was underway. After the service, later that night at the home where we were lodging, the pastor would tell us the particulars concerning this unexpected wedding.

A man and woman who had lived together for thirty-four years had come in the altar call the evening before to accept the Lord Jesus Christ as Savior. No one had said a word to them about never having been legally and officially married. However, after giving their hearts to the Lord the evening before, they went to the pastor and requested to be officially married. Hence a simple marriage ceremony was arranged for the following evening to accommodate their request and desire.

This couple's thirty-three-year-old son was there for his parents' wedding ceremony that night. And if memory serves me right, he, too, came to the altar and invited Jesus into his heart.

Following this Sunday through Sunday Pachuca crusade, we went to Progresso for a two-night "mini-crusade" in the same church I had ministered in two years earlier. For me, it was a rewarding and gratifying experience to return there and find many of the converts from the '57 Crusade still going on with the Lord. The same dedicated pastor was still there, shepherding the flock; a devoted Christian brother.

Following the mini-crusade at Progresso we divided up and went separately, with interpreters, to a number of cities in the region around Mexico City, preaching Christ as Savior, Healer, and Soon-Coming King of Kings and Lord of Lords. And the Lord added souls to the body of Christ (His Church) as we went forth preaching in various towns and villages there. Many sick and afflicted people received definite healings from the Lord, who confirmed His Word with signs and wonders.

Although Art Morlin and I have remained very close friends across the years since this time, that would be our last combined effort in evangelism. Since then, however, we have both pastored churches and have each, at times, been guest speakers at the other's church.

Bobbie, Sally, Joan, and Kim had stayed in Kansas, near my parents, while Art and I were ministering in Mexico. When we got back to Kansas, Art and Joan, along with their two-year-old daughter, Kim, returned to the State of Washington, where they have lived ever since. Shortly after returning to Washington Art began a long ministry of pastoring churches.

Bobbie, Sally, and I remained in the Midwest until mid-December 1959, ministering in churches in Kansas, Oklahoma, Missouri, Texas, and Colorado. We also returned to the Seattle area in December, where we would remain for a few years.

As much as we loved our darling Sally, we also desired to have another child, and the Lord would give us our desire. On September 16, 1960, our son, Andrew Lewis, was born. With both of our children, the Lord caused me to know, through a dream, what their gender would be before their birth. If there is a significance concerning this, I have not yet figured it out!

When Andrew ("Andy") was four months old, I accepted an invitation to work with world-renowned Missionary Evangelist T.L. Osborn, whose international headquarters were in Tulsa, Oklahoma. So, it was "on the road again" for Bobbie and me, along with our two children. During this tenure with T.L. Osborn, we traveled quite extensively, especially after being assigned to special duties by T.L and his wife, Daisy, which primarily consisted of preceding them in special three-day meetings throughout the country, making arrangements for their arrival, and doing "goodwill" ministry, promoting the special meetings that would occur in select cities. We began these special assignments in Harrisburg, Pennsylvania, then went on to a number of other cities, doing the same things.

Our last assignment would be in Seattle, after which we opted to discontinue that particular phase of ministry. Brother Osborn did appoint me to be a Regional Director of Co-Evangelism for the Northwestern Region (Washington, Oregon, Idaho, Montana, Wyoming, and Alaska). While this was a great honor, it soon became apparent that God had other plans with reference to the ministry He had called me to, thus I resigned this appointment.

The Osborns again contacted me, requesting us to go to the island country of New Zealand to represent their ministry there, which I strongly considered. However, after earnest prayer and wise counsel from trusted ministerial colleagues, I respectfully declined the appointment.

I loved Reverend T.L. Osborn, whose ministry had touched me deeply and whom I held in highest esteem, yet I knew God was calling me to a new phase of my own ministry—the pastorate. Brother Osborn had expressed to me his strong opinion that I should not consider pastoral ministry (citing, for his reason, that he had witnessed the ruin of many God-called evangelists who had settled down to pastor churches).

"You are an unspoiled, natural-born evangelist," he told me. "Don't spoil that ministry by settling down to pastor churches!" he admonished me.

I continued to consider, with caution, Brother Osborn's admonition concerning pastoral ministry, until my brother Dwane's wife came to our home in Federal Way, Washington, on Saturday, May 15, 1965, and asked me if I had talked to either Dwane or Lester as yet that day.

"No," I answered. "Was I supposed to?"

"You mean you don't know?" she asked cautiously.

"Don't know what?" I probed.

"Your mother passed away today," she told me painfully.

At that moment I was temporarily in a state of shock and disbelief. I had just talked with Mother by phone the previous Sunday, May 9th, Mother's Day. I had told my precious mother how much I loved her and how I was missing her. I had not seen her since December 31, 1963.

I was suddenly enveloped in a cloud of painful sorrow. She had been such a sweet, tenderhearted, loving mother, a mother who had prayed for me and pointed me to Jesus—who actually had caused me to want to be a Christian. *She was too young to just die suddenly*, I told myself. She had just turned sixty-three on the March 18th. I had expected to have her around for many years to come, but this was not to be. She was now in the Presence of the Lord, which I knew was far better, yet it was a *bitter pill* for me to swallow. I so keenly felt the sense of loss and the pain of sorrow at that moment that many things that had seemed important to me, at least for the moment, suddenly became insignificant and trivial.

Admittedly, I also struggled with disgust toward my two brothers, Lester and Dwane, when I learned that they had known for several hours that Mother had passed away and yet had not informed me of her death. A root of bitterness sprang up in me temporarily over this and I was ready to let them know that I really did not appreciate them not getting in touch with me. Thankfully, however, I "dumped" the resentment from my heart, realizing that they must be suffering the same pains of sorrow over Mother's death that I was experiencing. When I finally asked them why they hadn't told me about her passing, they both said that they assumed that I had gotten a call like they had.

Dwane and I would fly back to Kansas for Mother's funeral service while Lester, his wife Christine, and two sons, Bruce and Bryan, would drive there. It was hard to say goodbye to such a precious loved one as Mother was, but I knew I would not wish her back to this life now that she had tasted the world to come. At the gravesite—Mount Pleasant Cemetery, about four miles north of Norwich, Kansas, and one half mile from my birthplace—I had a wonderful spiritual experience. As Mother's casket was being lowered into the cold ground, I suddenly received a beautiful vision in which I saw the Lord coming in the clouds of the air and, simultaneously, that grave bursting open—my beloved Mother coming forth in mighty resurrection power with a majestic, glorified body. It was a truly a comforting and stabilizing experience for me. I know beyond a shadow of doubt that that vision will, one bright and glorious day, be swallowed up in reality!

It was shortly after Mother's passing away that I received a call about the pastoral vacancy at Meade Community Church in Meade, Kansas.

"Would you consider being a candidate for this church?" the voice on the other end of the line asked.

Called to Pastor?

By this time I was beginning to realize that there was a change forthcoming in the course of my ministry. With the death of my mother still fresh on my mind, I was now ready to consider something I had previously thought would never be—pastoral ministry.

"Let me pray about this," I told Brother Gilbert Wilson, a board member of the church. "I'll call you back tomorrow with an answer." We mutually agreed on that, thus I went before God in earnest prayer.

"Lord," I pleaded, "if this is Your will for me, You will have to make me know that it is You and not just something I want to do. You will have to give me a pastor's heart," I added.

After seeking God about this and then discussing it with Bobbie and our children, I decided to call Brother Wilson and tell him that we'd like to drive down to Kansas, come to the church, present our ministry to the congregation, and then allow the Lord to lead in the matter. The children were excited about the possibility of moving to Kansas, and Bobbie, although a bit apprehensive about such a decision, was resigned to "not my will, but Thine be done, dear Lord!"

We did make the trip to Meade, Kansas, presenting our ministry to the congregation there, after which they voted unanimously to invite us to be their next pastor. We thanked them for considering us and for the strong vote of confidence by which they decided to invite us to come be their pastors. We still wanted to be certain that this was God's will and not ours.

This was the first-ever invitation for me to serve in pastoral ministry, and admittedly, I had a lot to learn. After thirteen and a half years of evangelistic ministry, it would be a "different ballgame" if I decided to accept the church's invitation, and I knew it.

Meade, Kansas, population 2,800, was a beautiful little city in Southwest Kansas. It is the county seat of Meade County and thus a town of some prominence. And of course, I was not a stranger to the town, nor to the church. Ironically, my uncle Paul Bailey had served as pastor of that church in the mid '30s. It was his first pastorate. I had also attended a camp meeting held in the city park in Meade in the summer of 1947 at the age of fifteen. Art Morlin and I preached at this church on several occasions, also. I preached in a night service of another camp meeting in Meade on Monday night, August 2, 1954. Then too, Bobbie and I had been to that church in evangelistic ministry on several occasions previously.

A lady in that church, Sister Ethel Boyd, had been miraculously healed of total blindness in one eye in a service in which Art Morlin and I had ministered in 1954, just before Art departed by bus to return to Seattle to attend to "unfinished business." She had gone blind in one eye at age six and had never seen with it until sixty years later when, in response to believing prayer, she was completely healed and had her eyesight restored. Ironically, during my tenure there as pastor of Meade Community Church, Sister Boyd would be the first person for whom I would conduct a funeral service.

After a reasonable space of time we contacted the church and told them we would come to serve the congregation in pastoral ministry, but would need to have a space of time before we could arrive there. Our home in Federal Way, Washington, which I had built and in which we were living at the time, would have to be sold first.

The home sold in October of 1965 and we moved to Meade to begin a new phase in our family life as well as in my ministry. I would now become Bobbie, Sally, and Andy's pastor, an awesome but sobering thought for a relatively young husband and father.

Our children had won a pony, "Rusty," in a drawing at Federal Way and it was mandatory that he, too, make the move from Washington to Kansas, along with our tri-Collie dog, "Lassie." For the purpose of transporting such important cargo, a friend helped me prepare a special two-wheeled trailer. We finally got moved to Meade. Professional movers had moved our furniture and other household goods in late October, 1965, where we would begin pastoral ministry that would extend across thirty-five years serving in pastorates of five different churches in three different states.

Later pastorates included the Spearman Union Church in Spearman Texas; the Full Gospel Evangelistic Chapel in South Seattle, Washington; the Davenport Assembly of God in Davenport, Washington, where both of our children graduated from high school, and Hazel Dell Assembly of God in Vancouver, Washington (this one for a little over twenty-one years).

Ministry in Mexico and Beyond

While serving as pastor of the Spearman Union Church in Texas I was permitted a month's sabbatical in July, 1969, for the purpose of missionary evangelism in Central America.

After three nights of special services in Mexico City, arranged by my dear friend, Wayne Meyers, who also served as my Spanish interpreter, I ministered in churches in Guatemala City, Guatemala; San Salvador, El Salvador; Jinotega, and Yali, Nicaragua; San Jose, Costa Rica; and Panama City, Panama. I also spent two days in Tegucigalpa, Honduras, but did not minister there due to a misunderstanding with the missionary concerning dates. Most of this evangelistic tour was concentrated in the country of Nicaragua, where I ministered in a salvation and healing campaign in the mountain city of Yali. After we concluded the campaign in Yali, my missionary friend, Reverend Larry Schnedler, told me that it was a "landmark victory."

"What do you mean by that?" I asked.

"Well, every other minister who has attempted to pierce the spiritual darkness in Yali was killed," he replied. "This has been the first successful attempt at evangelism in that city," he exclaimed. For whatever reason that this was true, I could only thank my Wonderful Lord for His watchful care and protection during the Yali Crusade. With the exception of Mexico City, the city of San Salvador, El Salvador, was the only other Central American city I ministered in more than one night. It was a two-night mini-crusade there.

Once again, in each of these Central American countries I would see *"that face"* in the crowd while preaching or praying for the sick. This has always served as a confirmation of the Lord's special call on my life for missionary evangelism. By far, the greatest satisfaction that came to me through these open doors of ministry abroad has been the precious souls that have turned to the Lord Jesus Christ for salvation. That has been the driving force that has caused me to regard any and every sacrifice or inconvenience to be unworthy of consideration by way of comparison.

After serving as pastors of Union Church in Spearman, Texas, we accepted the pastorate of Full Gospel Evangelistic Chapel in South Seattle, Washington, where we served for three years before moving on to Davenport, Washington. We would spend the next six years (1973–1979) there. My uncle, Reverend Paul Bailey, had founded Evangelistic Chapel in Seattle and built the new church building there. Pastoring in a large metropolitan area was considerably different than it had been in the smaller towns of Meade, Kansas, and Spearman, Texas, but we were able, by God's grace and enablement, to adapt to the changes and thus lead many to Christ during our tenure there.

Our fourth pastorate would be with the Davenport Assembly of God Church in Davenport, Washington—another small town in a rural setting. During our six-years there, our church was able to build a beautiful new sanctuary, debt free. Both of our children, Sally and Andy, graduated from Davenport High School and went on to college—Sally to Northwest College of the Assemblies of God in Kirkland, Washington, and Andy to Southern California College of the Assemblies of God in Costa Mesa, California. After her first year at Northwest College, Sally decided to get married and married her high school sweetheart, Jay Nevin, on December 27, 1975. It was a beautiful wedding held in the new church sanctuary.

Since her husband, Jay, was serving a four-year term in the United States Air Force, Sally moved away from Davenport, first to Wichita Falls, Texas, and then to Jacksonville, Arkansas. While living in Jacksonville, Sally gave birth to our first grandchild, a beautiful baby girl whom they named "Jaynece Gail Nevin." She became the joy of our lives, although we didn't get to see her much until her dad had completed his four years in the Air Force. She was born in Little Rock, Arkansas, on January 18, 1978.

Our son, Andy, had been very active in sports at Davenport High School. He played football, basketball, and baseball all of his four years there, his teams making it to the state playoffs in all three sports (but never a state championship). He was also the "first chair" trumpet player in the high school band three of his four years in high school.

After graduation, Andy enrolled in Southern California College, where he would receive his B.A. degree in May, 1984. He had been recruited to play baseball at SCC, and pitched for the team. In April, 1979, we resigned the pastorate in Davenport after accepting an invitation to serve as pastors of the Bethel Assembly of God Church in Vancouver, Washington, where we would continue until retiring from pastoral ministry in June, 2000.

Our six years of pastoral ministry in Davenport were some of our most memorable as a family. We were well respected in the community and treated royally by the constituents of our church.

Our first Sunday at Bethel Assembly of God Church in Vancouver was Easter Sunday, April 15, 1979, hence our tenure with that church touched on four decades (the '70s, '80s, '90s, and '00s). My father, Floyd Lewis Ott, passed away on Saturday, April 14, 1979, thus making our debut at Bethel Assembly of God a "bittersweet" experience. We flew to Kansas on Monday, April 16th, to attend his funeral service.

After completing his four-year term in the Air Force, our son-in-law, Jay Nevin, and his family moved to Vancouver in September 1979. On September 23, 1979, our daughter, Sally, gave birth to our second grandchild, Clarence Douglas Nevin. Now we would have two grandchildren to love on and "spoil."

Exactly two years to the day after my father passed away at age 74, I received a phone call that my brother, Louie, had dropped dead of a massive heart attack. He was fifty-six years old. Because Louie had influenced my life so profoundly in the early 1950s, I was stricken with grief to learn of his sudden death. Bobbie and I flew to Gainesville, Texas, to attend the funeral service for Louie. He was laid to rest there in the Gainesville Cemetery.

After graduating from Southern California College in May 1984, our son, Andy, stayed in the Los Angeles area for a few months working in the accounting department of the Herbalife Company. But "homesickness" finally set in, so he resigned his job and returned to Vancouver,

Washington, where he has lived since that time. On August 22, 1987, Andy married his college sweetheart, Miss Tristeen Parker. They were married in the Hazel Dell Assembly of God Church on Bobbie's fifty-third birthday, with Dad officiating. To that union, God has given four beautiful children—Alyssa, Megan, Sidney, and Drew.

The Beginning of Sorrows

The deaths of Mother, Dad and Louie would be only the beginning of sorrows for my family and me. On February 18, 1987, just as we were about to leave our house to go to the church for our Wednesday mid-week family night service, we received a phone call that Bobbie's Dad had died quite suddenly of a heart attack. It was a sudden shock and a difficult thing to cope with. But knowing that he had entered into the Lord's Presence took the "sting" out of his sudden passing, and we consoled ourselves with this thought.

The next great sorrow came to our family in late April, 1991, when our son-in-law admitted to our daughter, Sally, that there was another woman in his life and thus he was leaving his family. This broke Sally's heart, as well as their children's hearts; Jaynece, age 13, and Doug, age 11. And, of course, it also broke Bobbie's and my heart. Up until this time we thought that something like this only happened to "other families." We never thought of or expected that it could or ever would happen to ours.

From that time on I had to take the place of their father for Jaynece and Doug, as much as I possibly could. But the toll on both of them was severe—so much so for Jaynece that she had the first of many grand mal seizures on Christmas Day, 1991. Needless to say, that awful seizure frightened all of us. It was the "beginning of the end" for our beautiful granddaughter. More about this later . . .

The Jewish Connection

While pastoring the Bethel Assembly of God, which was re-named Hazel Dell Assembly of God in 1982, a chain of events led to what I call *The Jewish Connection*. I had received an invitation to attend a "Travel Symposium" at the Neva Shalom Jewish Syna-gogue in Portland, Oregon, in April, 1983. By this time Bobbie and I had already hosted two pilgrimages to the Holy Land (in October of 1980, and September of 1982), thus I was interested in attend-ing this symposium.

The special guest speaker of the event was the Israeli government's Minister of Tourism, Mr. Schmuel Zurell. Several other pastors from the Vancouver/Portland area were in atten-dance at this early morning event that was geared to generate interest in visiting the country of Israel. It soon became appar-ent, however, that none of the other pastors was particularly in-terested in the subject and thus left the meeting early. Looking around, I was quick to notice that this left only me there at the synagogue with Rabbi Stanfer and Mr. Zurell. I expressed to Mr. Zurell and Rabbi Stanfer the fact that I had a special love in my heart for God's Chosen People, the Jews, and thus a very special interest in the nation of Israel.

Sometime earlier, while trying to find the headquarters for the Portland Jewish Community Center, I had stopped in at the Neva Shalom Synagogue to inquire about the location of the center. My mission on that occasion was to deliver a check in the amount of seven hundred fifty dollars from my church to the Center, specifi-cally designated to help the wives of slain Israeli soldiers who had been killed in ambush while on patrol duty. A very friendly and gracious Rabbi Stanfer had just stepped out of his office at the moment I entered the synagogue.

"Could I be of assistance to you?" he asked.

When I told him what my mission was and that the church, which I served as pastor, had decided to become a "Bless Israel" congregation, he received me warmly, commending me and my church for this thoughtfulness toward his people, the Jews. Not only did he tell me exactly where to find the Center I was looking for, but he also invited me to attend the upcoming travel symposium.

After arriving at the Jewish Community Center's office and relating my mission to the people in charge of planning and activities, the gentleman in charge asked me if I could come back a little later. The reason for this was that he wanted to have a photographer on hand to photograph me handing the check to him for the purpose of publishing a story about me and my church in their newspaper for the Jewish Community. Hence, "The Jewish Connection" was set in motion.

While attending a convention in Richland, Washington, a couple of weeks after the travel symposium in Portland, the phone rang in my hotel room at about 7:00 A.M. Because we had been up quite late the night before, we were still in bed asleep that morning.

When I picked up the telephone and said, "Hello," the voice on the other end of the call responded, in quite broken English.

"Hello, this is Schmuel Zurell from the Ministry of Tourism in Israel. I'm calling to invite you to come to Israel on an all-expense paid tour of our country." He continued, "Now, I'm sure you will need some time to discuss this invitation with your church board, so I'm not asking you for an answer right now. Just think it over and discuss it with your church board and then call me back."

At that juncture I interrupted Mr. Zurell by saying, "Oh, yes, sir, I accept your invitation right now. It won't be necessary to discuss it with my church board. I know they would want me to accept this invitation," I said. Thus the "trip of a lifetime" was set in motion. This journey would commence the first week in June.

Upon returning to Vancouver from the convention in Richland, I related to my congregation the invitation I had received to go to Israel on an all-expense paid excursion in June. The announcement was applauded with cheers, handclapping, and even tears of joy as the people of my church overwhelmingly approved my acceptance of that awesome invitation. In fact, they gave me an offering of two hundred dollars to purchase souvenirs with while there.

With the complete itinerary in hand, along with airline tickets, I departed from Portland International Airport on Monday morning, June 6th, for one of the most memorable weeks of my entire lifetime. After arriving at John F. Kennedy Airport in New York City, I would join over one hundred others who had also been invited to make this pilgrimage to Israel. There we would transfer to El Al Israeli Airlines for the nonstop flight to Tel Aviv aboard a Boeing 747 airliner.

While waiting for the flight to Tel Aviv, I made acquaintance with a number of my fellow "Holy Land Pilgrims," one of whom was Mrs. Bobi Hromas, the daughter of the late Robert Parham (referred to in an earlier chapter). Of course I had met Mrs. Hromas on numerous occasions in the past—once at her brother Charles's funeral service in 1957 and again at her grandmother Fowler's funeral service in 1966. I had served as a pallbearer for Grandmother Fowler's funeral service. However, I had not seen her for some sixteen years until that day. This trip was "old hat" for her as she had lost count of how many times she had visited the country of Israel.

Sitting beside me on the flight to Tel Aviv was a lady from Southern California, Mrs. Peggy Grimes. She was also a friend of Bobi Hromas' since they both now lived in the Los Angeles area. Making her acquaintance would prove to be a *key link* in the unfolding of a most rewarding experience for me.

Coming down to the large dining hall from my room on the 17th Floor of the Hilton Hotel in Jerusalem on our second day in Israel, I paused at the entrance of the room to look around for a table to be seated at. As I glanced across the hall I observed Mrs. Grimes beckoning to me to come to the table where she was seated, along with some distinguished Israeli friends, hence I joined them.

"Rev. Ott, I'd like you to meet some very dear friends of mine," Mrs. Grimes said. "Meet Colonel Yehuda Levy, his wife and son," she urged. Just then this tall, dark, handsome, and distinguished Israeli gentleman stood, extending his right hand.

"Pleased to meet you, sir!" he said. "Welcome to Jerusalem and to Israel." He then introduced me to his wife and one of his sons, who were seated at the table with him and Mrs. Grimes.

We all visited around the table for a few minutes and then Mrs. Grimes (Peggy) asked to be excused, heading back to her room.

Before leaving Vancouver for this trip I had challenged my church to give a sacrificial love offering for me to present to the Government of Israel while on this trip.

"I believe that I have heard from the Lord about this," I told my congregation. "Since there are twelve tribes of Israel (descendants of Abraham, Isaac, and Jacob), I feel that God would have us to give an offering of $1,200 for me to take to Israel—one hundred for each of the twelve tribes." I went on.

"If this is of God, then there will be $1,200 or more in the offering, which we will now receive. If not, then you will know that this was my notion, not an impression from the Lord."

We had already received our usual Sunday morning offering for the support of the church and its ministries, hence this would be an offering above and beyond that. After the offering was received, ushers went into a side room to count it while the congregation sang a few choruses. With a gleam of delight on his face, the head usher entered the sanctuary and preceded to the platform to hand me a note concerning the sacrificial "Bless Israel" love offering. It read: "$1,200.03!" When I announced the amount of the offering to the congregation, a veritable "ocean of praise" went up to the Lord, both for the amount given, but especially for the verification that this was indeed His leading.

Thus I had in my possession a check from the Hazel Dell Assembly of God Church in Vancouver, Washington, made payable to the Israeli Government to present in person while on this trip. Our church had also decided to have a special plaque made declaring our love and support for the Jewish State of Israel. Inscribed on the plaque was an engraving of the church building, a declaration of our love and support, and the names of the members and constituents of the church, with an asterisk beside the names of those who had visited the Nation of Israel at some time in the past.

While visiting with Col. Levy and his family, I suddenly felt a "holy boldness" come upon me, thus I related to the Colonel that I had a strong desire to go to the Prime Minister's office building to present the check and the plaque to the appropriate person there.

"In fact," I boldly exclaimed, "I would really hope to be able to present these things to Prime Minister Menachan Began in person." At that, to my surprise, the Colonel said to me, "I believe I can arrange for you to do that."

Needless to say, my heart was racing with excitement and exhilaration at the prospect of meeting with the Prime Minister of the country of Israel!

"Really!" I exclaimed. "Oh, that would be wonderful if you could do that for me. I would be most grateful to you if you could make that arrangement," I told the Colonel.

Rising to his feet, he said, "Let me see what I can do. I will call you at your room after I've made the arrangements. OK?"

"Yes, sir," I replied. "I will eagerly await your call." With that, Col. Levy, his wife, and his son departed the dining hall. I also returned to my room to get dressed in a suit for the possibility of meeting with the Prime Minister of Israel! I was so excited I could hardly stand still to shower and get prepared for this most special occasion.

In about an hour the phone rang in my room.

"I'm here in the lobby," the Colonel said. "Please come down and meet me here and I'll take you to the Prime Minister's office building."

"I'll be right down," I told him. Thus, with the check in my inside jacket pocket and the plaque in my hand, I hurried down to the hotel lobby to meet Col. Levy.

"My automobile is in the parking lot," he told me. "I'll drive you over to the Prime Minister's office building now." As we walked out to get into his car, the Colonel told me, "I have good news and I have bad news! The good news is that I've arranged for you to present your check and plaque to the Government of Israel. The bad news is that earlier this morning, Mr. Philip Habeb (President Ronald Reagan's Chief Envoy to the Middle East) showed up unannounced and unexpectedly in Tel Aviv, thus Prime Minister Began has gone to meet with him. However," he continued, "I have made arrangements for you to meet with our Deputy Prime Minister, Mr. Dov Shalensky. He will receive you into his office and you can make your presentations to him. OK?"

While feeling just a little disappointed, I was still very "upbeat" and excited at the prospect of meeting with the second-highest-ranking man in the government of the Jewish State of Israel.

Arriving at the compound where the Prime Minister's office building was located, Col. Levy and I got out of his car and started walking toward that building. As we passed by several sentries, I observed that each of the guards saluted Col. Levy even though he was not dressed in military attire. He was now a retired, reserve Colonel of the Israeli Defense Forces. It was clearly apparent that the gentleman with whom I was walking was a respected, retired Israeli military officer. Once inside the Prime Minister's office building we took an elevator to an upper level where the Deputy Prime Minister's office was located. Recognizing the Colonel, the receptionist said, "Mr. Shalensky is expecting you. Please go on into his office."

Once in Mr. Shalensky's office, Col. Levy spoke to him.

"Please welcome Rev. Gail Ott from the United States." At those words, a very gracious Deputy Prime Minister rose to his feet, extended his right hand to shake hands with me, and said (in somewhat broken English), "Pleased to meet you, sir! Welcome to Jerusalem and to our country, Israel. Won't you please be seated?" Once the Deputy Prime Minister and I were seated, the Colonel excused himself and left the room, to my surprise, leaving me there in the presence of the second-in-command of one of the most significant nations on the face of the earth.

Admittedly, I was a bit nervous, wanting to make sure that I was not infringing on Mr. Shalensky's time, thus I got right to the point as to why I had been so desirous to meet with him (in lieu of Menachan Began.) This kind, gracious gentleman showed

302

a sincere interest in what I had to tell him and also expressed heartfelt thanks to me and to my church for our thoughtfulness and generosity.

"I will let Prime Minister Began know of your visit and of your gifts to our nation," he told me. "He will also be touched by this great kindness, especially for this plaque and for its declaration of your love and support for our country."

Noticing that I was a bit nervous about the time, Mr. Shalensky said to me, "Please relax. I'm glad that you came to see me." Thus, we visited for several minutes.

"Would you like a soft drink?" he asked me at one point in our visit.

"Oh, that would be nice," I replied, "but I don't expect anything like that."

"Nonsense," he said as he called his secretary on the intercom. "Please bring us a couple of soft drinks," he instructed her.

"I'll be right in with them," she responded. In a moment or so she entered the room with two orange sodas. What a delightful, unbelievable occasion that morning was for me! Before leaving the Deputy Prime Minister's office, he summoned Col. Levy to come into the room since I had expressed the desire for a picture to be taken of me presenting the check and the plaque to him.

"Happy to oblige," the Colonel exclaimed as I handed him my camera. After several poses were snapped, Mr. Shalensky spoke to me.

"You have brought gifts for my country, now I'd like to present you with a personal gift from me," he said, as he handed me a copy of his book entitled, *The Musselmen* (by interpretation, "The Living Dead"). As Mr. Shalensky was only one of two survivors of the Holocaust out of his entire family, this book chronicled many of the cruel atrocities that the Nazi regime inflicted upon the Jewish people of Europe during their reign of terror in the late '30s and early '40s.

"I am honored to receive your book," I told Mr. Shalensky. "I will treasure it as one of my prize possessions for the rest of my life," I assured him as I requested him to personally autograph that copy for me. Col. Levy also photographed Mr. Shalensky presenting me with his book.

After bidding Mr. Dov Shalensky a fond farewell, Col. Levy drove me back to the Jerusalem Hilton Hotel. I got back just in time to change into casual attire, to eat lunch, and then to go on a tour of the City of Jerusalem.

Of course, getting to meet Col. Levy, who in turn introduced me to the Deputy Prime Minister of the Nation of Israel, was indeed the highlight of this never-to-be-forgotten trip to Israel (my fourth of six visits there). My heart was filled with gratitude to God for the events of that memorable day in June, 1983. I had to pinch myself a few times to be sure that I was not dreaming that all of this had really happened. This trip was so awesome, I sometimes refer to it "as if I had died and gone to Heaven" for a week!

I fully expected to have a roommate for our stays in the various hotels in Israel that week, and just prayed that whomever my roommate might be he wouldn't snore in bed, etc., but to my surprise, I enjoyed a private suite in each city (Jerusalem, Tiberius, Haifa, and Herzeleya, on the Mediterranean coast of Israel).

Since I was one of three hundred people from more than one hundred countries invited to be a part of this week's events in the country of Israel, I was equally surprised to be assigned to ride in the VIP bus: Bus #1, of five). By being on Bus #1, I was privileged to enjoy the services of the top guide in all of Israel, Mr. Mike Rogoff.

What did I do to deserve all of this VIP treatment? *Nothing!* It could only be explained in terms of the blessing of the Lord. Each day of that week in Israel was filled with sightseeing; abundant food, and interaction with other people, both from the U.S. as well as other countries around the world, who had converged on that tiny nation for this week of glorious experiences. In each of the four cities where the three hundred invited guests lodged we were honored with elaborate banquets in the evenings and were entertained by Israeli artists, musicians, dancers, and dignitaries.

Upon returning home to Vancouver from this wonderful week of being pampered and blessed in the Jewish State of Israel, I was made to realize the abundant reality of Proverbs 10:22 (NKJV), which declares, "The blessing of the Lord, it maketh rich, and He addeth no sorrow with it."

The *Jewish Connection* did not end with this trip to Israel as a guest of the Israeli Ministry of Tourism. Time and space will not allow for the many details, but in time I would make acquaintances and friendships with a number of Jewish people right in my own community of Vancouver, Washington.

In 1989, I invited the Jewish Community of Vancouver to allow my church to host their annual Seder Dinner in our activity room at the church. It was a night of splendor for my wife, Bobbie, and me, as well as for the people of my church. Our ladies had made beautiful cloth tablecloths with matching cloth napkins especially for this very special occasion.

Bobbie and I were honored guests and were thus invited to be seated at the head table for this very special Jewish event. It was both interesting and inspiring for our church and for us. There were over one hundred people seated in the room that night.

Our friendship with the Jewish Community of Vancouver resulted in this group using our church facilities for their Shabbat gatherings for about ten years. It was truly an honor and a blessing for the church to have our beloved Jewish friends meeting in our facility during those years. Although they were offered the facility free of cost, they did a number of special things for the church to express their appreciation, one of which was the purchase of special microphones for the choir loft in the sanctuary.

Since that memorable week in June 1983, I have hosted two more tours to the country of Israel. Most of my tour guests were family and friends. Four of my sisters (two now deceased) and two of my brothers have accompanied me on tours to Israel. My brother Lloyd and his wife, Erna, have gone to Israel with me on three different occasions (1982, 1990, and 1995). Brother Dwane and his wife June were with us on the 1990 tour, along with brother Lloyd, Erna and our oldest sister, Pauline.

Perhaps if the Lord tarries I will return to the country of Israel again one day, but if not, I will carry with me wonderful, fond memories of the six times I've been privileged to go there and to walk where my Blessed Redeemer, the Lord Jesus Christ, walked during His earthly sojourn of some thirty-three years here on planet earth.

Bobbie accompanied me on trips to Israel in 1980 and 1982, but since she is not really fond of the long flights, she declined to make the journeys in 1990 and 1995. Yet she, too, has fond memories of her two visits to the Holy Land.

Chapter 14

. . . .

SMALL WORLD, BIG GOD

B obbie has never relished long airplane trips, *unless* we're on a family flight headed toward Hawaii! But we did launch out, as a couple, to a *few* more international destinations— Japan, South Korea, and San Juan, Puerto Rico.

My wife and I celebrated our Twenty-Fifth Wedding Anniversary in December, 1979, by flying to Hawaii. It was a very enjoyable and relaxing experience for both of us. Then, again in 1994, our entire family flew to Honolulu during spring break for our respective schools. Of course, Sydney and Drew Ott were not yet born at that time and Sally was now single. But it was a memorable getaway for our family.

In 1987, shortly after our son Andy and his wife Tristeen's wedding, Bobbie and I were afforded a trip to Japan and Korea. What an unbelievable difference twenty-nine years had made in the country of Japan! During my six weeks of ministering in that country in late 1958 the Japanese were still digging out of the rubble and ruin of World War II. The only automobiles I saw in the country back then were small, three-wheel vehicles that looked like a cross between a motorcycle and a pickup truck. Of course, there were some American-made cars around, but they were few and far between.

During Bobbie's and my visit to Tokyo in October, 1997, we saw one of the most modern, up-to-date cities in the world! The cars and trucks we saw on the streets appeared to be very late models and we saw *very few* older vehicles.

From Tokyo we flew to Seoul, Korea, for a very enjoyable week in that country. A highlight of our visit to Seoul was the opportunity to attend a Sunday morning service at the largest church in the world—the Yodi Full Gospel Church, which was founded by its Senior Pastor, Rev. David Yongi Cho. This church had over 750,000 members at that time—with a pastoral staff of over two thousand ministers! Bobbie and I were afforded the very rare privilege of touring the church's administrative offices, including Dr. Cho's private office.

While visiting the capital city of Seoul, we took a bus tour to the famed DMZ (Demilitarized Zone) that separated North and South Korea, recalling the terrible war fought there and the loss of the lives of more than fifty thousand American soldiers.

We also flew to the southern Korean city of Pusan where we spent a couple of days. My brother Lloyd had been stationed at Pusan during the Korean conflict in the early 1950s, thus that area was of particular interest to me.

Remarkable Occurrences "Down Under"

In 1988, along with my brother Lloyd, his wife Erna, and our oldest niece, Delores Hall (who is Louie's eldest child), I made the long journey "down under" to Australia and New Zealand. The occasion, specifically, was to attend the World's Fair in Brisbane, Australia. This was not a ministry trip, but it was a very enjoyable and interesting excursion. Our niece Delores and Lloyd's wife Erna roomed together while Lloyd and I did the same. The idea of two seventeen-hour flights to and from Australia left Bobbie a little cold, thus she opted not to make this trip with the rest of us.

We did have some memorable moments! At the World's Fair in Brisbane, the four of us attended a performance at the *Pavilion of*

Promise. When the performing artist, whose first name was Mike, came out onto the stage, he suddenly stopped everything and with his index finger pointed at me, shouted, "There's Pastor Gail Ott from Vancouver, Washington, in the U.S.A!"

Of course, I had already recognized him as the Christian brother from Australia who had come to our Hazel Dell Assembly of God Church and performed his "acts" for the congregation. One of the acts this brother performed at our church on a Sunday night was to crack a large bullwhip down the center aisle in rapid succession. He was a master with his whip which made a piercing noise, resembling loud gun shots!

Although that performance highly pleased the younger set, it did not set well with some of the senior citizens of the church, thus he agreed to "do his thing" out in the parking lot following the service. This brother also played music on some very unusual instruments, which he himself had made. Most notable was his "digery-doo" instrument, a novelty indeed. He did, of course, present the gospel message during the course of that service, as well.

After the service had been dismissed and most of the older folks had left for home, a crowd gathered in the church parking lot for a bullwhip-cracking spectacle. Mike could crack that big whip with unbelievable rapidity that had the sound of a western gun battle! The people in an apartment complex next to the church came out on their porches to see what was going on. He certainly had mastered this performance, which was also the highlight of his act at the World's Fair in Brisbane.

You may wonder how Mike came to be ministering at Hazel Dell Assembly of God. Actually, I'd met this brother sometime earlier at a Full Gospel Businessmen's Convention in Portland, Oregon. At the urging of the emcee for pastors to invite him to their churches, I'd invited him to come. What a coincidence that Mike's three-day performance (during the six-month duration of the World's Fair) would take place at the exact time of our visit to the Pavilion of Promise!

"This is unbelievable" my brother Lloyd said, "that someone away down here in Australia would know you!" Yet as unbelievable as it may have seemed, it happened!

Now, to further extend the *unbelievable* factor of this episode, I recently met a man and his wife at a funeral service in Camas, Washington. While visiting with them I learned that they were the hosts for Trinity Broadcasting Network's Portland, Oregon, affiliate (Channel 24). Moreover, I learned that the wife was a native Australian who had served as a television anchorwoman for one of the networks in that country, but had taken a six-month leave of absence from that job to work at the Pavilion of Promise during the six months duration of the World's Fair.

When Mike finished his performance that day, he invited me and my small group to come to the Hospitality Room of the pavilion where the performers meet and wait to go on stage. We accepted his kind invitation and were treated to soft drinks, snacks, cookies, etc. When I related that incident to this former TV anchorwoman, she smiled.

"Well then, I probably was the person who served you on that day!" She distinctly remembered Mike and his three-day performance at the pavilion. Additionally, her husband, who was from Portland, Oregon, had also made a six-month commitment to travel to Brisbane and work at the Pavilion of Promise during the Fair. The two had met there, fallen in love, and were subsequently married.

An incident similar to this occurred in 1995 while I was hosting the most recent of my tours to Israel. My group had purchased tickets to attend the World Pentecostal Conference in Jerusalem, which was in session while we were there. The huge auditorium was packed, hence my group members and I all had to spread out throughout the auditorium in hopes of finding seats. Everyone eventually found a single slot, except my brother Lloyd and me. After roaming the auditorium for about ten minutes, we spotted an usher, who beckoned us to two seats in the balcony farthest from the platform. We followed his direction and seated ourselves in next-to-the-very-last row of seats in the highest seating area in the auditorium.

Since it was a very hot evening in Jerusalem, the house air-conditioning was not keeping up with the high temperatures, thus it was quite warm in that place! Lloyd and I quickly decided to shed our jackets. Having folded my jacket over the back of my seat with my name badge showing, the gentleman in the seat behind us tapped me on the shoulder.

"Are you Gail Ott?" he asked. He'd noticed the name badge on the lapel of my jacket.

"I am," I replied.

"Well, I'm Bob Forseth. I came to Davenport, Washington, many years ago and ministered in your church there [the Davenport Assembly of God]." Bob Forseth had also served as pastor of The Church by the Side of the Road in South Seattle that Bobbie had grown up in, where I'd surrendered to the Lord, and where Bobbie and I were married.

Since my brother Lloyd did not know Brother Forseth, he once again exclaimed, "You are unbelievable, Gail! We meet people all over the earth that know you. I can't believe this!"

Beneath the "Midnight Sun"

My brother Lloyd and his wife, Erna, joined Bobbie and me for a ten-day trip to the State of Alaska in July, 1991. We attended several services at an indoor camp meeting hosted by a church in Spenard, a suburb of Anchorage. The host pastor had been a long-time friend and acquaintance of my family. In fact, my brother Lloyd had sold Bob Palmer, its pastor, an airplane a few years earlier. We marveled at the "midnight sun"—a phenomenon of that northern region that meant it did not get dark until two or three in the morning!

Bobbie and I flew to San Juan, Puerto Rico, in July, 1998, for a two-fold purpose—ministry and vacation. While there, I preached in an Assembly of God church in San Juan. We also toured much of the island. Our time together was most memorable, especially since, following our return from Puerto Rico in August, I would undergo treatment for prostate cancer.

Another significant travel experience for me was a flight to Pensacola, Florida, to attend several services of the Brownsville Revival at the Brownsville Assembly of God Church. My youth pastor at that time, Dave Riley, accompanied me for this very special occasion. Our time at this world renowned revival concluded with a Sunday morning service on Father's Day, 1996—the one year anniversary of this mighty spiritual outpouring that continued for about two more years.

During our visit to this historic revival, Evangelist Steve Hill preached two of his most powerful sermons. One sermon was entitled "White Cane Religion," with a sequel to that sermon preached the next evening entitled "There is a Ditch!"

Attending the great revival at Brownsville stands out in my mind as one of the greatest "mountaintops" of my ministerial experience. While there, I had the privilege of meeting Pastor John Kilpatrick.

"Let me lay hands on you and pray for you right over here on this side of the platform," he said. We moved about ten or twelve feet to our right.

"This is exactly where I was standing on that Father's Day Sunday morning one year ago when the mighty outpouring, which continues to this day, began." He then laid hands upon me and spoke a prayer of blessing. Now I consider that a "blessed experience!"

If I could have desired anything more on that occasion, I suppose it would have been that my beloved friend and colleague in ministry, Art Morlin, could have been there with me to witness the awesome outpouring of the Spirit in that place, especially since our first visit to Pensacola was made together (and our young friend, Pub Roberts, and his sister, Joyce, back in early December, 1952). However, Art had other commitments at the time and was not able to accompany us there.

The "Still, Small Voice" Speaks Again

On December 14, 1990, while babysitting our newest grand-child, Alyssa Gail Ott (born April 17, 1990), in my church office, I had a very unusual and significant experience. The ladies of our church were having their Annual Christmas Dinner Party at the church that evening, thus I was keeping Alyssa so that Bobbie and Tristeen, our daughter-in-law, could enjoy the festivities. While watching a Trinity Broadcast Network Special on a small television set that evening, God spoke to my heart in a very definite way.

As a part of that special telecast, Paul and Jan Crouch, founders of TBN, were speaking from Red Square in Moscow, Russia. Snow was falling in Moscow as this live telecast was aired on TBN that evening. With tears streaming down her cheeks and the TV camera directly focused on her, Jan was appealing to ministers of the gospel to come to the country of Russia and preach Christ to a people "ripe for revival."

"They are hungry for the gospel here," she urged. "The doors are wide open now," she continued. "But who knows how long they will remain open?" she challenged.

It was at that instant on that Friday night in December, 1990, that God spoke a "word of knowledge" to my heart and spirit. The message was brief, but crystal clear.

"You will go to Russia and you will preach my gospel there!" At that instant, I felt the Presence of the Holy Spirit in a very powerful way. As I pondered what had just been dropped into my heart, I was both excited and *awed* by the thought of the "Rhema Word" that I had just received from the Lord.

Nevertheless, I kept all of this to myself for a few days, desiring to be certain that this was of the Lord and not something arising out of my own spirit. One of the ways it "checked out" was the fact that I had not, up until that instant, ever once even *thought* about going to Russia to preach Christ there.

When I finally realized that this thing was *truly* of the Lord, I divulged the matter to a few trusted friends and colleagues.

"Please pray with me about this," I urged them. "I do not have a single contact in Russia. I don't have a clue how this thing will play out," I admitted. "All I know is this: God spoke to my heart and revealed to me that I will go to Russia and will preach His gospel there; hence I will now have to trust Him to work this all out because there is no way that I can do it on my own!"

This started the *prayer wheel* turning on my behalf with regard to this awesome challenge. Eventually I divulged my mandate of the Holy Spirit to the church body, requesting their earnest prayer. A small group of us had been meeting at the church for morning prayer five days a week. I engaged the daily *prayer warriors* to bind together with me in agreement concerning this matter.

As the weeks and months went by I found myself increasingly preoccupied with the prospect of a missionary journey to Russia. *How will this scenario unfold?* I wondered. I found myself praying more frequently and more fervently about this great challenge. As time went by, I found myself contacting close friends and confidants, asking them to join me in prayer, asking God that I might be made to know how He would work this all out.

One of the first persons to whom I divulged this matter was Sister Lydia Swain, whom I had met at the Yodi Full Gospel Church in Seoul, Korea. At the time, Lydia was Dr. Cho's personal assistant. She happened to be home in the U.S. for the Christmas holidays, thus I invited her to come to Vancouver to minister in our church while she was stateside. She graciously accepted my invitation and thus was scheduled as our special guest speaker on Sunday, January 6, 1991.

During her stay in our home while in Vancouver, I shared how God had spoken to me about going to Russia, requesting that she agree with me in prayer concerning the matter, which she consented to do. Thus, Lydia became one of my committed prayer partners concerning Russia. She was especially interested in the call that God had placed on my heart since she was of Russian decent. She shared with me the story of how her father had built a church in Russia in the early years of the twentieth century and how that, after the Bolshevik Revolution of 1917, the church had been closed—its windows and doors boarded shut. Her father escaped from Russia with his family and came to America.

For this reason Lydia Swain became especially interested in the call of God I had received to go to Russia and preach His Gospel there. One morning before she left Vancouver Lydia spoke to me.

"You know, I was just thinking. My brother has hopes of going back to Russia to reopen the church that our father built, which was closed down by the Communist Government following the Revolution. Who knows," she continued, "maybe the Lord will send you there to minister in that very church after it opens up again!"

"Well," I said, "if that is His plan and His will, I'll be more than happy to do just that!" We stayed in touch after Lydia returned to Korea to continue her ministry at the world's largest church.

The reason Lydia had accepted my invitation to come to Vancouver was because of her longstanding friendship with one of the men of the church, Rev. Cecil Caruthers. They'd met in Southern Florida when they were both quite young. Cecil was serving in the United States Navy at that time, during World War II, and was temporarily stationed in Miami, where they'd met on a city bus. During the bus ride, Lydia invited Cecil to come to a revival meeting at the First Assembly of God Church in Miami that evening.

"You will be blessed, I promise you," she told Cecil. "Rev. Loren Fox and his evangelistic party are conducting a revival crusade at our church, and it is wonderful. Why don't you come out to the service tonight?" she urged.

"I just might do that," Brother Caruthers replied. And do so he did. He sat near the back of the church—"just in case things got too scary for him." After all, he was of a different, much more conservative religious persuasion at that time. The end result of Cecil Caruthers's acceptance of Lydia's invitation to attend a revival service that night in Miami was that he would later become a member of the Fox Evangelistic Party and would travel with the Ministry as song leader for some five years.

Of course, Cecil and Lydia parted ways after the Fox Party's revival meeting in Miami, but they remained friends. Lydia and her husband would later head to Korea as Assemblies of God missionaries. After the death of Mr. Swain, Lydia continued missionary service in Korea, eventually becoming involved with Dr. Cho and the Yodi Full Gospel Church in Seoul.

Cecil, a native of Kentucky, came back to Washington State, where he had been with the Fox Party in the town of Naselle, Washington, for a revival crusade a few years earlier and married a Finnish girl, Miss Aimee Wirkkala, thus becoming a Washingtonian.

After Bobbie and I returned from our visit to Korea, which included a thrilling Sunday morning service at Yodi Full Gospel Church, I gave a report on the journey to our church and mentioned Lydia Swain. Brother Cecil Caruthers came immediately to the platform at the close of that service.

"Did I hear you correctly?" he asked. "Did you say that you met Lydia Swain at Dr. Cho's church in Korea?"

"Yes, I did," I replied. "Why do you ask?" It was then that I heard the whole story from Brother Cecil. Shortly after speaking with him about our meeting Lydia Swain in Korea, he contacted her, renewing an old friendship. This ultimately resulted in her coming to our church to minister in January, 1991.

Nothing had developed with reference to Lydia's brother returning to Russia to reopen the church their father had built early in the twentieth century. I did, however, receive a call from Lydia a few months after she was with us in Vancouver.

"I'm calling from Korea," she said. "The purpose of my call," she continued, "is to ask if you might be interested in going to India to preach. Dr. Cho has been invited to preach there, but is unable to accept the invitation at this time, so I thought about you. Would you be interested?"

I thanked her for thinking of me, but respectfully declined.

"I've been to India before and had a wonderful ministry there," I told her, "but I just can't think of going anywhere else as long as this call to go to Russia to preach is still burning in my heart. Unless God lifts this call from me," I said, "I can't go elsewhere first."

"I understand," she responded. "I admire you for sticking to the call that the Lord has given you to Russia. I will continue to agree with you in prayer that the Lord of the Harvest will open a door to you for the fulfillment of that call," she added.

A few weeks later I received a telephone call from a Jewish evangelist friend, Rev. Randy Lechner of Lakeland, Florida.

"Gail," he said, "I'm going to be going to Korea for some ministry there. Why don't you come go with me on this trip?" Just as I'd responded to Lydia Swain, so I now responded to Brother Lechner.

"Thank you, my dear brother," I replied. "I'd love to accept your invitation to Korea, but right now I'm waiting on the Lord for a door to open in Russia as He has told me that I will go there and will preach His Gospel. Hence I must respectfully decline your gracious invitation."

"I understand," he responded. "But before we hang up, let me pray a prayer of agreement with you concerning this call, OK?"

"I'd love it," I responded. Brother Randy prayed a powerful prayer for me concerning my call to Russia to preach the message of Jesus Christ.

"Now before we hang up," I added, "would it be OK if I put you in touch with Dr. Cho's personal assistant in Korea? Her name is Lydia Swain and she is now a personal friend of mine. I'm sure she could be a great blessing to you," I told him.

"Oh, that would be great!" he responded. "Please do."

"I will see what I can do and then will get back in touch with you, OK?" With that we concluded our phone conversation. Shortly thereafter, I called Lydia Swain and mentioned my friend Randy to her.

"I'm sure you could be a great blessing to him and would hope that he might also be a blessing to you," I told her.

"By all means," Lydia responded, as she gave me information to pass on to my friend, Brother Lechner.

Randy did make the trip to Korea and did contact Mrs. Swain after arriving in Seoul. By all reports the Lord made each a great blessing to the other during his stay in Korea. Shortly after Brother Lechner left to come back to America I received another phone call from Lydia, who was sobbing as she spoke with me.

"Brother Ott," she said, "I want to thank you from the bottom of my heart for arranging for your Jewish minister friend, Brother Randy Lechner, to come here and meet with me. What a tremendous blessing this dear brother has been! I've been going through some difficult trials of late and this brother ministered to me in the power of the Holy Spirit in such a marvelous way. I feel like I've had a *personal revival* in my soul," she added. "How can I say thank you enough for sending him my way?"

"I am blessed, too," I told her, ". . . just to know how God has coordinated these things so that everybody is blessed and *He* gets the glory for it all."

Brother Lechner called me after he returned home from his trip to Korea to thank me for putting him in contact with Lydia and to report how the Lord had blessed both of them spiritually through the contact. Oh how good, gracious, and kind our Wonderful Lord is!

More time had passed and now it was late September, 1991. Still no doors had opened with reference to the call to Russia to preach His Good News. I often found myself praying for the *entire* hour of our daily Morning Prayer meetings at the church for God to open the door before me for the fulfillment of His call.

". . . When You Search for Me with *All* Your Heart."

Finally, on Friday morning, October 24, 1991, I found myself beseeching the Lord to either open a door for me to go to Russia or else to lift the burden on my heart to do so. On that particular morning at prayer I was so engrossed with this burden that I never got around to praying for any other need. I literally "groaned in the spirit" for the full hour of our prayer time that morning.

Shortly after the others who had come to the church for intercessory prayer had left that for the day, the phone in my office (next to the prayer room) began ringing. I picked up the receiver and a familiar voice greeted me on the other end of the line.

"Gail, this is your friend, Randy Lechner. Listen to me now . . .," he urged. "This is of God! After you hang up from talking with me, I want you to call this number in Dallas, Texas. This man is another Jew and is a friend of mine. I believe this is the door God will open for you to go to Russia," he exclaimed emphatically.

My first thought as Brother Randy said these words to me was of the promise of God recorded in Jeremiah 29:13 (NKJV), which declares: "And you will seek Me and find Me, when you search for Me with all your heart."

Could it really be that at the conclusion of my most earnest, fervent prayer concerning the call to go to Russia to preach Christ, the answer had finally come? Indeed, it had, although it had come in a totally different manner than I would ever have imagined—once again confirming that, "His ways are not our ways and His thoughts are not our thoughts!" (Isaiah 55:8).

Although I did not fully understand all that my Jewish friend and colleague related to me in that conversation by phone, I sensed in my spirit that this truly was of the Lord, thus I was cautiously excited. Hanging up the phone after speaking with Brother Lechner I looked at my watch, then suddenly remembered I had promised my thirteen-year-old granddaughter, Jaynece, that I would take her to a studio in Portland that afternoon, where she was scheduled to audition for a modeling contract.

Jaynece had been modeling clothing since the age of eight. There was barely enough time for me to pick her up at home and drive her to the studio for her audition; thus I would now have to wait until Monday to make the call to Dallas, Texas.

Incredibly, Jaynece and I walked into the studio at the exact time of her appointment—not a minute early, not a minute late! Following her interview it was apparent that this modeling opportunity was not the will of God for her at that time in her life, but at least she made it there for the audition!

On Sunday morning, October 27th, I related to my congregation that quite possibly a door was finally opening for me to fulfill the call to go to Russia to preach the gospel there. The entire church had been praying for me and *with* me to that end for ten months. The membership was in total agreement about my going when the Lord opened a door for it to happen. Thus a volume of spontaneous praise arose at my announcement that morning.

"All I'm asking of you, dear people, is that you agree with me in prayer that if this is indeed God's doing, it will come to pass. I will know tomorrow after I make a phone call to Dallas, Texas," I told the congregation.

Just then a lady stood to her feet, weeping as she said to me, "My husband and I want to give you one hundred dollars to help with the expense of your trip."

"Oh, no," I responded. "I was not asking for financial support, just for your earnest prayers."

"But God just spoke to both of us to give you one hundred dollars for your trip," she insisted.

"OK," I said, "If you feel God spoke to you to do that, I will gratefully accept your financial help, but that was not my motive when I asked this church to pray with me about the contact Brother Lechner had given me." By the time I had spoken those words there was no stopping what had already begun. One after another people stood, pledging various sums of money to help me with the financial need for this trip—a trip that had not even materialized at that time!

It seemed that things sort of got out of hand and I was embarrassed about it, wondering what visitors in the service would think about what had taken place, even though it was totally spontaneous and unsolicited. Yet I was made aware, once again, of just how good and gracious the Lord God is to us. By the time the "pledging" had ended that morning, more than enough money to cover all of the expenses of the trip, including the purchase of a video camera, had been promised. I was overwhelmed at the outpouring of kindness and love bestowed upon me by the gracious people whom I served as pastor. And, most certainly, my heart was filled with gratitude to my Wonderful Heavenly Father for His abundant provision. Now all that needed to take place was for all the arrangements to unfold!

On Monday morning, October 27th, I made the phone call to the Jewish gentleman in Dallas, Texas, whose business was a travel agency. My friend Randy had learned that this man was putting together a "familiarization tour" to Russia for ministers and, knowing of my desire to go to there to preach the gospel, had phoned me about the special tour. After my conversation with this travel agent, Sam, by phone that morning, I put together all of the necessary documents, photos, and a cashier's check and sent them by overnight express mail. He received them the next morning, just under the deadline to be included in the tour.

The entire tour, including round-trip airfare from New York City, all hotels, meals, guided tours of Moscow and St. Petersburg, as well as a couple of days and nights in Helsinki, Finland, were included in the unbelievable price of $1,050.00. My round-trip airfare from Portland, Oregon, to New York City was the only other expense.

On Wednesday, October 30th, an overnight package from Sam, the travel agent, was delivered to me. Here were all the necessary documents, airfare tickets, etc., for the trip. I was all set to go, with the exception of purchasing round-trip airfare to and from New York City. I soon took care of that!

Now all of the travel arrangements were in place. *But what about contacts in Moscow and St. Petersburg to arrange opportunities for preaching the Gospel of Christ? How would this part of the trip play out?* I did not know the "how" of the matter, but I did know the "Who" that I would have to look to for the answer to this—the Lord of the Harvest. In earnest, fervent prayer I besought the Lord once more to somehow provide me with the necessary contact inside Russia. Just as the travel portion of the tour had come about by the providence of God, I somehow knew that this aspect of the tour would unfold in the same manner. Indeed it did!

To Russia . . . *with Faith*

A friend who had heard that I was going on a tour of Russia contacted me to suggest that I get in touch with a certain local gentleman who was in charge of an agency of the Lutheran Church denomination that assisted Russian emigrants coming to Portland, Oregon. I was able to get in touch with this brother in Christ and thus told him of my travel plans to Russian. He was at once very interested and invited me to come to the agency to meet him for lunch the next day. This sounded like "music to my ears" as I sensed that the Holy Spirit was at work pulling all things together so that my mission might be fulfilled. I spent a very enjoyable and profitable hour or so with this brother as we visited over lunch.

"When are you going on this trip?" he asked me.

"This coming Monday, November 11th," I replied.

"How about contacts there?" he asked, "Do you know anyone who could arrange services for you to minister in?"

"Not yet," I replied. "That is what I've been earnestly praying to the Lord to provide."

"Great!" he said. "I know just the person for you to contact. He lives here in Portland. His dad is a Pentecostal pastor in Moscow. I'm sure he could help you with arrangements to preach both in Moscow and in St. Petersburg since his dad is the President of the Pentecostal Churches in Russia."

My new friend gave me the name and phone number of this young Christian Russian man in Portland, whom I contacted that same evening. We agreed to meet at the Lutheran Agency the next morning at 10:00 A.M. I could hardly wait for the next morning, when I would meet this young Russian Christian.

Contacts Come Calling

Upon arrival at the agency that morning, after we were introduced, we sat down together in a vacant conference room. He was just as excited as I was that I was going to his native country and to Moscow, where he had lived prior to coming to America.

"I will call my family in Moscow today and let them know you are coming. They will arrange for you to preach in one of our churches while you are in Moscow." He went on.

"They will also arrange for you to preach in one of our churches in St. Petersburg. My uncle, Demetrius, is the pastor of the church there, and a sister whose name is Tamara will be able to interpret for you. My family will also arrange for an interpreter for you in Moscow."

"Wonderful," I exclaimed. "I'm very excited about all of this because the Lord spoke to me ten months ago that I would go to Russia and preach His Gospel there. Now it is about to become a reality!"

I gave this young man the name and address of the hotel where we would be staying in Moscow so that he could, in turn, give that information to his family when he called them later that day.

Later that evening, this gracious young Russian Christian called saying that he had made the call to his family and they were excited that I was coming to Moscow! They would contact me at the hotel on the day of my arrival there.

I bade farewell to Bobbie and our family on Monday morning, November 11th, 1991, and departed for New York City, where I would meet Sam and the other ministers going on this tour of Russia. Since I had never met Sam or any of the others, I would do so at JFK International Airport in New York. Four of the pastors were Assemblies of God ministers, as was I. There was also a Baptist minister from Texas, who would be my roommate on this trip—a very gracious, congenial, and pleasant brother. One clergyman from the state of Illinois was accompanied by his wife on the trip.

Besides Sam, the tour host, there was also a lady who was an agent for Finair (the airlines we traveled on) who would be with us for the entire tour. It so happened that I was the only one of these pastors who had any contacts for ministry in Russia, but they were all equally happy that one of us did have contacts and were thrilled that I had invited all of them to accompany me to the services I would be preaching in. I apologized to the group that they would have to listen to me preach as I reasoned, *How would I be able to share the opportunities for ministry with each one when they are so limited?*

"Oh, no!" they all said back to me. "God provided these contacts for *you*. We *want* you to do the preaching. We're just thrilled that we will get to be in these services while in Russia for none of us knew in advance that we would be afforded such an opportunity!"

Unlike other countries I had ministered in, only two services were arranged for me to minister in while in Russia. I would have hoped that there could be special services every night, but since there were only two, I cherished the opportunity that had been afforded me. It was the fulfillment of the thing God had spoken to my heart on that Friday evening, December 14, 1990, while watching my infant granddaughter, Alyssa, in my office.

On the evening of our first day in Moscow, a sister of the young Russian Christian gentleman I had met in Portland, Oregon, came to the beautiful, new hotel where we were staying. Former President George Bush, Sr., had stayed at this hotel when in Moscow. Accompanying this lady was one of the officials of the Pentecostal Churches of Russia, an assistant to her father, who was away in another city in a remote area of the country at the time.

"We are happy to meet you," the young lady said to me in broken English. "And we are happy that you have come to Moscow. We have arranged for you to preach in one of our Pentecostal Churches here tomorrow night," she told me. "Perhaps you can hire the bus and driver that is taking you on the tours of Moscow to take you and your group to the church," she suggested. "We will come here early tomorrow evening to meet you again and ride on the bus with you to the church. It is a fair distance from this hotel," she added.

I had introduced each member of our tour group to these people. And each of them gave to the young lady a gift they had brought from America (candy bars were some of the gifts I remember seeing—a real delicacy that these people were not accustomed to having very often, if ever.) We were able to contract for the tour bus and driver to take us to the church I would be preaching in that next night. Every member of the group volunteered to pitch in some dollars to pay for the bus and driver.

The excitement was high amongst all of us. For years most of us had prayed that the power of Communism over the Russian people would be broken and that there might once again be religious freedom in that country. Now we would both witness and be a part of the answer to those prayers. It was truly a rewarding experience for all of us!

The Russian people in attendance at the service sang several songs in their language and then our group sang a few songs in English before I was introduced as the one who would preach the Word of God. My message was, *"The God of Might and Miracles Lives Today."* The anointing of the Holy Spirit on the ministry of the Word of God was very real and precious. The Holy Spirit also anointed the young man who interpreted for me, thus we worked well together as a preaching team.

At the conclusion of the preaching, we gave an invitation to accept Jesus Christ as Lord and Savior. Several responded, with whom we prayed the "Sinner's Prayer of Repentance and Acceptance." When we began praying for the sick, almost *every* person in the audience came forward for the laying on of hands and prayer. At this point in the service I invited all my fellow pastors from America to get involved in praying for the people, which they were happy to do and were blessed of the Lord as they did so.

One young man I had prayed for (one of the first to come forward for prayer), had left the building, but later returned, just shortly before the service was dismissed. He told my interpreter that part of his foot had been cut off in an accident and that he had realized after we had prayed for him that this foot was beginning to grow out again. Since we did not ask him to remove his shoe so as to prove his testimony, I cannot say with any assurance that this kind of miracle of healing had actually been performed by the Lord. But the young man was very excited and felt that he was the recipient of a *divine, supernatural miracle.*

It was snowing lightly when the service was dismissed as we went out to board our bus to return to the hotel. However, the snow and much cooler temperature did not dampen any of our spirits. All hearts were warmed and filled with praise and gratitude to God that we had been privileged to worship with and minister to our brothers and sisters in Moscow, for whom we had prayed for many years during the long era of oppressive Communist rule and domination. We had experienced *answered prayer* in the form of renewed religious freedom in Moscow, Russia.

Although my primary purpose for being in Russia was to preach "His Gospel" there, our guided tours of the City of Moscow were very interesting experiences for me and the group. On Friday afternoon, November 15th, we checked out of our hotel in Moscow. We would be boarding a train about midnight for the 400 mile trip to St. Petersburg. However, before going to the train station we went to an old theatre building that had been turned into an evangelistic center to attend a service there.

It was conducted primarily by young Russian Christians and thus was much more upbeat and energetic than the Pentecostal church I had ministered in on Wednesday night, two days prior. Most of this service was in the Russian language, which none of we Americans could understand, but we were especially blessed by the orchestra that accompanied the singing. A young man who played a trombone in the orchestra especially blessed me. He was really in the spirit of things and played a very lively trombone.

The train ride from Moscow to St. Petersburg was not comfortable but was unique. The sleeper cars we rode in were very small and cramped. There were four bunk beds in each cubicle, one on each side of the aisle, with upper and lower bunks. I was a little disappointed that the train ride was at night; hence we were not able to see the countryside as we traveled along.

The train arrived in St. Petersburg in the early morning hours of Saturday, November 16th. A bus waited to take us to our hotel before the day's sightseeing tour began. After an early lunch at the hotel, we left for a tour of the Winter Palace of Paul the Great, one of the czars of bygone days. To me, this palace, which covered an area of some ten acres, was one of the most interesting sights we visited in Russia. The beauty and elegance of that palace was simply indescribable. To say that it was a luxurious structure would indeed be a vast understatement.

We visited other sights in St. Petersburg that afternoon before returning to our hotel for dinner and a night of rest.

Everyone in the group was up early on Sunday morning, excited about the service we would attend in another Pentecostal church in Russia. I was on the phone making contact with Tamara, the Russian lady who would serve as my interpreter for the upcoming service. I copied down the information she had given me for our bus driver, who would drive us to church.

After a good breakfast in the hotel dining room everyone returned to their respective rooms to get dressed for the church service we would be going to that morning. I spent time in prayer, beseeching the Lord for the anointing and blessing of the Holy Spirit. I would be preaching through an interpreter, an experience I had had on many past occasions throughout the world.

The church was full of eager worshippers and seekers when we arrived there. We sensed the anticipation of the audience, who knew that an American minister would be preaching that day. Tamara, my interpreter, met us as we got off of the bus outside the church.

"Which one of you is Rev. Ott?" she asked.

"That's me," I replied as I extended my right hand for a handshake. I quickly introduced the group of ministers who'd accompanied me, after which we were led into an annex-type building next to the church sanctuary where we would meet Pastor Demetrius. Christian greetings were exchanged before we entered the sanctuary through a side door on the right. Tamara and I were invited to sit on the platform with the pastor while my brethren were seated on the front row, requiring a few of the parishioners to relocate. It was *standing room only* in the sanctuary that morning.

The preliminary part of the service seemed to be quite traditional, a choir singing old gospel hymns accompanied by a pianist.

When the time came for me to be introduced, Pastor Demetrius gave a warm welcome speech to me and my fellow American ministers through Tamara, the interpreter. Coming to the pulpit, I, too, gave words of greeting to the audience and to all in attendance, after which I had each one of my fellow ministers stand and say a few words of greeting as they were introduced.

After all the introductions were completed, I again led our group in singing a gospel chorus in English for the congregation. A round of applause expressed their appreciation.

Finally the moment of truth had come! Once again I would read a scripture text, pray a prayer for the Holy Spirit's anointing upon the preaching of the Word as it was being declared. I then read Hebrews 13:8—"*Jesus Christ the same yesterday, today and forever.*" as my text for the sermon. I then began declaring the *unsearchable riches of Christ* to saints and sinners alike. I keenly sensed a special anointing of the Holy Spirit as I preached in English and Tamara interpreted God's message to the group into Russian.

A sense that this was the fulfillment of the *word of knowledge* God gave me in my office on Friday night, December 14, 1990, eleven months prior, seemed to almost overwhelm me at times while I was preaching. It certainly caused me to feel a deep sense of humility as I realized that this was not my doing, but rather an event carefully orchestrated by the Holy Spirit. Oh, how good and gracious the Lord is—especially when we realize that we have done nothing to be made worthy of such blessings!

At the conclusion of the sermon, as always, I extended an invitation for lost sinners to turn to Jesus for forgiveness and salvation. Several responded, with whom personal workers, joined by my ministerial colleagues from America, spent time in prayer. We also invited the sick and afflicted to come forward for believing prayer for the healing of their bodies. Many responded, and truly the power of the Lord was present to heal the sick!

Following the service my group and I were invited to go back into the annex building for an authentic Russian meal, which everyone enjoyed. That morning service in St. Petersburg was the second and final preaching engagement for me in the country of Russia. It might seem strange that after all the arrangements that preceded this ministry/familiarization tour to Russia, I would be afforded only two opportunities to minister, yet among my fondest and most treasured missionary memories, this experience ranks high. I say that because of the remarkable things that transpired in order to make this Russian trip a reality. These can only be explained in terms of the miraculous!

One Tract to Give

On our last day in Russia our guide took us to a restaurant near the St. Petersburg Airport, out of which we would fly to Helsinki, Finland. We ate lunch and had about an hour of free time before departing to the airport. My roommate, Steve, and I were the first two to return to the bus. Having boarded, we sat discussing how wonderful our experience had been in Russia. Suddenly Steve noticed a beautiful young Russian woman crossing the street and heading toward the restaurant.

"I think I will go and give this last Russian tract that I have to that young lady," Steve said. The tract was entitled, "Four Things God Wants You to Know." Just as Steve approached the young lady, our interpreter emerged from the restaurant, thus he enlisted her services to explain the tract to the young woman. I watched in amazement as that young lady stood still on the sidewalk and read the entire tract before moving one step away.

When Steve returned to the bus his face shined with delight as he explained to me that this young woman had been led to the Lord just four days previous by a born again Christian, therefore she was thrilled to get her hands on anything that might help her in her newfound joy of salvation!

Besides the two church services I had been privileged to minister in, my group and I had done considerable one-on-one ministry using New Testaments and various tracts, all in the Russian language. The minister from the State of Illinois, had brought along a considerable supply of these tools for evangelism. To my amazement, not once did I ever see anyone throw one of the tracts down. Only a couple of times did I see anyone decline to accept a piece of gospel literature when it was offered to them. On the streets, in the hotels, on the subways, and elsewhere people seemed eager to read the gospel literature we handed to them.

At the Tolstoy Mansion in Moscow, the guard that stood watch over the property was handed a New Testament by one of the ministers just as we were entering the grand mansion. When we emerged from the building nearly an hour later, he was still standing in the same spot, his black Labrador dog lying right beside him, as he eagerly read from the New Testament that had just been given to him. The spiritual hunger of the Russian people was one of the most significant observations of all the things I saw in that country.

Man's Thought versus God's

On our first night at the hotel in Helsinki, Finland, I found myself praising and worshipping the Lord in our bathroom after our evening meal.

"Oh, Lord," I said, "how I thank and praise You for the awesome experience of going to Russia and for the manifestation of Your supernatural power in the two services that I was privileged to ministered in; for the anointing of the Holy Spirit—not only upon me, but also upon my interpreters. You are an awesome, mighty God!

"But, Lord . . .," I continued, "You spoke to my heart just before I left from home on this trip that I would witness the manifestation of *Your Glory* while in the country of Russia. Was that young man who came back into the church in Moscow declaring that his foot that had been severed above his toes was growing back again . . . was that the manifestation of *Your Glory* that You promised I would witness?"

Just at that instant, in that still and small voice of the Spirit, I heard the Lord say to me: "No, *that* was not it. But you did indeed witness My glory being manifested *in the heart-hunger of the Russian people.* This is the work of My Spirit, not the work of man!"

That was exactly what I needed to hear, for upon receiving that Word from the Lord a sense of fulfillment and satisfaction swept over my spirit as tears of joy trickled down my cheeks. There was nothing that I had done to deserve such joy and blessing; I had again been the recipient of the wonderful grace of Jesus, my Lord and Master!

San Paolo and Buenos Aires

In the fall of 1996, while still serving as pastor of the Hazel Dell Assembly of God church in Vancouver, Washington, the Lord opened the door for me to return to the country of Brazil for missionary evangelism. It had been over thirty-nine years since my first ministry trip to Brazil, which was concentrated in three northeastern cities of that country—Fortaleza, Natal, and Recife. This time my ministry would be in three cities in the southern part of the vast country—Sao Paulo, Rio de Janeiro, and Santos. Unlike my ministry in Northeastern Brazil in 1957, in the three cities I would visit this time I would preach in churches rather than in tents, stadiums, and open-air meetings. I was especially blessed to have my brother Lloyd accompany me on this month of evangelistic ministry—not only in Brazil, but also in Argentina.

Two other significant blessings for this evangelism tour would be to have my dear Jewish friend and fellow minister, Robert Spectes, the President of Rock of Israel Ministers in Cincinnati, Ohio, join us for our ministry in Sao Paulo and Santos, as well as two wonderful interpreters, the Alancar brothers. Gedalchi and Geneton Alancar, native Brazilians who lived in Sao Paulo, were friends of Robert Specter and of his late father and founder of Rock of Israel Ministers, Rev. Hyman Specter.

After attempts to secure the services of veteran missionaries in Brazil to do the interpreting from English to the Portuguese language failed, Robert was able to arrange for Gedalchi and Geneton to serve in that capacity. These young, energetic, and admiring Brazilian brothers were among the very best interpreters I've ever had the privilege of serving with in this capacity.

Most of the churches I ministered in on this ministry tour were large—including one in Rio de Janeiro, which had over 12,000 members. Souls were saved in every service we ministered in. Most of my preaching engagements were in the City of Sao Paulo, the second largest city in the world. Not only did I minister in several churches in Sao Paulo, I also was a guest evangelist on a television program in that city. The TV station was owned and operated by Geneton Alancar. I preached, through an interpreter, on six different daily programs and my brother Lloyd, an automobile dealer in Cheney, Kansas, was interviewed on the seventh day. It was a very special experience for both of us.

The pastor of a large Pentecostal church in the costal city of Santos in Southern Brazil who was also a medical doctor—a surgeon whose specialty was restoring severed body parts (fingers, hands, toes, feet, arms, legs, etc.). Geneton Alancar was my interpreter for the service I spoke in there, which was videotaped in its entirety. Geneton later testified of being personally blessed by the sermon I preached in that service, entitled, *"When You Consider!"* It was based on Jesus' healing of the Roman Centurion's servant in Capernaum (Matthew 8:5–11).

My friend, Robert Specter, did not stay for the entire time we were in Rio de Janeiro but had to return to America. He was with us long enough, however, to enjoy a helicopter tour of the City of Rio, my first and only ever flight by a copter!

When the ministry meetings in Southern Brazil were concluded, Lloyd and I flew to Asuncion, Paraguay, where friends, twin brothers Adolf and Rudolf Loewen, who lived there, met our flight. Their brother, Erich, had emigrated to the United States many years ago and had lived in Vancouver, Washington for many years. He was a member of Hazel Dell Assembly of God, the church of which I was the pastor. Rudolf and his family had been in Vancouver to visit Erich and were guests in our home a year earlier.

The Loewens were of German decent and were Mennonites who had settled in an area of Paraguay known as Polendon (Erich's birthplace). Erich was to have flown to Paraguay to meet Lloyd and me in Asuncion, but had to cancel his trip at the last minute. He was to have arranged preaching engagements for me there, both among the Spanish-speaking sector and in the German community, and would have served as my interpreter for both languages. Since no ministry opportunities developed in Paraguay, Lloyd and I were shown around by the family, both in Asuncion and in the German community in and around Polendon, a small German village in the interior of Paraguay.

Adolf Loewen was a private pilot (as was my brother Lloyd). Adolf flew us in his small plane to his cattle ranch along the Paraguay River. He had a cabin on the banks of the mighty Paraguay River, where we spent a couple of nights. To say the least, it was a different, but interesting experience for both of us. We also visited in the homes of two of Erich's sisters in the capital city of Asuncion before flying on to Buenos Aires, Argentina.

A dear friend and Assemblies of God missionary in Argentina, Rev. David Ellis, met Lloyd and me at the airport in Buenos Aires upon our arrival there. He took us to an apartment in Buenos Aires for an overnight stay before we traveled by automobile to the Central Argentine City of Cordoba (a 400 mile drive), where I would be engaged in preaching ministry for a few days.

That evening in Buenos Aires was an opportunity to attend an ongoing revival in a large church. The main speaker that evening was a converted "Drug Lord," known and once feared by most everyone who knew him. The anointed service was a refreshing experience for all of us before driving to Cordoba the next day. The four-hundred-mile drive across the countryside in Argentina was especially interesting to Lloyd and me since we had grown up on a farm in South Central Kansas. Vast fields and pastures with herds of cattle reminded us of our upbringing on the farm.

We arrived in Cordoba, where Dave Ellis and his family lived, on a Saturday afternoon. His parents, Rev. and Mrs. Richard (Dick) Ellis also lived in Cordoba. They were veteran missionaries from Seattle, Washington, and were serving their final term before retiring. Lloyd and I were guests in the home of these gracious people during our stay in Cordoba.

The next day we were taken to the Pentecostal church in Cordoba where I would serve as guest speaker in the morning worship service. Dave Ellis served as my Spanish interpreter for that service. That evening I was spoke in a large Pentecostal church in Cordoba. The pastor, "Poncho," had come to Cordoba from the country of Chile. He informed me that he had visited friends in the City of Vancouver, Washington, where I made my home. His friends in Vancouver had served as missionaries in Chile when he was a child and thus a lasting friendship had been established.

Poncho's church had some 1,700 members and was packed out on the Sunday night that I ministered there with Dave Ellis again as my interpreter. A number of people responded to the invitation to accept Christ as Savior and many in attendance responded to the invitation to come forward for believing prayer for healing, subsequently testifying to receiving the Lord's healing power to remove their infirmities.

For the next four days, Monday through Thursday, I preached in the chapel services at the Assemblies of God Bible School in Cordoba, founded by Missionary Dick Ellis. Again Dave Ellis served as my interpreter for those speaking engagements.

On Friday morning, Lloyd and I bade farewell to both the Ellis families before flying back to Buenos Aires on Saturday. There we again lodged at the missionary apartment in Buenos Aires, shared mutually by several missionaries in the country of Argentina.

Early on Saturday morning we boarded a United Airlines 747 jetliner for the trip from Buenos Aires to Miami, Florida, and then on to Wichita, Kansas, where Lloyd lived at the time. (He has since moved to the City of Derby, Kansas, south of Wichita).

I couldn't end the story of this latter venture to South America without mentioning the fact that while ministering in churches there, I again saw "*that face*" that has spurred me on again and again to proclaim the "Unsearchable Riches of Christ" to various people groups around the world. As we were leaving the hotel in Sao Paulo, to go to a service where I would be preaching one night, a small boy peeked around the left rear corner of the minivan that was there to pick us up. As I turned to look at him, all of a sudden, I saw "*that face*" that I had seen so many times in so many places of the world. He only appeared for a moment and then was gone. As always when I would see "that face," it was confirmation of the special calling I had received from the Lord in the beginning days of my ministry.

Although I did not minister in the country of Paraguay, I also saw "*that face*" there, though only for a fleeting moment. It happened while Lloyd and I walked and mingled among the people on the street, wandering in stores, and moving along the sidewalk. This was also the case in Argentina. I saw "*that face*" that I will never forget on several occasions while ministering in the large church pastored by Poncho in Cordoba.

Upon returning to Wichita, Kansas, I would fly back home to Vancouver, Washington, to again be reunited with my family and also to pick up the reigns of the church. How very grateful to God I was that my church would allow me the freedom to go abroad on many occasions, especially those occasions during which time I would be preaching the gospel to "other sheep" of the Lord's fold in far away places.

Hence, while serving as senior pastor of the Hazel Dell Assembly of God Church in Vancouver for over twenty-one years, I traveled to the Holy Land, Northern Africa (Egypt), and Europe on five different occasions; to Japan and Korea once, to Russia and

Finland once, and then once each to Brazil, Paraguay, and Argentina. Some of my most memorable experiences and fondest memories occurred during that twenty-one year span.

....

Chapter 15

THROUGH THE VEIL: ENROUTE TO VICTORY

D uring my tenure as pastor of the Hazel Dell Assembly of God Church in Vancouver, Washington, I lost my Dad, my beloved brother Louie, and then my dear sister Janice, who had traveled with me in revival crusades in the summer of 1954. Sadly, Janice died of cancer at the age of sixty-two.

I had just returned from a funeral service for my youth pastor's sister held in Tacoma, Washington, on Monday, October 26, 1998, when Bobbie met me at the door.

"Gail," she said, with a hush in her voice, "your brother Lloyd called while you were gone to say that your sister Janice passed away today." And although it did not come as a surprise, it was a shock to learn that she was gone. Her funeral service was set for Monday, November 2nd.

Bobbie and I began making plans to fly back to Wichita to attend her funeral service. Our oldest grandchild, Jaynece Gail Nevin, then age twenty, begged us to let her go with us to Janice's memorial service. She wanted to see my brother Gary's youngest daughter, Valerie Ott, who also lived in Wichita. We finally convinced Jaynece that it was not really in her best interest to go with us to Kansas. However, had we known what lay ahead, we would have sacrificed anything we owned to make it possible for her to accompany us to Wichita on that occasion . . .

My Greatest Sorrow

Nothing that had ever happened in my life had prepared me for what would happen just seven weeks later. During my tenure as pastor of the Hazel Dell Assembly of God Church several tragedies had happened. Aimee McGraw and her twelve-year-old daughter, former members of my church, burned to death in a house fire. I preached their memorial service. Susan (Collier) Hosler, granddaughter of one of the ladies of our church, was ruthlessly murdered (stabbed to death and her body dumped behind a farm building. It was not discovered for many weeks because a heavy snow had fallen and covered it.) I had officiated for the wedding of Susan and her husband Chip Hosler a few years earlier.

Other senseless tragedies tore at our minds. Rev. and Mrs. Michael Alvarado, retired from the ministry and now members of my church, got up early one morning to leave for Southern California. Mary Alvarado knocked on the bedroom door of their son, Michael Jr., to bid him goodbye. When he didn't respond, she slowly opened his bedroom door. The covers were pulled up over his head. When Mary pulled the covers back, to her utter shock and disbelief, there lay the motionless body of their beloved son with the barrel of a .22-caliber rifle in his mouth and the index finger of one hand still on the trigger. He had committed suicide.

Brother Alvarado called me shortly after discovering Michael's lifeless body in his bed. By the time I arrived at their home his body had been taken to the morgue for an investigative autopsy. Needless to say, there was unbelievable shock, pain, and heartbreak etched on the faces of these dear, loving parents. I prayed with them for grace, comfort, and most of all, *faith* to accept that which they could not possibly understand. Again it fell my lot to preach the funeral service for one more person who had died a tragic death.

Still, none of these experiences prepared me for what *my family and I* would experience on Friday morning, December 18, 1998. Our granddaughter, Jaynece, a sweet, loving, and beautiful young woman had moved in with Bobbie and me just three weeks earlier. She was having a struggle trying to get along on her own in a rented house with another lady, so Bobbie and I made a suggestion.

"Jaynece, why don't you move back in with us? You wouldn't have to pay us anything for room and board, and you can get on your feet a little financially, while you decide what you want to do next." Our granddaughter, her mother, and brother, Doug, had moved in with us for a while after her parents' divorce and had moved out after Sally remarried the previous month of June.

At the time Sally's new husband, a Ph.D.-level physicist, had a job change coming up that would require a family move to Bethlehem, Pennsylvania. All of this was weighing heavily on Jaynece. She had lived in Vancouver since she was sixteen-months-old. Her extended family all lived in this area, as well as her many friends from elementary, middle, and high school. She'd graduated from Prairie High School on June 7, 1996. She also had many close friends in our church, especially in the youth group. Additionally, she was struggling to maintain some kind of relationship with her father, Jay Nevin, and his new wife, Gloria.

Undoubtedly the pressure of all of the above-mentioned factors weighed heavily upon her. She wanted to be with her mother, but was very unsure about making the move to Pennsylvania. All of this seemed to have a direct affect upon Jaynece because she had started having seizures, an earlier life-problem, more frequently and severely.

On Thursday evening, December 10th, while Bobbie and I were preparing to go out for dinner at a nice restaurant to celebrate our forty-fourth Wedding Anniversary, I heard Jaynece fall in the downstairs bathroom. I literally leaped from landing to landing, covering fifteen steps in three leaps, then rushed to the bathroom—finding her crumpled on the floor next to the vanity cabinet. It was at that moment that I screamed out loud to Satan, saying, "Devil of hell, you cannot have my granddaughter! Get your filthy hands off of her! I rebuke you devil in the name of Jesus Christ my Lord!"

While I was rebuking the devil over Jaynece's crumpled form, she opened her eyes and just stared at me for a few seconds. As I helped her to her feet, she began crying with pain. When the seizure hit her, she fell to the floor just as if a bullet had been shot through her brain. This had been the case on many occasions in the weeks preceding this incident.

As she had crumpled to the floor once more in a heap, the middle finger of her right hand struck the solid oak front of a drawer on the vanity cabinet, literally tearing the fingernail completely off. There remains, to this day, a notch in that oak drawer front caused by her fingernail catching on it as she went down.

Typically after one of these grand mal seizures, Jaynece would be back to normal again in about thirty minutes or so, though she was usually somewhat disoriented immediately after regaining consciousness. We called our daughter Sally, who came as quickly as she could to be with Jaynece while we went out to eat. Needless to say, this ordeal cast a "wet blanket" upon our celebration.

The worst was yet to come. Jaynece and her relatively new boyfriend, Nathan, had gone with Bobbie and me on Thursday night, December 17th, to the Lloyd Center Shopping Mall in Portland, Oregon. We all had a nice time that evening, doing some Christmas shopping. One of the items we were never able to find was an accompaniment music tape for a song entitled, "Who Would Have Thought?" which Jaynece wanted to sing at our church's Annual Christmas program on Sunday morning, December 20th.

As we were returning home from the mall that evening, for some reason I looked in the rear-view mirror of our minivan and saw our precious granddaughter sitting in one of the middle seats. I was angry at the devil, thinking *unless she is healed by the power of the Lord or helped with this disease by medical science, what does she have to look forward to in life?*

After we arrived home that evening, Jaynece and Nathan wanted to stay up for a while to watch a movie on television. The TV was in our family room on the upstairs level our house. A guest bed-room was next to the family room, in which I had been sleeping some of the time after treatment for prostate cancer a few months earlier. As I was going to bed I spoke to the kids.

"Now don't you two stay up too late. Remember, you have to get up early in the morning to go to work, Jaynece." She had been working for the Nordstrom Department Store in the Vancouver Mall for a few weeks and seemed to really like her job. So, after telling them goodnight, I went to bed. Nathan went home after the movie was over and Jaynece went to bed in her room downstairs.

At 6:20 A.M. the next morning (Friday, December 18th) I got up, went downstairs, knocked on Jaynece's door, and then slowly opened it.

"Jaynece, honey," I said, "you'd better be getting up and ready for work. Your ride will be here pretty soon."

"Yes, I know, Grandpa," she responded. "I'll be up in a few minutes." With that, I went back upstairs and got back into bed. By this time, Bobbie had gotten up and was upstairs preparing to go to work at Harney Elementary School, where she had worked for several years as a staff assistant. It was the last day of school before the Christmas break, thus a Christmas party was to be a part of the day's activities at her school.

In a few minutes Bobbie came to the bedroom where I was and spoke worriedly.

"Gail, maybe you should go downstairs and check on Jaynece. The water has been running for quite a while." By that time I was a little groggy, half asleep again.

"Don't worry. I'll hear her if she drops (i.e., has a seizure)." So I waited a minute or two. Then, suddenly, it dawned on me: *Maybe she's already had a seizure!* I jumped out of bed and quickly bounded down the stairs and rushed to the bathroom door.

"Jaynece, are you OK?" I asked.

No answer came, so I decided I'd better open the door and go in to see if she was OK. The door was locked, so I rushed to find a screwdriver to unlock the bathroom door. To my utter horror and dismay, there was Jaynece, slumped over the edge of the bathtub with her head submerged in eight inches or more of water. She had on her pajama bottoms and a bra.

At that moment I panicked. As I pulled her limp body out of the tub and dragged her out into the hallway I screamed to Bobbie.

"Call 9-1-1 immediately! I'm afraid Jaynece has drowned!" Bobbie quickly called 9-1-1 and then called our daughter Sally (Jaynece's mother), who also worked in the Special Education program at one of our public schools here in Vancouver. She, too, was preparing to go for the last day of school before the Christmas break.

The medics arrived at our house quickly with an ambulance. After attempting to revive Jaynece several times, they took her limp body out of the house on a stretcher and placed her in the ambulance. Sally had arrived at our house just in time to ride in the ambulance to the hospital, where Jaynece was taken to the Emergency Room. The last words the medic said to me were, *"Don't get your hopes up."*

As the ambulance raced away to the hospital, Bobbie and I quickly made several phone calls. I was to meet fellow pastors for a Morning Prayer Meeting at eight o'clock, thus I called one of them, alerting him to our crisis and urging them to pray. Calvin, Sally's husband of five months, drove Bobbie to the hospital and I came in our minivan shortly afterwards.

There are no words to describe the thoughts that raced through my mind as I sped along State highway 14 headed for Southwest Washington Medical Center. *How could this be? Has this really happened, or am I in a daze?* But it *had* happened.

When I walked into the Emergency Room where Jaynece's body lay, Sally came over to me.

"Dad, she's gone," she said. That was when I literally fell apart and started weeping uncontrollably. I dearly loved all five of our grandchildren—Sally's two and Andy's three (at that time—*four* now as of April 23, 2002). Yet for some reason I had an extra special love in my heart for our first-born grandchild, Jaynece. I would gladly have given my life for her that morning, had that been possible, and now she was gone—exactly one month before her twenty-first birthday!

Soon three of my fellow pastors were at the hospital Emergency Room praying for me and my family, trying to console us in that, our saddest moment. One of my dear pastor friends, Rev. Bo Melin, had lost his wife and the mother of his four children in the fall of 1996, a little over two years earlier. I had tried to be a comfort to him in his darkest hour of sorrow. Now, here he was by my side, standing with me in prayer, offering to help in any way that he might be able to.

"Just hold us up in prayer," I told him, along with the other two pastors that had come to the hospital. A fourth pastor friend called and talked to me there at the hospital, assuring me of his earnest prayers.

Jaynece's dad, Jay, also came to the hospital that morning, just one week shy of seven years since he had come to the same hospital after she had had the first of many grand mal seizures on Christmas Morning, 1991. My heart went out to him also on that tragic Friday morning as we all were grasping for some kind of meaning to this tragedy.

Needless to say it was a sad day for me and my family—without question, the saddest day of my entire lifetime.

It wouldn't get any easier in the days to come as we were forced to deal with issues we had not given any prior thought to—like planning a memorial service, picking out a casket, deciding on a burial site, and many other painful decisions that had to be made. There were also many relatives and friends to call both near and far.

Friends Minister to Us

The day for Jaynece's memorial service was set for Wednesday, December 23rd at our home church, Hazel Dell Assembly. Her body would be laid to rest in a temporary crypt at the Northwood Park Cemetery near Sally's home to the north of

Vancouver. A new mausoleum was on the drawing board to be built in the near future, thus the temporary crypt. The new mausoleum was eventually built on the cemetery grounds, and Jaynece's casket moved into it on September 28, 2000.

Several ministers were asked to take part in the memorial service, including former youth pastors and friends as well as Bobbie's two brother-in-laws, Rev. Don Duncan and Rev. Art Morlin.

The youth of our church, whom Jaynece dearly loved, sang Jaynece's favorite song, "Shout to the Lord." Bobbie's niece and nephew, Susan Clark and Rev. Doug Duncan, sang the song, "If You Could See Me Now!" and then Susan Clark's daughter, Allison, sang "Amazing Grace." We had obtained a tape recording of the song, "Who Would Have Thought?" (sung by the author of the song, David Jeremiah). It was played as a prelude to the service. We also found a tape recording of the song, "I Am a Promise," which Jaynece had sung in church and in pageants on numerous occasions when she was just a little girl. It was played as people walked past the open casket saying their final good-byes to a precious young lady who would soon be laid to rest.

That Wednesday, December 23, 1998, was the coldest day of the entire winter of 1998–1999. It had snowed in the early morning hours then wind blew, making it severely cold. The church was totally packed out when the service began. There was standing room only even though the adjacent Fireside Room had been opened to accommodate the overflow crowd.

At my request, Rev. Don Duncan, who had preached the funeral sermon, led the congregation in singing an old gospel song entitled "I'll Meet You in the Morning" just before the casket was opened for viewing. Fighting back tears, I proudly stood at the head of Jaynece's casket as perhaps four hundred people passed by to view her body.

After the committal service at the cemetery, conducted by yet another youth pastor, most of the people who had gathered at the crypt where her casket was placed returned to the church, where the gracious ladies of the church had prepared a lovely sit-down dinner. About one hundred were served, mostly family and close friends. My brothers Lloyd and Gary had come from Wichita for the funeral. Brother Dwane and his son, Mike, had driven down from Seattle. My brother Lester, who lived in Gainesville, Texas, was unable to make it as was the case with my three remaining sisters, Pauline, Beulah ("Boots"), and Vera Jane.

After the funeral service was concluded and everyone had gone back home (Christmas was just two days away), the pain of sorrow and sense of loss lingered. It didn't seem to get any easier as time went on. I was unable to control my weeping in the days, weeks, and months that followed. I wept for so many consecutive days until I wondered if there would ever be a day, for the rest of my life, that I would make it through without crying. But, it did happen. After five-hundred-and-fifty-five consecutive days in which I wept, I finally made it through a day without shedding tears. However, the ache didn't go away. And, now, five years later, I still struggle to fight back tears of sorrow if I try to talk to someone about my precious granddaughter's death.

It has also been very hard for my wife, Bobbie, and especially for our daughter, Sally, to deal with the stark reality of Jaynece's death. Only recently, in a phone conversation with Sally, she got quiet and then began to sob.

"It doesn't seem to get any easier after all this time, does it, Dad?" to which I was compelled to answer, through sobs, "No, Sally, it really doesn't. But . . .," I went on to say, "we must look ahead now instead of looking back so much. There is hope ahead, for I expect to see our precious Jaynece again one glad day in that Heavenly Home where there will be no more death, heartache, tears, or pain—in the Glory World, where we will live forever and forever with our Wonderful Lord!"

Christ's Victory, Even in Death

Just a few more observations concerning the death of Jaynece. Upon arriving back at our home, after leaving the hospital on that fateful Friday morning of December 18, 1998, I went back into the bathroom where Jaynece had drowned in the bathtub while attempting to wash her hair earlier that morning. Standing there in deafening silence, trying to find some clue as to the awful event of that morning, I suddenly heard the devil mocking me for the words of rebuke I had shouted at him eight days earlier when I'd said, "Devil, you cannot have my granddaughter!"

There I stood as I heard Satan mocking me.

"Who says I can't have your granddaughter? I've got her now!" Then, at that same instant, I heard another voice, One I had heard on a number of occasions in the past. It was that still, small, sweet voice of the Holy Spirit saying to me, "Oh no, the devil doesn't have Jaynece. I have her now!" And, of course, this ministered comfort to my aching heart at that moment in time.

A few days after we laid Jaynece to rest, I found myself crying out to the Lord in agony of soul, saying, "Lord, I don't understand. Is this my reward for serving you all these years?" I was ashamed later as I realized that I had uttered those words in unbelief. But, my wonderful Lord again answered my cry tenderly, speaking His words into my spirit.

"I don't ask you to understand, my son; only to *trust Me*. No, this is not your reward for serving Me. Eternal life will be your reward when you come to the end of your journey." This again ministered volumes of comfort to my troubled, aching heart.

My church was very kind, understanding, and gracious, giving me a month off during the darkest days of our grief and sorrow. Bobbie was also given "as much time as needed" off from her job at Harney Elementary School.

Another encouragement came one Sunday morning in August, 1999, at a church in Clearwater, Florida, where I had been invited to preach in the worship service by a dear friend, Pastor Garnet Blakely. Pastor Blakely and his family were singing one of Dottie Rambo's songs entitled, "I've Never Been this Homesick Before!" While they were singing that song, I suddenly had a very brief vision in which I saw Jaynece, as she come running up to me, throwing her arms around my neck, and saying, *"Grandpa, what took* you so long?" That was it—the vision ended, but the comfort of that moment has not ceased to bring hope and joy to my heart whenever I call it to remembrance.

On a final note concerning our loss, Jaynece's brother, Doug Nevin, was on a tour of Europe at the time of his sister's death. Our son, Andy, knowing that Doug frequently checked the Worldwide Web on computers throughout Europe, put out a distress message for him to call home immediately. When Doug found Andy's e-mail note on the Internet, he said, "I turned to my friend Travis and said, 'I'll bet that my sister Jaynece is either in the hospital or else has died. I'd better call home as soon as I can get to a phone.'" Call home he did, and, indeed, heard the worst possible news.

"Your sister had a seizure and drowned in the bathtub this morning," came the shocking communication.

"My heart began to pound and continued for several hours," Doug said as he quickly made his way to the London Heathborough Airport for the flight home. On this end, a date for the memorial service could not be set until we knew that Doug could be here to attend it. All agreed, there was no way to hold that service without him there.

The airline agents were very understanding and Doug was able to get a flight out of London, arriving home the evening of December 20th at the Portland International Airport. The first stop, heading to our house from the airport, was the funeral home where Jaynece's body was lying in state in a viewing room. That was an extremely difficult, traumatic moment for a nineteen-year-old young man who had to deal with the untimely death of his only sibling—Jaynece, his beloved sister.

To sum up this chapter (for I suppose volumes more could be written about this dearly beloved, precious granddaughter whom I loved with all of my heart), her passing from this life has indeed made me more homesick for Heaven than I've ever been before. I am truly thankful to my Wonderful Lord, however, for allowing us to have her to love and to cherish for twenty years and eleven months, for she truly "lit up our lives" during her brief lifespan.

I "Retire," then Get Busy!

After serving as senior pastor of the Hazel Dell Assembly of God Church in Vancouver, Washington for over twenty one years, I began to sense that it was time for me to step down. Since I wanted to be sure that to retire from the pastorate was the will of God for my life and not just my own will, I sought the Lord diligently through prayer that He would confirm my decision by giving me a peace concerning the matter.

It was while attending the Annual District Convention of the Assemblies of God, Northwest District, in Everett, Washington, from April 25–28, 2000, that I finally felt a peace in my heart about retiring. Returning to Vancouver from this convention, I called a special meeting of the church board for Saturday evening, April 29th, to inform the board members of my decision to retire. The meeting was held in my office and was somewhat of an emotional affair. I gave my letter of resignation to the Secretary/Treasurer of the Board, Mrs. LaVone Hallo, to read to the other five members.

As LaVone began reading my letter she paused momentarily as she "choked up," starting to sob. Regaining her composure, she continued reading the balance of the letter. A moment of silence followed before I shared more deeply with the members of our board that it had not been an easy decision for me to make and that only after *praying through* on the matter had I finally made it. Of course I had discussed this decision with my wife, Bobbie, before notifying the church board of same.

A somber mood pervaded the congregation during the morning worship service on Sunday, April 30th, when my letter of resignation was read from the pulpit. Our final service as senior pastors of the church would be Sunday morning, June 25th. It would be the *"end of an era"* for that church body. They would now be dealing with a situation that had been unnecessary for over twenty-one years—that of securing a successor for the pastorate of that parish.

The gracious people of the church began planning a retirement celebration to honor Bobbie and me for our twenty-one years of service. It would be held on a Sunday afternoon following the morning worship service. Friends and relatives from far and wide were invited to attend this event, many of whom came. My brother Lloyd and his grandson, Philip Heasley, from Derby, Kansas, came the farthest distance to be there for the festivities of that very special day.

Many greeting cards, cash gifts, and spoken words of appreciation were expressed by people whose lives we had touched in some way during our tenure as pastors. A very generous love offering was also given to us as a farewell gift from the church, which enabled us to fly to Central Florida for a brief period of rest and relaxation, as well as reflection upon both the past and the future.

It was by mutual agreement that we decided we would continue to live in our home here in Vancouver. I offered to be of help in any way I could in the selection process for the new pastor.

Bobbie and I will always be grateful to the people whom we served as pastors during our twenty-one years and four months at the Hazel Dell Assembly of God Church; for their cooperation, generosity, and understanding during our times of grief.

In 1983, our fourth year as pastors there, the church board decided to sell the church-owned parsonage and in turn, lend the equity from the sale to Bobbie and me for the purpose of buying or building a home of our own. Of course, that proposal was brought before the church membership for approval before any action was taken. The parsonage sold in April of 1983, after which Bobbie and I moved into a rented house while deciding what course of action we would take. After deliberating for a short while, we decided to look for a suitable vacant lot on which to build a new home.

Finding a corner lot in a nice area of the City of Vancouver, another wonderful, pleasant surprise was in store for us. My sister "Boots," a career schoolteacher, had sold her home in Santa Anna, California, for a considerable profit. She was moving to Colorado Springs, Colorado, to continue and complete her career there. Thus, Boots gave Bobbie and me a gift of $10,000 to help with the building of our new house. What an awesome blessing! In addition to the interest-free loan from the church in the amount of $50,000 and this gift from my sister, yet another financial "shot-in-the-arm" was to come from the sale of my Dad's house in Cheney, Kansas.

Each of my brothers and sisters elected to give me their share of $1,000 from the sale of that house, hence we had another $8,000 to apply to the building of our new home. Within a period of ten months I had drawn the blueprints for and built the home we still live in—a 2,750-square-foot, two-story house. Although not completely finished, we moved into this house near the end of January, 1984. Looking back, I don't know how I accomplished all of this while pastoring a church at the same time, especially since I was past fifty years of age!

Ten years after selling the church parsonage and subsequently lending us the $50,000 equity, the church body had yet another awesome surprise blessing for us. We had just returned from attending the National Convention of the Assemblies of God in Minneapolis, Minnesota, in mid-August, 1993. A very special Sunday morning service had been planned to welcome us back home in which the Chairman of the church board announced that the membership of the church had decided to "forgive us" the debt of $50,000 lent to us for the purpose of building our own home!

We were overwhelmed by the thoughtfulness and generosity of the gracious congregation of our church! The original agreement concerning the $50,000 loan was that upon our resignation as pastors we would have two years to repay it, after which 8% interest would be added to the balance until paid.

In addition to the kindness and generosity of the congregation in canceling this large loan, consideration was taken into account that during those years I had been able to negotiate the purchase of 14.88 acres of prime property for the church. Compared to the value of property in general, the purchase price of $200,000 for this parcel was a "real estate steal." Of course, the purpose for purchasing that property was in hopes of someday relocating and building a new church facility there. That dream never materialized due to a myriad of technical difficulties. Eventually, two-plus acres of the property were sold for $480,000, with the church still owning some twelve acres of it.

At the time of my retirement, God had enabled us to leave the church entirely debt-free, with over one-and-a-half million dollars of assets, plus over $30,000 in a savings account. But, regardless of the above, it was a *tremendous* act of kindness and generosity on the part of Hazel Dell Assembly of God church body to bestow such an awesome blessing upon us. We will be forever grateful to the people of that church and especially to our Wonderful Lord for such a great blessing which, although undeserved, came to us just the same.

Many memories—most of which are happy ones, mingled with a few sad and bitter ones—are etched in our minds and hearts from our years of serving that church in the capacity of senior pastors.

Faith with a Mission—and "Working Clothes" on

Although retirement from the "pastoral" phase of my ministry was concluding after some thirty-five years, I would not be retiring from the ministry as such. Since leaving the church, the Lord has led in a variety of ways and has opened many doors of ministry for me.

In addition to speaking engagements (often "fill-ins" for pastors who are away from their pulpits), since retiring I have traveled abroad again—*twice*. Shortly after I retired from pastoring, my brother Lloyd called me to ask if I would be interested in going to China on a ministry trip.

"Oh, yes!" I told him. "I'd love to be able to do that."

"Well," he said to me, "a group of men from my church (in Wichita, Kansas) are going to Wuhan, China, in October (2000) to do repair work on a church building there. It will be a 'work' ministry trip, and if you will go with us I'll 'pick up the tab' for you, OK?"

"Sign me up," I replied. "I'm going!" *And go I did!* We flew into Beijing and, after an overnight stay there, flew on to the City of Wuhan, population 7,300,000.

This would be an entirely new experience for me. Whereas I had always gone abroad to *preach* in evangelism crusades in the past, this time I would be one of twelve men from the U.S.A. who would install plywood over the rough, old wood floor in this large church building. We also did repair work on the balcony, platform, and some doors. After installing the plywood floor covering (with screws brought from Wichita for this purpose), we painted the entire area. By Sunday, the church was readied for a glorious morning worship service.

Lloyd's pastor, Rev. Jonathan Hollis (pastor of Colonial Heights Assembly of God in Wichita), preached in that service, with missionary Mike Baldree interpreting his English words into Chinese. Approximately four hundred Chinese people attended that service, at the conclusion of which several responded to the invitation to accept Christ as Savior. Many also came forward to be prayed over for healing. All of us joined in for the prayer service, and many testified to *instantaneous* healings. Others received the Baptism of the Holy Spirit, as well.

Following the service, we all went to eat at a restaurant that catered to foreigners, especially Americans. We then went to an area of Wuhan where we saw a sight I had never seen before nor since in my life. Probably one million people or more were milling in a huge area of the main business district of the city. It was the single-greatest mass of human beings I had ever seen in one place at one time.

After completing the repair work on the church building in Wuhan we flew back to Beijing, where we spent a couple of days sightseeing before flying back to the U.S. Among the points of interest in and around Beijing were Tienamen Square, The Forbidden City, and The Great Wall of China.

I was very thankful to my brother Lloyd for making this adventure possible to me and to the Lord for allowing me the opportunity of going. Another great blessing was the beautiful hotel we stayed in while in Wuhan: the Shangri-La. It is immensely elegant; one where heads of state would no doubt stay when in Wuhan.

Nova Scotia and 9/11

While preaching at an indoor camp meeting in Clearwater, Florida in the spring of 2001, a Christian gentleman from Nova Scotia, Canada, was in attendance, along with his wife. During one of the services in which I was preaching, the Lord spoke to this brother, Gary Dunham, a businessman from Lower Sackville, about a church out in a rural area of Nova Scotia. His uncle had built this church and pastored there until the time of his death. Eventually this "Church in the Pines" was closed, the doors and windows boarded over. It had remained unopened for twelve years.

In the camp meeting service on that particular evening, the Lord spoke to Gary's heart about reopening that church. He came forward during the altar service requesting that I pray with him about this. We joined hands and prayed in agreement for divine guidance with reference to this burden that the Lord had placed on Gary's heart. Following the concluding service of the camp meeting, Gary asked me if I would consider coming to Nova Scotia to preach in that church after he opened it again.

"I'd be happy to do that," I said. "Just let me know when you want me to come." Sure enough, Gary went back to Nova Scotia and began the process of reopening that little country Pentecostal church. During the summer of that year I received a phone call from Brother Dunham.

"How about coming to preach at the 'Church in the Pines' this September?"

"I've just been waiting for a call from you," I told him. "When do you want me to come?" We agreed that I would begin preaching in Nova Scotia on Sunday, September 9, 2001.

With my airfare and reservations made, I was set to leave from Portland International Airport at 5 A.M. on Monday, September 7th.

However, on the evening of September 6th, while we were stopped at a traffic signal on a controlled-access highway in Vancouver, a young woman hit our car from behind at a considerably high speed. She had upset an open can of Coke and was attempting to upright it; thus she'd failed to notice that traffic ahead of her was at a standstill. The impact was terrific, causing several thousand dollars of damage to our car and also sending Bobbie to the hospital by ambulance, a precautionary measure in the event that her neck might be broken. After the ambulance left for the hospital, I drove the car on home, then got into another vehicle and drove to the hospital, praying for Bobbie all the while.

By the time I arrived at the Emergency Room of the hospital, Bobbie was being X-rayed. Thankfully, she had no broken bones, but she was somewhat bruised. Worst of all was the "whiplash" to our necks from the tremendous force of the external vehicle's impact, from which we both still suffer at times. I also was X-rayed to check for cracked and/ or broken bones, and, again, thankfully had none.

After finally arriving back home we discussed my trip to Halifax, Nova Scotia, and both agreed that I should go ahead and make the trip. Hence I bade farewell to Bobbie and flew out on the morning of September 7. It was necessary to change planes and airlines at Boston's Logan Airport that afternoon.

Upon arriving at the Halifax International Airport, I was met by Gary Dunham and his wife, Carolyn, who drove me to their home in Lower Sackville, where I would be lodging for the next ten days.

Early on Sunday morning, September 9, the Dunhams drove me to the rural area where the Church of the Pines was located, probably seventy miles from their home. The people at this newly restored country church seemed to be very eager and excited about the special services I would be preaching in and were very responsive to the preaching of God's Word. Several backsliders came for prayer to be restored spiritually and others came for healing. As I had witnessed so many times before and in so many different areas of the world, once again the power of God was present to heal the sick. The God of Miracles would again show Himself to be "alive and well" and a "rewarder of those who diligently seek Him!"

It was "dinner on the grounds" following the morning service, after which I was invited to the home of one of the parishioners for a time of rest and relaxation before returning to the church for the evening service. The following Tuesday morning, September 11th, after having breakfast with the Dunhams, I went out to a chapel that Brother Dunham had had built on one end of his place of business, which was adjacent to their home. It was a really nice room where one could pray and study, thus I was taking advantage of the opportunity.

About 9:50 A.M., Brother Dunham came hurriedly to the chapel where I was praying and called to me.

"Come quickly to the house, Brother Ott. An airliner has just crashed into one of the World Trade Center Towers in New York City and it is on fire and burning!" Halifax and vicinity are in the Atlantic Time zone, hence one hour ahead of the Eastern Time Zone. We hurried to the Dunham's house where I quickly became "sick inside" at what I was witnessing on live television.

I had seen those magnificent towers on many occasions, but this time the South Tower had black smoke billowing out of it all around its top floors. While watching in disbelief at what I was viewing on live television, at about 10:05 local time I saw *another* airplane approaching the towers. In horror, we watched as that plane crashed into the North Tower, somewhat lower than the first plane that had crashed into the South Tower. Upon impact the aircraft burst into a massive ball of fire.

At that point in time, it had become clearly evident that a horrific terrorist attack had been launched against my beloved nation, the United States of America. Then came the awful news that yet another hijacked airplane had crashed into the Pentagon in Arlington, Virginia, at about 10:40 A.M. Atlantic Time. The shock and gravity of these unthinkable atrocities being committed against innocent fellow Americans caused me to cry out in anguish of soul to God.

"What is happening to my beloved country, Lord?" I began to breathe out prayers of protection for President George W. Bush and for our nation's capital.

While still watching in shock and disbelief at what was going on in my beloved country, yet another report came on the news that a *fourth* airliner had crashed in a field near Shanksville, Pennsylvania, at about 11:05 A.M., Halifax time. It soon became evident that this, yet another intentional attack, had been foiled by some of the brave passengers onboard that flight. It was soon learned that *this* plane's target was to have been the White House in our nation's capitol.

For the rest of that day and into Wednesday, September 12th, many airliners bound for New York City were diverted to Halifax. A total of sixty-six airliners were grounded at that airport and all air traffic to and from Halifax had come to a halt. As a result of these diverted airplanes, every hotel, sports arena, and public building soon filled to capacity. Hundreds of homes were also opened up to stranded travelers, some from abroad and others returning home to America from Europe, Africa, and the Middle East.

Brother Dunham and I, along with many local pastors, went to some of the sites where stranded travelers were put up offering to pray and counsel with frightened and troubled passengers. Many expressed gratitude for our concern.

Scarcely would I ever have expected the events of 9/11, 2001 to take place—especially while I was in relatively close proximity to the atrocities that took place in New York City on that day of infamy!

After the special services were concluded at The Church in the Pines, airlines were flying again and thus I took flight for home. However, my return was by way of Montreal and Vancouver, British Columbia, Canada, as no flights were being allowed into the U.S. yet. Once in Vancouver, B.C., I had to take a bus from Canada to the Seattle International Airport for my flight on to Portland, Oregon.

I was thankful to be home again, but along with most everyone else was still trying to adjust to the reality of the awful events that had happened while I was away. I was also thankful to the Lord for the privilege of going to Nova Scotia, Canada, to preach the unsearchable riches of Christ at "The Church in the Pines" in a rural area of that Province.

After being home from Northeastern Canada for just over two weeks, I would fly away once again, this time to the City of Santa Cruz, Bolivia, in South America. It would be my *third* missionary venture to South America. This time would be different, however, as it was another "work/ministry" excursion.

Bricklaying in Bolivia

Once again my brother Lloyd challenged me to go on a mission abroad, this time to build a church in Santa Cruz, Bolivia. I was "neither a bricklayer nor the son of a bricklayer," but in just five days of hard work a crew of seventeen men (sixteen from Lloyd's church in Wichita and myself) completely built and dedicated a church in that city. In those five days I personally laid over one thousand bricks!

The pastor and his congregation had been meeting and worshipping in a makeshift structure consisting of wood poles and tarpaulins. Since Bolivia is the second-poorest country in the Western Hemisphere, we witnessed a lot of poverty and dire human need. The little children in Santa Cruz especially touched my heart. Many of them came around the building site to see what was going on. Some offered to help, handing up the bricks to us, etc. On the night of the dedication service of the church, the place was packed out. Approximately half of those in the crowd were children!

While working on the structure, as well as in the dedication service, I saw "*that* face" numerous times. I also had the privilege of preaching in a large church in Santa Cruz on the one Sunday night we were there. There again, I would see "*that face*" in the audience while preaching through an interpreter. As had been the case so many times in the past while ministering abroad, the Lord of the Harvest again confirmed his call on my life to "go into all the world" and preach His Gospel. It was always a humbling experience for me and this time would be no different.

Both going to and returning home from Bolivia, we experienced very strict security procedures at airports, especially the Miami International Airport in Florida. This was largely due to the terrorist attacks on New York City and Washington, D.C., which had taken place a few weeks earlier. These delays were taxing, but we appreciated the strictness as it meant our safety, as well as that of so many others.

Once again I was very thankful to the Lord for allowing me yet another opportunity to go abroad for ministry in yet another country. I was also very grateful to my brother Lloyd for "picking up the tab" for me to be able to make the trip.

After arriving back home from the trip to Bolivia I became quite ill with a massive infection that took three months—plus 56,000 units of Cipro—to recover from! Thanks be unto God for the victory over that illness, which undoubtedly was due to eating food in less-than-sanitary conditions while in Bolivia.

Sawdust in South Africa? The Journey Continues

God willing, in August, 2004, I will be journeying to South Africa for yet another missionary evangelism outreach. Plans are now being made for me to preach in gospel tent meetings in that country. I am excited and am eagerly looking forward to it! Who knows? This could be my final missionary venture. If so, then I will be most grateful to my Wonderful Lord for yet another opportunity to go abroad to preach the "Unsearchable Riches of Christ" to yet another people group in yet another area of the world!

Looking back now on the awesome experience I had with the "stranger in the storm" on the morning of August 19, 1952, in Northwest Missouri, I believe I can truthfully say with the Apostle Paul, ". . .I was not disobedient unto the heavenly vision" (Acts 26:19) that God gave me that day, nor was *He* ever unfaithful to me.

A New Venture . . .

On February 8, 2002, I would reach that biblical milestone of "threescore years and ten" (Psalm 90:10). My family honored me with a special "Seventieth Birthday Party" at our home, with many friends and relatives invited to join the celebration.

It was at this gathering that the concept of me joining a men's quartet as a lead singer and preacher started to emerge. The minister who had filled that position previously had decided to resign in order to pursue other interests, and I was invited to consider joining *The Gladtimers* to fill the vacancy he'd left. Within a couple of months I was a full-fledged member of *The Gladtimers*, a group of retired Christian men who had gotten together and started singing for the glory of the Lord.

At present, I am still with the group. We do approximately sixty concerts per year. When asked to take the entire service, I do the preaching, which has opened numerous doors of opportunity for me in that aspect of ministry. In April of 2003, *The Gladtimers* recorded their fourth album—and this time I was privileged to be a part of that project.

The average age of *The Gladtimers* is seventy-three-and-counting, which proves that you are *never too old* to do something for the Kingdom of God if you are willing and obedient to God's calling!

EPILOGUE

Although this writing has been autobiographical in nature and chronological in order of the events recounted, it has not been the aim of this author to write about himself. As stated in the *Preface* of this book, my aim has been to glorify the Lord and to give testimony to His Matchless Grace in my life, as well as to chronicle the miracles and supernatural manifestations of which He has allowed me to be witness and sometimes partner. My sincere prayer and desire is that you, the reader, will have sensed His glory and greatness as you have read the accounts of those *"deeds of the Lord"* chronicled in this book.

When I stop to think about it; *who am I that I should attempt to write a book, setting in order the "Deeds of the Lord" that I have witnessed and experienced? Are there not many great men whose shoes I am not worthy to tie the strings of? Men like Billy Graham, Oral Roberts, T.L. Osborn, and today's "man of the hour," Benny Hinn. . . . These are men who have filled large auditoriums, vast outdoor stadiums, and open fields and have ministered to thousands upon thousands of people throughout the world!*

Yet, when I ask that question, *Who am I?* I cannot help but recall a simple yet profound maxim I once read in a little Amish prayer book. It says this:

"I am only me, but I'm still someone.
I cannot do everything, but I can do something.
Just because I cannot do everything
does not give me the right to do nothing."

So it is with this conviction of heart that I have put into print *I Have Been Young*. Moreover, it is with great desire of heart that *I Have Been Young* might be made a distinct blessing to all who *have* and those who yet *will* read this true story of God's faithfulness to one small "somebody!" If that deep-seated desire of my heart becomes a firm reality, then the writing of this book shall not have been in vain. *God bless you!*

In His Grip,
Gail B. Ott

To order additional copies of

I Have Been Young

Have your credit card ready and call

Toll free: (877) 421-READ (7323)

or send $19.95* each plus $6.95 S&H** to

WinePress Publishing
PO Box 428
Enumclaw, WA 98022

or order online at: www.winepressbooks.com

*WA residents, add 8.4% sales tax

**add $2.00 S&H for each additional book ordered